Monetary Stability as a Common Concern in Inter

World Trade Institute Advanced Studies

VOLUME 7

The titles published in this series are listed at *brill.com/wtia*

Monetary Stability as a Common Concern in International Law

Policy Cooperation and Coordination of Central Banks

By

Lucía Satragno

TUTA SUB AEGIDE PALLAS · 1683 ·

BRILL
NIJHOFF

LEIDEN | BOSTON

Open access publication of this book has been made possible by the Swiss National Science Foundation.

The Library of Congress Cataloging-in-Publication Data is available online at https://catalog.loc.gov
LC record available at https://lccn.loc.gov/2021059492

Typeface for the Latin, Greek, and Cyrillic scripts: "Brill". See and download: brill.com/brill-typeface.

ISSN 2405-9331
ISBN 978-90-04-50872-9 (hardback)
ISBN 978-90-04-50873-6 (e-book)

This book is printed on acid-free paper and produced in a sustainable manner.

For Alejandro, Felicitas, Emilia and Celina

Contents

Acknowledgments

This book is a revised version of the doctoral monograph that I defended at the World Trade Institute (WTI), University of Bern in May 2020. During the process of completing my DPhil thesis, which was mostly enjoyable but at times challenging and lengthy, I have acquired many debts. Above all, I owe special thanks to my two outstanding doctoral supervisors, Professor Thomas Cottier from the WTI, University of Bern and Professor Rosa Lastra from the Centre for Commercial Law Studies, Queen Mary University of London, both of whom I truly admire. I am extremely grateful for their intellectual guidance, constant support and personal friendship. Professor Cottier, my main supervisor at the University of Bern, has not only given me great guidance along the journey towards completing my doctoral thesis but also expanded my knowledge on international public law, encouraged me to think beyond the *status quo* and embrace the project of Common Concern of Humankind in the special case of monetary affairs. Professor Lastra, my co-supervisor, has been a constant source of inspiration for my research on monetary and financial law, on which she is one of the leading scholars worldwide.

My thesis has greatly benefited from the work of the team under the project on Common Concern of Humankind at the WTI (the Project on Common Concern), led by Professor Cottier and comprised by my doctoral fellows: Zaker Ahmad, Alexander Beyleveld, Iryna Bogdanova and Judith Schali. This Project on Common Concern and my doctoral studies were funded by the generous grant provided by the Swiss National Science Foundation. My time as visiting scholar at the Swiss Institute of Comparative Law and at the Centre for Banking and Finance Law, National University of Singapore Faculty of Law has also been the most enriching in the gradual development of my thesis. I would also like to thank Claus Zimmermann and Federico Lupo-Pasini for their valuable comments to some key aspects of this book during the workshops and seminars conducted in connection with the Project on Common Concern. I am very grateful to the staff at Brill, in particular Marie Sheldon and Kelley Baylis, for overseeing the publication process.

Last but not least, a very special thanks to my husband Alejandro for his constant love, support and encouragement to pursue and complete this thesis, and to our three daughters: Felicitas, Emilia and Celina (the last two were born during this process), who overwhelm me daily with their joy and enthusiasm. I am also indebted to my parents and my mother-in-law.

The final manuscript of this book was completed on 22 October 2021. All efforts were made to keep this book up to date as of that day. However, a few exceptions could not be considered.

Lucía Satragno
Singapore, 22 October 2021

Abbreviations and Acronyms

ABF	Asian Bond Fund
ABMI	Asian Bond Market Initiative
AJIL	American Journal of International Law
APPS	Asset Purchase Programmes
ASEAN	Association of Southeast Asian Nations
BCBS	Basel Committee on Banking Supervision
BIS	Bank For International Settlements
BoC	Bank of Canada
BoE	Bank of England
BoJ	Bank of Japan
BRICS	Brazil, Russia, India, China and South Africa
BSAS	Bilateral Swap Agreements
CBVC	Central Bank Issued Virtual or Digital Currencies
CFMS	Capital Flow Management Measures
CJEU	Court of Justice of the European Union
CMI	Chiang Mai Initiative
COFER	Currency Composition of Official Foreign Exchange Reserves
CUP	Cambridge University Press
DLT	Distributed Ledgers Technology
DN	Danmarks Nationalbank
EC	European Communities
ECB	European Central Bank
EE	Edward Elgar Publishing
EEA	Exchange Equalisation Account
EJIL	European Journal of International Law
EMES	Emerging Markets Economies
EMEAP	Executive Meeting of East Asia-Pacific Central Banks
EMU	European Monetary Union
EPG	Eminent Persons Group
ESCBS	Euroepan System of Central Banks
ESF	Exchange Stabilisation Fund
EUROSTAT	Statistical Office of the European Communities
FDI	Foreing Direct Investment
Fed	Federal Reserve
FG	Forward Guidance
FSAP	Financial Sector Assesment Programme
FSB	Financial Stability Board

FSF Financial Stability Forum
FSIA Foreign Sovereign Immunities Act
G20 Group of Twenty
GATT General Agreement on Tariffs and Trade
GFC Global Financial Crisis
GFSN Global Financial Safety Net
GPG Global Public Goods
IBRD International Bank For Reconstruction and Development
ICJ International Court of Justice
IEL International Economic Law
IFA International Financial Architecture
IFDP International Finance Discussion Papers
IFIS International Financial Standards
ILC International Law Commission
IMF International Monetary Fund
IMS International Monetary System
IOSCO International Organisation of Securities Commissions
ITO International Trade Organization
JIEL Journal of International Economic Law
LOLR Lender of Last Resort
Los Expanded Lending Operations
NBER National Bureau of Economic Research
NIRP Negative Interest Rate Policy
OECD Organisation for Economic Co-Operation and Development
OMT Outright Monetary Transactions
OUP Oxford University Press
PCIJ Permanent Court of International Justice
QE Quantitative Easing
R2P Responsibility to Protect
RFAS Regional Financing Agreements
ROSCS Reports on the Observance of Standards and Codes
SDRS Special Drawing Rights
SIA State Immunity Act
SNB Swiss National Bank
TFEU Treaty on The Functioning of The European Union
UK United Kingdom
UN United Nations
UNCJIS United Nations Convention on Jurisdictional Immunities of States and their Property
UNDP United Nations Development Programme

UNFCCC	UN Framework Convention on Climate Change
UMPTS	Unconventional Monetary Policy Tools
US	United States of America
USD	US Dollar
VCS	Virtual Currencies
WTO	World Trade Organisation

Table of Cases and Legislation

Cases

Barcelona Traction, Light and Power Company, Limited, ICJ Reports 1970, 3, 32.
Case of Certain Norwegian Loans (*France v Norway*) [1957] ICJ Rep 9.
Case C-370/12 *Thomas Pringle v Government of Ireland* EU:C:2012:756.
Case C-62/14 *Peter Gauweiler and Others v Deutscher Bundestag* EU:C:2015:400.
Fisheries Jurisdiction (United Kingdom v Iceland) Merits, Judgement, ICJ Reports 1974 p 3.
NML Capital, Ltd. v Banco Central de la Republica Argentina 652 F.3d 172, 175 (2nd Cir. 2011).
Serbian and Brazilian Loan Cases, Judgment of 12 July 1929, PCIJ, Series A nos. 20–1, 44 and 122.
S. S. Lotus (*France v Turkey*), Judgement of 7 September 1927, PCIJ, Series A, No 10.

Legislation

International Legislation, International Organisations and other International Fora and Related Instruments

Adoption of the Paris Agreement (2015) FCCC/CP/2015/L.9/Rev.1, 21.
Convention on Biological Diversity (1992) 31 ILM 818, 822.
Convention for the Safeguarding of the Intangible Cultural Heritage (2003) 2368 UNTS 3, 35.
International Monetary Fund, 'Articles of Agreement of the International Monetary Fund'.
International Monetary Fund Executive Board, 'Unenforceability of Exchange Contracts: Fund's Interpretation of Article VIII, Section 2(b)' (Decision No 446-4, 10 June 1949).
International Monetary Fund Executive Board, 'Payments Restrictions for Security Reasons: Fund Jurisdiction' (Decision No 144-(52/51), 14 August 1952).
International Monetary Fund Executive Board, 'Article VIII and Article XIV' (Decision No 1034-(60/27), 1 June 1960).
International Monetary Fund, 'IMF Executive Board Adopts New Decision on Bilateral Surveillance over Members' Policies' (Public Information Notice, PIN 07/69, 15 June 2007).

International Monetary Fund Executive Board, 'Decision on Bilateral and Multilateral Surveillance' (Decision No 15203-(12/72), 18 July 2012).
International Monetary Fund, 'By-Laws Rules and Regulations' (November 2019) rule K-1.
International Treaty on Plant Genetic Resources for Food and Agriculture (2001) 2400 UNTS 303, 379.
Statute of the International Court of Justice, Article 38.
United Nations Charter (full text).
United Nations Convention on Jurisdictional Immunities of States and Their Property.
United Nations Framework Convention on Climate Change (1992) 31 ILM 849, 851.
United Nations Educational, Scientific and Cultural Organization, 'Declaration of Ethical Principles in relation to Climate Change' (13 November 2017).

EU Legislation

Protocol (No 4) on the Statute of the European System of Central Banks and of the ECB [2010] OJ C326/230 Art 2.
Treaty on the Functioning of the European Union [2008] OJ C115/47 Art 127.

National Legislation

Bank of England Act 1998, Section 11.
Bank of England Act 1998, Section 15.
Constitución Argentina Art 75.
Federal Constitution of the Swiss Confederation of 18 April 1999 Art 99, para 1.
Federal Reserve Act, Section 2 A (12 U.S.C. 226).
Federal Reserve Act, Section 10 (12 U.S.C. 226).
Foreign Sovereign Immunities Act of 1976, Pub L 94-583, 90 Stat 2891.
State Immunity Act 1978.
US Constitution Art 1, §8.

Introduction

> The international monetary system to which we aspire is one that preserves the gains of the past sixty-five years, without succumbing to its own instability. It is a system that maintains freedom of trade and current payments and that allows sharing more widely the benefits of financial globalization, appropriately regulated. It is a system where all countries recognize their stake in global stability and accept that near-term national objectives may, if needed, be constrained by the global interest. International cooperation is, in the long run, a necessary ingredient in the search for national prosperity. This should lead every country to look with a renewed sense of responsibility and discipline to the system as a whole. The G20 or a "G" of similar limited size, under the proposed renovated architecture, would be in a powerful position to promote the global common good, and to make it prevail, including, at times, against a narrow, short-term interpretation of national Zinterests. The opportunity for the emergence of a fully fledged international monetary order is here at stake.
>
> 'Rapport Camdessus', February 2011[1]

In the last decade, the study of international monetary law has regained relevance. The 'free market paradigm' that promoted self-adjusting and efficient markets for the last 30 years was abandoned with the onset of the global financial crisis of 2007–2009 (GFC),[2] which gave rise to a more interventionist approach to the economy with increased regulation. The GFC not only revealed

1 Palais-Royal Initiative, 'Reform of the International Monetary System: A Cooperative Approach for the Twenty First Century' (2011) <http://global-currencies.org/smi/gb/telechar/news/Rapport_Camdessus-integral.pdf> accessed 21 October 2021. This report was written by a group of leading economists convened together under the direction of Michel Camdessus, Alexandre Lamfalussy and Tommaso Padoa-Schioppa.

2 Lastra and Wood considered that the core of the global financial crisis was between 2007 and 2009. See Rosa M Lastra and Geoffrey Wood, 'The Crisis of 2007–2009: Nature, Causes, and Reactions' (2012) 13 JIEL 531.

the structural weaknesses of the international monetary system (IMS) but also stressed the need for reform with the intention to promote global stability.

Methodologically, this book takes a specific legal approach. It is based on a combination of public international law, regulatory law and the interdisciplinary interchange between law, history and economics. This volume studies in particular the role of law and institutions in the pursuit of monetary stability.[3] In doing so, it argues that monetary stability is both an indisputable public good at the domestic level and an essential global public good (GPG) for the international community.[4] Hence, this book recognises that there are overlapping jurisdictions dealing with monetary stability at the different levels of governance (national, regional and international) and that they intersect and influence each other.

This book also remarks that since the collapse of the rule-based system of 'Bretton Woods'[5] in the 1970's, there has been an imbalance among the different domains dealing with monetary stability. That is, policies on national and regional levels prevail over multilateral and international solutions in monetary affairs. The main causes of this imbalance are attributable to the current design of the international monetary order, a system mainly based on monetary sovereignty attributes of the states and soft international governance. The role of public international law in monetary affairs seems to have reached its limits since the entry into force of the second amendment to the articles of agreement of the International Monetary Fund (IMF or the Fund).[6] While

3 This volume acknowledges that there is no universally-accepted definition for monetary stability. At the domestic and regional levels of governance, monetary stability has two dimensions: internal and external. While 'internal monetary stability' refers to the stability of domestic prices and is generally measured by the consumer price index calculated by a public agency, 'external monetary stability' is understood as the stability of the value of a specific currency vis-à-vis other currencies. At the international level, global monetary stability refers to the stability of the whole IMS. That is, the stability of the key elements of the system: exchange rate agreements, international payments system, international capital movements, and monetary reserves and access to liquidity. In other words, international monetary stability refers to the stability of the countries' balance of payments position. For detailed analysis on the concept of monetary stability from a multilevel governance perspective, see chapter 2, section 2 of this book.

4 For a detailed study on the theory of public goods and in particular the study of monetary stability as a local public good and GPG, see chapter 3, section 1 of this book.

5 The 'Bretton Woods' system is named after the Bretton Woods Conference that was held in Bretton Woods, New Hampshire, United States of America in July 1944. For a description of the 'Bretton Woods Period' (1944 – 1973), see chapter 1, section 3 of this book.

6 The Articles of Agreement of the International Monetary Fund (hereinafter, Articles of Agreement) were adopted as a result of the United Nations Monetary and Financial Conference, Bretton Woods, held in New Hampshire, United States of America on 22 July 1944 and were entered into force on 27 December 1945. They were amended on six occasions.

the IMF is still the central international monetary institution, this book claims that a reconsideration of the role of the states in the pursuit of international monetary stability, through their monetary authorities, is required.

This state of affairs makes the case for the application of the novel doctrine of common concern of humankind (Common Concern).[7] This book argues that the conduct of monetary affairs is not only limited but also assisted by the rules of public international law through specific treaty provisions and also by rules of customary international law. It is in this context that this book introduces the emerging doctrine and potential principle of Common Concern. This book argues that Common Concern provides an adequate methodological approach to address the under-provision of the GPG of international monetary stability and the debate on global cooperation and unilateral measures in monetary affairs.

Common Concern refers to 'an important shared problem and shared responsibility, and for an issue which reaches beyond the bounds of a single community and state as a subject of international law'.[8] Departing from that notion, the incipient doctrine promotes Common Concern as a new principle in international law that redefines the responsibilities of states concerning the promotion and protection of GPGs by adding an extra layer of responsibility beyond their jurisdictional domains. The nature of problems associated with Common Concerns calls for a collective action response and demands cooperation among states. Under this doctrine, international cooperation among states is the preferred approach to solve the problems associated with Common Concerns, and unilateral lawful action stands as the second best approach.

The emerging doctrine of common concern of humankind is well established in the fields of natural resources and environmental law and has recently attracted a debate about its applicability to other areas of international law. There are references to common concern of humankind in international treaty language in relation to climate change, biodiversity protection, plant genetic resources and cultural goods in a broad sense. Notwithstanding these treaty

---

See IMF, 'Articles of Agreement of the International Monetary Fund' <www.imf.org/external/pubs/ft/aa/> accessed 21 October 2021.

7 Hereafter, the term 'Common Concern' or 'Common Concern of Humankind' in capital letters will be used to describe the doctrine and emerging principle as proposed to be applied in this book and the term 'common concern of humankind' or 'common concern' in small letters will be used to describe the general principle as used in international instruments and most of literature. Cottier develops the emerging doctrine and principle in Thomas Cottier, 'The Principle of Common Concern of Humankind' in Thomas Cottier (ed), *The Prospects of Common Concern of Humankind in International Law* (CUP 2021).

8 ibid.

references and existing literature on the topic, the normative concept and implications of the emerging doctrine are not yet specified.

Acknowledging that common concern of humankind has so far mainly been a source of inspiration in the search for adequate normative solutions to overcome the under-provision of GPGs of magnitude, Professor Thomas Cottier together with a group of four doctoral students at the World Trade Institute, University of Bern embarked in October 2015 on a project funded by the Swiss National Research Foundations and with the support of the Swiss State Secretariat for the Economy.[9] The main purpose of this project was to develop further and in detail the foundations and normative implications of the emerging doctrine and potential principle of Common Concern. In doing so, the project undertook several seminars and workshops and culminated in an edited volume published by Cambridge University Press in 2020, *The Prospects of Common Concern of Humankind in International Law*.[10]

The opening chapter of the volume written by Professor Cottier[11] describes the historical foundations of common concern of humankind by providing a comprehensive recount of the existing scholarly work on the topic and detailing the expression in treaty language. It continues by expanding on the emerging doctrine of Common Concern and stating its potential to emerge as a principle of international law, by shaping rights and obligations in international cooperation, domestic commitments, possibilities and limits of extraterritorial effect, and its impact on the law of sanctions and countermeasures in seeking compliance with international obligations undertaken. In doing so, it proposes to apply a process of claims and responses to global problems that may amount to being Common Concerns. It concludes by claiming that the potential principle of Common Concern of Humankind will not only deploy effects globally, but also operate as a general principle of law within today's realities and multilevel governance.

The above-mentioned chapter by Cottier sets the foundations and normative basis for a more refined and detailed doctrine of Common Concern to be tested in different regulatory areas. On that basis, the four doctoral students involved in the project developed subsequent chapters on the book in the areas of human rights, income inequality, transfer of technology of renewable energy and monetary stability. The latest of my authorship provides a departing point

9 For more information on the project on Common Concern of Humankind under the auspices of the World Trade Institute, University of Bern see the institute webpage on the topic: <www.wti.org/research/res/#open-83766-sustainability> accessed 21 October 2021.

10 Cottier (ed), *The Prospects of Common Concern of Humankind in International Law* (n 7).

11 Thomas Cottier, 'The Principle of Common Concern of Humankind' (n 7).

for this book on the question of whether international monetary stability can amount to a Common Concern.[12] Hence, this book builds upon and expands on the doctrine of Common Concern in the field of international monetary law. From a methodological perspective it tackles the three main components of the doctrine: (i) international cooperation, (ii) domestic commitments and (iii) securing compliance, and uses them to analyse the issue of monetary stability as a Common Concern and also to give structure to the book as follows:

Chapter 1 provides the necessary background to the main theme of the book. It examines the IMS, describing its key features since the collapse of the 'Bretton Woods System' in the 1970's: exchange rates, international payment system, international capital movements, and monetary reserves and access to liquidity. It reviews the term IMS and how it is complementary but different from the international financial system. The chapter also points out how the characteristics of today's IMS were challenged and modified by the events of the GFC. The chapter ends by arguing that there is a clear trade-off between the pursuit of domestic goals and the stability of the overall system that demands a profound reform.

Chapter 2 examines the relationship between the stability of the IMS and the attributes of the monetary sovereign powers of the states while also arguing that domestically- and regionally-oriented monetary policies have spillover effects beyond its jurisdictions. In doing so, the chapter studies the concept of monetary stability at the different levels of governance (domestic, regional and international). It also explores the modern notion of monetary sovereignty and its main attributes for the issuance and regulation of money in a given jurisdiction. The chapter continues by arguing that in a world of highly interconnected financial and monetary systems, locally- and regionally-oriented policies have effects beyond their intended borders. Hence, it considers the collection of international spillovers of monetary policy (both conventional and unconventional) as the main channel of influence of the IMS and provides a description of the main unconventional monetary policies in place since the start of the GFC. The chapter concludes by considering that the promotion and protection of monetary stability from a multilevel governance perspective requires a collective action response. Thus, the chapter argues that the emerging doctrine of Common Concern can be a valid methodological approach to overcome this issue.

12 Lucía Satragno, 'International Monetary Stability as a Common Concern of Humankind' in Cottier (ed), '*The Prospects of Common Concern of Humankind in International Law*' (n 7).

Chapter 3 describes the key aspects of the theory of public goods (both local and global) and considers monetary stability as an indisputable public good at the domestic level and an essential GPG for the international community. It recognises monetary stability as an under-provided GPG that demands urgent solutions. Hence, the chapter introduces the emerging doctrine and potential principle of Common Concern of Humankind as a valuable method to deal with collective action problems. It provides a review of the scholarly work and evolution of the emerging doctrine to date and also describes the salient features of the refined doctrine proposed by Cottier in the above-mentioned book.[13]

Based on this more advanced doctrine, the chapter continues by offering a preliminary consideration of the application of the three-dimensional approach proposed by the doctrine to the case study of international monetary stability. It starts with the duty to cooperate in monetary affairs both from a *top-down* approach and a *bottom-up* approach. It continues with an examination of the domestic obligations concerning monetary stability with an emphasis on the special role of central banks and also discusses some cases of unilateral actions and issues of extraterritoriality in the pursuit of monetary stability. Lastly, it offers some remarks on securing compliance with obligations that may emerge from an accepted Common Concern of international monetary stability. The chapter concludes by highlighting the complexities that the Common Concern preliminary analysis exposes for the pursuit of monetary stability. It also offers some guidelines for the following three chapters that are devoted to the analysis of this three-dimensional approach in detail.

Chapter 4 studies the duty to cooperate internationally as the best solution to solve the problems associated with Common Concerns. It recognises that there is no general duty to cooperate, consult and negotiate under current international law. Hence, this duty would apply only to matters that are considered Common Concerns of Humankind after being scrutinised by a process of claims and responses. Concerning monetary affairs, the chapter acknowledges that international cooperation for the pursuit of monetary stability lacks an appropriate international regulatory framework and instead rests on soft governance arrangements and on the goodwill of the states to promote monetary policy coordination. The chapter also analyses the duty to cooperate in monetary affairs both from a *top-down approach* (international level of governance) and a *bottom-up approach* (central banking cooperation).

13 Cottier (ed), *The Prospects of Common Concern of Humankind in International Law* (n 7).

The study of the *top-down approach* in monetary affairs considers the IMS as being an integral part of the so-called global or international financial architecture (IFA). It describes the key governance and normative aspects of the IFA and the main challenges and deficiencies evidenced by the GFC. Under the key governance aspects of the IFA the chapter gives special mention to the salient role of the IMF as the central international monetary institution. It describes the Fund's key functions and evolution over time. On the normative aspect of the IFA the chapter examines the system of international standard-setting (mostly soft-law). The study of the *bottom-up approach* of the duty to cooperate focuses on the cross-border cooperation among countries with a special focus on monetary policy coordination among monetary authorities. It briefly examines central banking cooperation throughout history and it provides a description of the main examples of effective central bank involvement in international coordination since the collapse of the Bretton Woods system and ends with an analysis of the responses provided by central banks during and after the GFC to date. The chapter continues by offering some examples of possible enhanced cooperation based on the premises of the new 'obligation to act' proposed by the potential principle of Common Concern. The chapter ends by considering that the enhanced duty to cooperate proposed by Common Concern will have a positive impact on the promotion of international monetary stability both from a *top-down* and *bottom-up* approach. A *top-down approach* would require a reinforcement of the role of the IMF as the central international monetary institution and a *bottom-up approach* would entail enhanced cross-border cooperation among states.

Chapter 5 focuses on the second element of the emerging doctrine of Common Concern: *the obligations at the domestic level* or *obligations to do homework*. This element comprehends two levels of commitment: the duty to promote and protect the Common Concern at the local level and the duty to implement international commitments assumed in international agreements and in customary law. For monetary stability considerations the *first level of commitment* encompasses the pursuit and maintenance of monetary stability as a domestic public good and a local Common Concern. The chapter studies this first level of commitment with special focus on the role of central banks as the preferred institutional arrangement in the promotion and protection of monetary stability. The chapter also examines the institutional framework of central banking. In doing so it studies the main functions and objectives of central banks and monetary authorities in relation to monetary stability. The chapter continues by analysing the special characteristics of the system of exchange rate controls and the management of a country's foreign reserves and its impact on exchange rate stability. The chapter concludes by stating that while central banks have a unique position in the pursuit and maintenance of domestic monetary stability both in crisis and in regular times, the new obligation at the domestic level promoted by Common Concern will reinforce this unique position by expanding it not only to local concerns but also to global considerations in relation to monetary stability.

Chapter 6 studies the *second level of commitment* regarding the obligation to do homework of the emerging doctrine of Common Concern. This second level of commitment entails compliance with international commitments assumed in international agreements and in customary law. The doctrine is not intended to affect the existing obligations under international law but to confer them with the foundations of the emerging principle of Common Concern. That is, encouraging the timely and effective implementation of international commitments. In this regard, the emerging doctrine also aims to inspire autonomous domestic policy-making to address the issues underlying the Common Concerns. Accordingly, the chapter analyses this dimension of the obligation to do homework by considering salient examples of domestic unilateral actions with extraterritorial effects in the realm of monetary affairs. It provides a description of the key unilateral measures in monetary affairs: exchange restrictions and capital controls, with special mention to the case of exchange rate manipulation. The chapter also analyses the accumulation of reserve assets as a unilateral measure of precautionary nature and contains a note on the proliferation of regional financing agreements as an alternative to manage volatility caused by monetary policy spillovers.

The chapter also offers some remarks on the most controversial element of the emerging doctrine of Common Concern, the third element: *securing compliance* with the obligations that may emerge from an accepted Common Concern of international monetary stability. The emerging doctrine of Common Concern suggests that there is a fundamental difference between the discretionary right of states to act under the existing mechanism of international law of sanctions and countermeasures and the new obligation to act as suggested by Common Concern. This new obligation to act might be applicable only in the case of a fully fledged doctrine of Common Concern, determined within the process of claims and responses that is subject to the principles of proportionality and accountability. For monetary affairs, the key international rules are laid down in the Articles of Agreement and they apply to the Fund's members. The chapter also examines the legal nature of the rights and obligations contained in such Articles of Agreements with special focus on the obligations detailed in Article IV and the sanctions contemplated in Article XXVI.

The conclusion of this book provides a summary on the key findings of the *process of claims and responses* as proposed by the doctrine of Common

Concern of Humankind and applied to the case study of international monetary stability. It also provides some alternative proposals on how to enhance the pursuit and maintenance of monetary stability at the different levels of governance with Common Concern lenses and under the parameters of international monetary law. As reminded by Proctor:

> Yet in the monetary field, as in any other, sovereignty is not unlimited. International law sets certain minimum requirements as to acceptable conduct in this sphere and these must be explored. Furthermore, concepts of sovereignty do not merely involve a collection of rights which a State may enjoy; they also connote a set of corresponding obligations which are owed to other States. If a State has the right to establish and to regulate a monetary system, then it must respect the right of other States to do likewise. Such rules of customary international law as may exist can, of course, be varied by treaty, and States can agree to submit to additional obligations by that means.[14]

14 Charles Proctor, *Mann on the Legal Aspect of Money* (7th edn, OUP 2012) 523.

CHAPTER 1

The International Monetary System in the Post-Crisis Era

This initial chapter examines the international monetary system (IMS), describing its main features since the collapse of the 'Bretton Woods System' in the 1970's and how it was challenged by the events of the 2007–2009 global financial crisis (GFC).[1]

The IMS deals essentially with the rules that govern the balance of payment relations among states and accordingly, 'public international monetary law' is at the core of this study. However, this chapter indicates that since the entry into force of the Second Amendment to the Articles of Agreement (Second Amendment) of the International Monetary Fund (IMF or Fund) in 1978 the legal and institutional arrangements for the pursuit of monetary stability favour the national dimension with the central banks as preferred actors. The central international monetary institution, the IMF, has since then shifted the centre of its activities from a rule-based system monitoring the 'par value' regime to a surveillance-based function (that coupled with the other key IMF functions, namely conditional financial assistance, provides the post-Second Amendment *raison d'etre* of the IMF).[2] Therefore, this chapter ends by arguing that this clear trade-off between the pursuit of domestic goals and the stability of the overall system demands a profound reform of today's IMS.

1 See Rosa M Lastra and Geoffrey Wood, 'The Crisis of 2007–2009: Nature, Causes, and Reactions' (2012) 13 JIEL 531. On the causes of the GFC see also Herman M Schwartz, *Subprime Nation: American Power, Global Capital and the Housing Bubble* (Cornell University Press 2009); Raghuram G Rajan, *Fault Lines: How Hidden Fractures Still Threaten the World Economy* (Princeton University Press 2010); Nouriel Roubini and Stephen Mihm, *Crisis Economics: A Crash Course in the Future of Finance* (Penguin Press 2010).

2 In 2010 the IMF published two documents to clarify the role of the IMF in the promotion of international stability. See IMF, 'The Fund's Role and Mandate – An Overview' (2010) <https://imf.org/external/np/pp/eng/2010/012210a.pdf> accessed 21 October 2021; IMF, 'The Fund's Mandate – The Legal Framework' (2010) <http://imf.org/external/np/pp/eng/2010/022210.pdf> accessed 21 October 2021.

 | DOI:10.1163/9789004508736_003

1 Definition and Purpose of the International Monetary System

The term 'international monetary system' was introduced for the first time in the Articles of Agreement of the IMF[3] by its Second Amendment, which became effective in April 1978. With its inclusion into international treaty language the term acquired legal importance in the context of international monetary law with the IMF as the central international monetary institution. A definition of the term was neither provided by the Second Amendment nor by any Fund posterior decision. Hence, this *lacuna* made room for different interpretations about the scope and limits of the term.

As clearly summarized by Sir Joseph Gold, general counsel of the IMF from 1960 to 1979, there are two extreme understandings about the meaning of the term:

> At one extreme is the view that the international monetary system consists of all the rules and practices that apply to the transactions of both monetary authorities and private parties that affect the balance of payments. At the other extreme is the view that the international monetary system consists solely of those rules affecting the balance of payments that monetary authorities have undertaken to observe by international agreement in the strict sense.[4]

There is also a position in between, preferred by Gold as he stated that:

> The intermediate view means that the international monetary system consists of a complex of relationships among countries on matters affecting the adjustment or financing of the balance of payments that are governed by rules and understandings that are more extensive than international monetary law as a branch of public international law.[5]

This intermediate view recognizes that 'public international monetary law' is at the core of the 'international monetary system' with special focus on the

3 The Articles of Agreement of the International Monetary Fund (hereinafter, Articles of Agreement) were entered into force on 27 December 1945. They were amended on six occasions. See IMF, 'Articles of Agreement of the International Monetary Fund' <www.imf.org/external/pubs/ft/aa/> accessed 21 October 2021.

4 Joseph Gold, 'Public International Law in the International Monetary System' (1984) 38 Sw LJ 799.

5 ibid.

rules that govern the balance of payment relations among states.[6] In addition, and due to the complexity of such relations, the international monetary system also considers the agreements among the national monetary authorities that are usually in charge of those relations but excludes the agreements between monetary authorities and private actors that are covered by 'private international monetary law'.[7] The borders of 'public international monetary law' (dealing with the relations among sovereigns) and 'private international monetary law' (dealing with the relations among private parties and private parties with sovereigns) are not always clear and there are some crossing points. However, this book focuses on the public international law aspect of monetary affairs leaving aside the private international law considerations.

Adopting this 'intermediate view', a policy paper released by the IMF states that the term 'international monetary system' covers:

> (a) the rules governing exchange arrangements between countries and the rates at which foreign exchange is purchased and sold; (b) the rules governing the making of payments and transfers for current international transactions between countries; (c) the arrangements respecting the regulation of international capital movements; and (d) the arrangements under which international reserves are held, including official arrangements through which countries have access to liquidity through purchases from the Fund or under official currency swap arrangements.[8]

According to this interpretation of the term, the IMS is about arrangements between countries and the rules governing such arrangements. These official

---

6 It was only after the entry into force of the Articles of Agreement on December 1945 that the field of 'international monetary law' acquired relevance as a separate discipline within the confines of public international law. Hence, it can be stated that this is still a rather new field of law. Recent leading legal studies on the topic include, among others, Thomas Cottier, John H Jackson and Rosa M Lastra (eds), *International Law in Financial Regulation and Monetary Affairs* (OUP 2010); Mario Giovanoli and Diego Devos (eds), *International Monetary and Financial Law* (OUP 2010); Charles Proctor, *Mann on the Legal Aspect of Money* (7th edn, OUP 2012); Annamaria Viterbo, *International Economic Law and Monetary Measures* (EE 2012); Claus D Zimmermann, *A Contemporary Concept of Monetary Sovereignty* (OUP 2013); Thomas Cottier and others (eds), *The Rule of Law in Monetary Affairs* (CUP 2014); Rosa M Lastra, *International Financial and Monetary Law* (2nd edn, OUP 2015).

7 For an excellent study on private international monetary law see Proctor, *Mann on the Legal Aspect of Money* (n 6), pt II.

8 IMF, 'Modernizing the Legal Framework for Surveillance – An Integrated Surveillance Decision' (2012) <http://imf.org/external/np/pp/eng/2012/071712.pdf> accessed 21 October 2021.

arrangements are about the four elements that constitute the core of the IMS at the present: exchange rates, international payments system, international capital movements, and monetary reserves and access to liquidity. The stability of the IMS relies on the smooth operation of each of these four core elements or, in other words, the stability of the countries' 'balance of payments' position. Therefore, the legal and institutional arrangements in place for the operation and functioning of these four elements are at the core of this book.

The *Oxford Dictionary of Finance and Banking*[9] states that the phrase 'balance of payments' means:

> The accounts setting out a country's transactions with the outside world. They are divided into various sub-accounts, notably the current account and the capital account. The former includes the trade account, which records the balance of imports and exports. ... Overall, the accounts must always be in balance. A deficit or surplus on the balance of payments refers to the level of purchases or sales of the currency by the national government, usually through its central bank. The conventions used for presenting balance-of-payments statistics are those recommended by the International Monetary Fund.[10]

After delimiting the scope of the IMS to the four core elements mentioned above it is essential to consider the purpose or objective of the IMS as the global order for monetary affairs. In this sense, Article IV, Section 1 of the Fund's Articles of Agreement expressly states that 'the essential purpose of the international monetary system is to provide a framework that facilitates the exchange of goods, services, and capital among countries, and that sustains sound economic growth'.[11] The main objective of this framework is to provide order to the underlying conditions that are essential for financial and economic stability.

9 Jonathan Law and John Smullen (eds), A Dictionary of Finance and Banking (4 rev ed, OUP 2008).

10 The balance of payments coding system was developed by the IMF in cooperation with the Statistical Office of the European Communities (EUROSTAT), the Organisation for Economic Cooperation and Development (OECD), and the European Central Bank (ECB). This coding system was designed to assist the exchange of data in balance of payments, international investment positions, international trade in services, and foreign currency liquidity among these organizations, their member states, and other interested organizations or entities.

11 Articles of Agreement (n 3) Article IV, Section 1.

The main reason for this is that the stability of the IMS is intrinsically and reciprocally linked with the stability of the global economic and financial system. The history of international economic governance, in particular the Bretton Woods system, presents a very close interaction between trade, finance, investment and monetary affairs.[12] When the IMF was created, trade imbalances and the balance of payments were the main preoccupations, and monetary related issues were discussed closely related to trade policy concerns. Monetary interests and policies were mainly designed in line with the trade interests of a specific country.[13] This intrinsic relationship would have reasonably converged on the creation of a single international organization to deal with trade and monetary affairs. However, due to the constrains of the global politics at the time of their creation two separated international organizations were established: the IMF in charge of overseeing the IMS on the one hand and the International Trade Organization (ITO) in charge of the liberalization of international trade on the other hand. The ITO was never established and instead the framework of the General Agreement on Tariff and Trade (GATT) was enacted in 1947 which become later the World Trade Organization (WTO) in 1994.[14]

Consequently, it can be highlighted that the design of the Bretton Woods system did not foresee a comprehensive international economic order integrating trade, finance, investment and monetary affairs based on the rule of law.[15] International financial stability was not addressed by the Bretton Woods institutions, with the exception of provision on Article VI (section 3) of the Articles of Agreement of the IMF that provides for the possibility of control of capital transfers. Financial affairs were considered a national domain and therefore left to the entire discretion of states. As remarked by Tietje, global financial markets were not a relevant player in the international economic system until after 1945. Restrictions on capital movements limited international financial transactions. However, the situation started to change by the end of

12 See, Jan Wouters and Jed Odermatt, 'Comparing the 'Four Pillars' of Global Economic Governance: A Critical Analysis of the Institutional Design of the FSB, IMF, World Bank, and WTO' (2014) JIEL 17 (1) 49. Further detail on the Bretton Woods system is provided at the last section of this chapter.

13 On the IMF and WTO historical relationship see, Deborah Siegel, 'Legal Aspects of the IMF/WTO Relationship: The Fund's Articles of Agreement and the WTO Agreement' (2002) 96 AJIL 561 and Benn Steil, *The Battle of Bretton Woods: John Maynard Keynes, Harry Dexter White, and the Making of a New World Order* (Princeton University Press 2014).

14 Claus D Zimmermann, *A Contemporary Concept of Monetary Sovereignty* (OUP 2013) 39.

15 Christian Tietje, 'The Role of Law in Monetary Affairs: Taking Stock' in Thomas Cottier and others (eds), *The Rule of Law in Monetary Affairs* (CUP 2014) 17.

1960's with a more visible role of financial markets in the international economic system. Because of the intrinsic relationship of monetary and financial affairs, this new role of financial markets had an impact on the IMS.[16]

In spite of the intrinsic relationship among financial and monetary affairs, the IMS is different from the 'international financial system'. In the words of Lastra:

> The phrase 'international monetary system' covers the official arrangements relating to the balance of payments – exchange rates, reserves, and regulation of current payments and capital flows, while the 'international financial system' encompasses the international financial institutions – formal and informal – and the various public and private actors of the so-called 'global financial market'.[17]

The Fund makes this difference very clear by stating that 'the international monetary system is *not* synonymous with the international financial system. Rather, it is comprised of, and limited to, those arrangements that directly control the balance of payments of members'.[18]

Although the IMS and the international financial system are not the same, financial and monetary affairs go hand in hand and the developments in one affect the other and *vice versa*. As stated by a policy paper released by the IMF:

> Global economic and financial instability may arise due to factors that could be: (i) related to the elements within the IMS (e.g., disorderly exchange rate adjustments, excessively volatile capital flows, etc.);

16 Tietje also remarks that the introduction of the 'eurobonds' in 1963 marked a radical change in the conduct of monetary and financial affairs globally. The 'eurobonds' are: 'bonds issued in a currency other than that of the country of issuance which are usually placed on different domestic financial markets simultaneously by big banks or banking consortiums ... Eurobonds had the effect that the international financial market, until the 1960's almost totally controlled and restricted by States, was opened up to the private sector'. Christian Tietje, 'The Role of Law in Monetary Affairs: Taking Stock' in Thomas Cottier and others (eds), *The Rule of Law in Monetary Affairs* (CUP 2014) 19.

17 Lastra, *International Financial and Monetary Law* (n 6) 433. Because of the remarkable differences between the IMS and the international financial system, this book only addresses monetary stability as a Common Concern. For a consideration on international financial stability as a Common Concern, see Federico Lupo-Pasini, 'Financial Stability as a Common Concern of Humankind' in Thomas Cottier (ed), *The Prospects of Common Concern of Humankind in International Law* (CUP 2021).

18 IMF, 'The Fund's Mandate – The Legal Framework' (n 2). It aimed to clarify the role of the IMF in the promotion of international stability.

(ii) other economic and financial factors outside the IMS (e.g., regulatory changes in a globally systemic financial center, commodity price shocks, interest rate shocks, sovereign debt defaults, collapse of a global systemically-important financial institution); and (iii) non economic or financial factors (e.g., wars, natural disasters).[19]

Therefore, while the contours of the IMS continue to be a matter of debate it is also the difference between monetary and financial stability. Consequently, the IMS is considered as an integral part of the international financial architecture (IFA), as it is explained in detail in chapter 4 of this book. Also, while there are differences between the two systems, they are both considered to be interrelated branches operating under the umbrella of the rapidly evolving field of international economic law (IEL) together with international trade and investment law.

Thus, my book assesses the rules of public international monetary law (covering the relations among states). It also considers the growing relevance of domestic and regional policies (national and regional monetary regulation with cross-border effects) and of the rules and standards of a soft-law nature (emerging from the IMF and other standard-setting bodies) in the field. In this sense, I follow the 'intermediate approach' to the study of the IEL disciplines recently suggested by Viterbo.[20] She argues that the traditional and strict public international law approach to the study of the IEL disciplines (monetary, finance, investment and trade) should be combined with a more comprehensive approach that incorporates the elements of national and private law and the soft-law codes and standards that have an impact on these rapid-evolving fields.[21]

19 IMF, 'Strengthening the International Monetary System – A Stocktaking' (2016) 5 <www.imf.org/external/np/pp/eng/2016/022216b.pdf> accessed 21 October 2021.

20 This 'intermediate approach' to the study of IEL follows the same arguments described by Gold on the interpretation of the term 'international monetary system' as mentioned above. See Viterbo, *International Economic Law and Monetary Measures* (n 6) 35–38.

21 On the study of IEL see, inter alia, Joel P Trachtman, 'The International Economic Law Revolution' (1996) 17(1) University of Pennsylvania Journal of International Economic Law 1; John J Jackson, Sovereignty, the WTO and Changing Fundamentals of International Law (2006 CUP); Andreas Lowenfeld, *International Economic Law* (2008 OUP); *Elgar Encyclopedia of International Economic Law* (EE 2017).

2 The Global Financial Crisis and the Fragility of the International Monetary System

The characteristics of today's IMS are influenced by the course of history, financial and monetary innovations and also by economic and financial meltdowns. Since this is not a historical study, my book does not include an extensive description of the crises that have happened since the collapse of the Bretton Woods System to date but it mentions them as examples.[22] The most recent crisis, the GFC, has had and continues to have a particular impact on the core elements of the IMS and that is why my study revisits the events of this particular crisis frequently.

The GFC was triggered by a combination of government and market failures with inappropriate implementation and enforcement of the existing regulations.[23] As remarked by the Jacques de Larosière Report, 'the present crisis results from the complex interaction of market failures, global financial and monetary imbalances, inappropriate regulation, weak supervision and poor macro-prudential oversight'.[24] Neither the local regulations at the state and regional level nor the international financial architecture at the global level were capable of preventing the GFC from happening because they did not adequately reflect the reality of the financial markets at that time. The 'free market paradigm' that promoted self-adjusting and efficient markets prevailed for the previous 30 years but was abandoned and gave rise to a more interventionist approach to the economy with increased regulation.[25]

The GFC not only drew attention to the deficiencies of the international financial system but also showed the fragility of the IMS. As highlighted by both

22 Lastra dedicates an entire section of her book to the developments of the international monetary system at the international level. See Lastra, *International Financial and Monetary Law* (n 6) ch 12–14.

23 On the causes of the GFC see, inter alia, Lastra and Wood (n 1); Viral Acharya and others, 'The Financial Crisis of 2007–2009: Causes and Remedies. Financial Markets, Institutions & Instruments' (2009) 18 Financial Markets, Institutions & Instruments 89; James Crotty, 'Structural Causes of the Global Financial Crisis: A Critical Assessment of the "New Financial Architecture"' (2009) 33 Cambridge Journal of Economics 563.

24 Jacques de Larosiere and others, 'Report of the High Level Group on Financial Supervision in the EU' (2009) <https://ec.europa.eu/economy_finance/publications/pages/publication14527_en.pdf> accessed 21 October 2021.

25 On this point Charnovitz argues that 'the world economy needs a better law of financial markets and such law needs to be responsive to the problems of both market and government failure'. Steve Charnovitz, 'Addressing Government Failure through International Financial Law' in Cottier and others, *International Law in Financial Regulation and Monetary Affairs* (n 6) 205–221.

the 'Rapport Camdessus'[26] issued in February 2011 by a group of worldwide leading economists and the IMF paper on 'Strengthening the International Monetary System: Taking Stock and Looking Ahead'[27] published almost simultaneously in March 2011, the GFC revealed the manifold weaknesses of the IMS. These reports agreed that the weaknesses of the system are manifested in four fundamental problems which demand urgent responses:

- The *first problem* is about 'global current account imbalances'[28] and the 'inadequate global adjustment mechanisms to prevent inconsistent or imprudent policies among systemic countries'.[29]
- The *second problem* considers the 'financial excesses and destabilizing capital flows'[30] highlighting the absence of a 'comprehensive oversight framework for growing cross-border capital flows'.[31]
- The *third problem* observes the 'inadequate systemic liquidity provision mechanisms'[32] together with the 'excessive exchange rate fluctuations and deviations from fundamentals'.[33]
- Finally, the *fourth problem* observes the 'structural challenges in the supply of safe assets'[34] with a special focus on the 'excessive reserves accumulation and reliance on few reserve currencies'.[35]

These flaws have a direct impact on the smooth operation of the core elements of the IMS and consequently on the stability of the global monetary order. According to the Fund's view:

26 Palais-Royal Initiative, 'Reform of the International Monetary System: A Cooperative Approach for the Twenty First Century' (2011) <http://global-currencies.org/smi/gb/telechar/news/Rapport_Camdessus-integral.pdf > accessed 21 October 2021.

27 IMF, 'Strengthening the International Monetary System: Taking Stock and Looking Ahead' (2011) < https://imf.org/external/np/pp/eng/2011/032311.pdf> accessed 21 October 2021.

28 As explained by Viterbo, 'Global imbalances are characterized, on one hand, by large and persistent current account deficits in a group of systemic countries (notably the United States) and, on the other hand, by corresponding surpluses in another group of States, which includes emerging economies (like China and India) and the oil exporters'. See Viterbo (n 6) 8.

29 IMF, 'Strengthening the International Monetary System: Taking Stock and Looking Ahead' (n 27) 1.

30 Rapport Camdessus (n 26) 3.

31 IMF, 'Strengthening the International Monetary System: Taking Stock and Looking Ahead' (n 27) 1.

32 IMF, 'Strengthening the International Monetary System: Taking Stock and Looking Ahead' (n 27) 1.

33 Rapport Camdessus (n 26) 3.

34 IMF, 'Strengthening the International Monetary System: Taking Stock and Looking Ahead' (n 27) 1.

35 Rapport Camdessus (n 26) 4.

> The international monetary system is considered to be operating effectively when the areas its four elements govern do not exhibit symptoms of malfunction such as persistent significant current account imbalances, an unstable system of exchange rates including foreign exchange rate misalignment, volatile capital flows, or the excessive build up or depletion of reserves.[36]

I analyse in deep the four key weakness evidenced by the GFC in the chapters that follow in this book, in particular in chapters 5 and 6.

Beyond stressing the specific problems connected to the functioning of the IMS, the GFC evidenced two central loopholes in the current structure of the system. These are: the lack of appropriate global institutions and the lack of adequate international cooperation. In this context, there is a widespread consensus on the need to reform the international monetary and financial systems with the intention to promote global stability. Notwithstanding that, most of the regulatory changes that have been triggered since the GFC are focused on addressing financial stability considerations with a predominant macro-prudential approach.[37] The monetary stability considerations have been mostly tackled at the domestic and regional level with conventional and non-conventional policy tools and unilateral reactions. Soft-law standards and calls for governance reforms prevailed for the international dimension of the monetary system. Consequently, there is a clear trade-off between domestically-oriented monetary policies and international monetary stability.

3 Key Aspects of the Core Elements of the International Monetary System

As explained by Gold, the elements of the IMS can change or evolve over time and thus a definition of the system with an enumeration of the elements is not static and should be revisited from time to time.[38] Consequently, for the

36 IMF, 'Modernizing the Legal Framework for Surveillance – An Integrated Surveillance Decision' (n 8) 7.

37 On the macroprudential approach see, *inter alia*, Daniel Heath, 'International Coordination of Macroprudential and Monetary Policy' (2013–2014) 45 Geo J Int'l L 1093; Kern Alexander, 'International Economic Law and Macro-prudential Regulation' in Thomas Cottier and others (eds), *The Rule of Law in Monetary Affairs* (CUP 2014) (n 6) 519.

38 For example, Gold cited the case of 'reserve assets' with the inclusion of the SDR as a new reserve asset by the First Amendment to the Articles of Agreement and the elimination

purposes of this study I analyze these elements in the present context. That is, the four core elements – exchange rates, international payments system, international capital movements, and monetary reserves and access to liquidity – with the legal and institutional arrangements in place and also with the challenges that emerged since the GFC as highlighted in the previous section. In this setting, a policy paper issued by the Fund explains that the characteristics of today's IMS are the 'options on the choice of exchange rate regime, a *de facto* central role of major reserve currencies, in particular the US dollar in international finance, the increased openness of trade and capital flows'.[39]

These characteristics are the result of four decades of evolution since the collapse of the previous regime named 'Bretton Woods System' in the 1970's, through the impact of recurrent economic and financial meltdowns, with the GFC as their peak expression.[40] The IMF Staff included in the previously mentioned paper a comprehensive and detailed table about the historical evolution of the four elements of the IMS and the salient features of the system that I adjunct as Annex I of this chapter for further reference.[41]

In this table the Fund divided the historical evolution of the IMS into three crucial periods: starting with the period of the Classic Gold Standard (1819–1914) and the Gold Exchange Standard (1925–31), continued by the Bretton Woods System (1944–73) and closing with the ongoing Post-Bretton Woods Period (1973-present).[42] As explained by Borio and Toniolo these historical periods are coincident with the evolution of central banking cooperation as it is explained in detail in chapter 4 of this book.[43]

---

of gold as the main reserve asset of the system by the Second Amendment to the Articles of Agreement. See Joseph Gold, (n 4).

39 IMF, 'Strengthening the International Monetary System – A Stocktaking' (n 19) 9.

40 Since the end of the Bretton Woods System in 1973 there have been a series of large financial crises such as the so-called Latin American sovereign debt crisis in the 1980's, the tequila crisis in the 1990's, the Asian crisis by the end of the 1990's, the dotcom bubble at the beginning of the 2000's, the most recent GFC and the European sovereign debt crisis of 2009–2012.

41 IMF, 'Strengthening the International Monetary System – A Stocktaking' (n 9) 8.

42 For an excellent historical study of the evolution of the IMS see Lastra, *International Financial and Monetary Law* (n 6) 407–427; for a very interesting book on the emergence of the Bretton Woods System see Benn Steil, *The Battle of Bretton Woods: John Maynard Keynes, Harry Dexter White, and the Making of a New World Order* (Princeton University Press 2014).

43 They consider the main factors that have determined the level of central banking cooperation on each of these periods are the following ones: (i) the overall conditions in international relations; (ii) the prestige enjoyed by central banks with the public at large, which also affects their institutional relationship with the political authorities (i.e. the allocation

'Gold Standard Period' (1819–1931): This period comprehends both the Classic Gold Standard (1819–1914) and the Gold Exchange Standard (1925–31). The classic gold standard was a *de facto* monetary arrangement between mayor economies from 1819 until 1914. In this informal arrangement gold was the anchor and countries guaranteed the gold convertibility of their currencies at a fixed price. Hence, gold become the main reserve asset that offered monetary stability until the beginning of the First World War. The war marked the abandonment of the classic gold standard and the imposition of exchange controls. International efforts to restore the standard were made in the inter-war period with an increase of central bank cooperation that led to the creation of the Bank for International Settlements (BIS) in 1930 as an institutionalised vehicle for multilateral cooperation.[44] However, the Great Depression of 1930's[45] affected central bank cooperation and the role of the BIS was limited to research and exchange of information among central banks.

'Bretton Woods Period' (1944–1973): This second period is named after the Bretton Woods Conference that was held in Bretton Woods, New Hampshire, United States of America in July 1944. As a result of the conference three international institutions were established: the International Monetary Fund (IMF), the International Bank for Reconstruction and Development (IBRD) and the International Trade Organization (ITO) with the aim to create a framework for international economic cooperation in monetary affairs, investment and trade respectively. While the IMF and the IBDR (World Bank) started its operations in the 1940's, the ITO did not prosper and instead the General Agreement on Tariff and Trade (GATT) was created in 1947.

As remarked by Lastra, there are two key differences between the 'Gold Standard' and the 'Bretton Woods Period'. Firstly, from an economic perspective is the assets into which national currencies could be convertible. While gold was the only asset during the first period, the second period counted with

of tasks in monetary policymaking, including provisions for central bank independence); and (iii) the technical nature of the problems requiring cooperation.

Claudio Borio and Gianni Toniolo, 'One Hundred and Thirty Years of Central Bank Cooperation: A BIS Perspective' (2006) BIS Working Papers No 197 <www.bis.org/publ/work197.htm> accessed 21 October 2021.

44 On the creation of the BIS see chapter 4 of this book.

45 As noted by Lastra, the BIS was to act as a centre for international central bank cooperation. But by the time the BIS started operations, the world was sliding into depression. The Great Depression, that is, the economic contraction from 1929 to 1933, was the most severe and widely disused international contraction in modern times and an unprecedented financial catastrophe.

Lastra, *International Financial and Monetary Law* (n 6) 411.

gold and also the fixed US dollar value of gold. Hence, during this second period of fixed but adjustable exchange rate regimes the gold acted only as a soft limit on the system that *de facto* evolved to the dollar standard or 'par value' regime (each currency had a par value with gold or with the US gold dollar standard). Secondly, from a legal perspective the international monetary system evolved from a *de facto* informal agreement among countries during the Gold Standard Period to a *de iure* international legal system governing the monetary relations among states in the Bretton Woods Period.[46] The IMF was entrusted with the management of the exchange rates and the Articles of Agreement imposed legal obligations on the member states. During this period central banking cooperation was focused on re-establishing the conditions for current account convertibility and sustaining fixed exchange rates through the provision of emergency liquidity lending and the so-called 'gold pool'.[47]

'Post-Bretton Woods Period' (1973 onwards): Liquidity problems and shortage of reserves during the 1960's led to the collapse of the gold pool in 1968. In August 1971 a declaration by former US president Richard Nixon to temporarily suspend the US Dollar convertibility into gold started the *de facto* end of the 'par value' regime. Despite some efforts to restore the system, the major currencies began to float against each other by March 1973.[48] The Bretton Woods system was ended *de iure* with the Second Amendment to the Articles of Agreement adopted in 1976 and effective in 1978. This amendment allows Fund's members to choose their exchange rate agreement and determine the external value of their national currency, as explain in detail in the next section

46 ibid, 409.

47 With the creation of the gold pool the European central banks acted together to match a US contribution to a pool of gold offered for sales on the London gold market. The Bank of England acted as the pool's operative branch. The pool functioned well until about 1965 and it stopped operating with the free market in 1968. The sterling group agreement entailed of a line of credit opened to London by nine central banks and the BIS in order to create a stability buffer for sterling given its role as reserve currency. With the devaluation of the pound in 1967 a second sterling group arrangement was negotiated between the Bank of England and the BIS (on behalf of 12 central banks) with the aim to keep a new fixed parity. This second arrangement was done through a facility consisting of foreign-currency swaps made available by the BIS to the Bank of England for a three-year period. Borio and Toniolo, 'One Hundred and Thirty Years of Central Bank Cooperation' (n 43) 14.

48 For an excellent description of the events from 1971 to 1978 see Joseph Gold, 'Law and Reform of the International Monetary System' (1975) 10 Journal of International Law and Economics 371; for an economic study about the collapse of the 'fixed exchange rates' regime see Peter M Garber, 'The Collapse of the Bretton Woods Fixed Exchange Rate System' in Michael D Bordo and Barry Eichengreen (eds), *A Retrospective on the Bretton Woods System: Lessons for International Monetary Reform* (University of Chicago Press 1993) 461.

of this chapter. Hence, the IMS mutated from the rule-based system of fixed exchange rates during the Bretton Woods Period to the free floating exchange rates regime that we still have nowadays. Borio and Toniolo characterize this new Post-Bretton Woods period as a market-led system in opposition to the government-led system that operated under the Bretton Woods Period.[49]

The described changes of the IMS have been a result of structural alterations in the global economy with a concomitant instability that triggered the tensions between domestically-oriented monetary policies and policies promoting the global monetary order. The GFC was not an exception and the events during the crisis and in its prolonged aftermath continue to evidence the existing trade-off between the pursuit of domestic goals and the stability of the overall system.

3.1 *First Element – Exchange Rates*

During the Bretton Woods System of 1944 the member states of the IMF (a nearly universal institution) committed themselves to maintaining the external value of their currencies. Hence, the *first element* of the IMS ('exchange rates') was expressly regulated by Article IV of the original Articles of Agreement of the IMF by setting the 'par value regime' (each currency had a par value with gold or with the US gold dollar standard).[50] This system of 'fixed exchange rates' was abandoned *de facto* in the early 1970's and *de iure* in 1978 with the entry into force of the Second Amendment.

---

49 Borio and Toniolo remarked that: The new "system" that emerged in the 1970's was one in which exchange rates, liquidity and adjustment became largely determined by decentralised financial markets, with governments playing a more indirect role. Exchange rates among the main currency areas were left to float; the financing of external positions was predominantly driven by private capital flows; and adjustments were induced by either the threat or the reality of a market reaction. Needless to say, this evolution from a government-led to a market-led system (...) did not take place overnight. In fact, it had started well before the breakdown of Bretton Woods, in part contributing to its demise. But by the mid- to late 1990's it was largely complete. The underlying force driving the change was financial liberalisation, both within and across national borders, together with the quickening pace of financial innovation, supported by technological advances in the elaboration and transmission of information.

Borio and Toniolo, 'One Hundred and Thirty Years of Central Bank Cooperation' (n 43) 17.

50 The original text of the Article IV, Section 1(a) of the Articles of Agreements stated that, 'The par value of the currency of each member shall be expressed in terms of gold as a common denominator or in terms of the United States dollar of the weight and fineness [sic] in effect on July 1, 1944'.

With the Second Amendment the Fund's members can decide their preferred exchange rate regime and the era of 'floating exchange rates' began. The revised Article IV, Section 2(b) reads as follows:

> Under an international monetary system of the kind prevailing on January 1, 1976, exchange arrangements may include (i) the maintenance by a member of a value for its currency in terms of the special drawing right or another denominator, other than gold, selected by the member, or (ii) cooperative arrangements by which members maintain the value of their currencies in relation to the value of the currency or currencies of other members, or (iii) other exchange arrangements of a member's choice.

With this Second Amendment the Fund's members can decide freely on their preferred exchange rate arrangement, except pegging their currency to gold.[51] There are a wide variety of options, and the Fund has identified so far ten different exchange rate systems.[52] The most widely used arrangements are: free floating and floating regimes, pegging exchange rates to one currency or to a basket of currencies, using the currency of another state, and participating in a currency bloc arrangement, among others. Notwithstanding this total freedom

51 The Second Amendment of the Articles of Agreement eliminates the so-called 'gold-dollar standard' that was a two-tier system of convertibility. As explained by Lastra, 'According to this par value regime, the value of currency of each participating member was defined in terms of gold or alternatively in terms of the US dollar of 1 July 1944, which had a fixed gold value'. See Lastra, *International Financial and Monetary Law* (n 6) 416–419.

52 Since 1950 the IMF publishes the 'Annual Report on Exchange Arrangements and Exchange Restrictions' which provides a yearly description of the foreign exchange arrangements, exchange and trade systems, and capital controls of all IMF member countries. The classification system is based on the members' actual *de facto* arrangements which may differ from their *de jure* arrangements. The system classifies exchange rate arrangements primarily on the basis of the degree to which the exchange rate is determined by the market. Since February 2009 this system differentiates among four main categories including ten different systems: hard pegs (such as exchange arrangements with no separate legal tender and currency board arrangements); soft pegs (including conventional pegged arrangements, pegged exchange rates within horizontal bands, crawling pegs, stabilized arrangements, and crawl-like arrangements); floating regimes (such as floating and free floating); and a residual category, other managed. For a complete description of each system see IMF, 'Annual Report on Exchange Arrangements and Exchange Restrictions 2018' (2019) <https://www.imf.org/en/Publications/Annual-Report-on-Exchange-Arrangements-and-Exchange-Restrictions/Issues/2019/04/24/Annual-Report-on-Exchange-Arrangements-and-Exchange-Restrictions-2018-46162> accessed 21 October 2021.

in the choice of their exchange rate regime the new Article IV, Section 1 created obligations on the conduct of members' policies with the intention to promote exchange rate stability.

This Article IV, Section 1, also known as 'IMF Code of Conduct', aims to provide guidance to the Fund's members in the conduct of their exchange rate policies. In its introduction the article states that 'each member undertakes to collaborate with the Fund and other members to assure orderly exchange arrangements and to promote a stable system of exchange rates'. It is interesting to note that this provision states the duty to 'promote' exchange rate stability but not to 'maintain' exchange rate stability. Accordingly, Proctor affirms that since the Second Amendment 'there is at present no positive treaty or other obligation on States to ensure the international stability of currencies, nor does the creation of any such obligation appear to be all likely'.[53]

This general duty to collaborate and promote exchange rate stability is followed by a non-exhaustive list of specific obligations concerning the members' domestic and external policies. The provision reads as follows:

> (i) endeavor to direct its economic and financial policies toward the objective of fostering orderly economic growth with reasonable price stability, with due regard to its circumstances; (ii) seek to promote stability by fostering orderly underlying economic and financial conditions and a monetary system that does not tend to produce erratic disruptions; (iii) avoid manipulating exchange rates or the international monetary system in order to prevent effective balance of payments adjustment or to gain an unfair competitive advantage over other members; and (iv) follow exchange policies compatible with the undertakings under this Section.

These obligations are drafted in a manner so that they are considered of a 'soft' nature and would only require the best efforts of the members, with the exception of Article IV, Section 1(iii), which is considered of a 'hard' nature and requires the members to achieve results beyond their best efforts.[54] I further discuss the scope and interpretation of the 'IMF Code of Conduct' in chapter 4.

53 Proctor, *Mann on the Legal Aspect of Money* (n 6) 595.

54 For an overview of the legal framework of Article IV of the Articles of Agreement see IMF, 'Article IV of the Fund's Articles of Agreement: An Overview of the Legal Framework' (2006), para 3.2 <https://www.imf.org/external/np/pp/eng/2006/062806.pdf> accessed 21 October 2021.

3.2 *Second and Third Elements – International Payment System and International Capital Movements*

The *second element* ('international payments system') and *third element* ('international capital movements') of the IMS are intrinsically related and have been subject to challenges imposed by the liberalization of current international payments and increased openness of trade and capital flows.[55] Despite the interface between these two elements, the Fund took two opposite directions in the regulation of international payments and capital flows under the revised Articles of Agreements.

According to the institutional view on the liberalization and management of capital flows launched by the Fund in 2012 (Institutional View),[56] the main reason for the asymmetry in the regulation of international payments and capital movements comes from the historical positive attitude towards liberalization of trade and the negative perception of capital flow movements at the moment that the IMF was created. The historical attitude toward these elements has evolved over time and the Fund expressly recognized both the benefits and the risks arising from international capital movements and reaffirmed the importance of capital flows for global stability. Both the Institutional View and the Integrated Surveillance Decision contain expressions in this regard.[57]

On one hand, Article VIII, Section 2(a) of the Articles of Agreement prohibits IMF members, without the approval of the Fund, from imposing restrictions on the making of payments and transfers for current international transactions – 'no member shall, without the approval of the Fund, impose restrictions on the making of payments and transfers for current international transactions'. The Article XXX(d) provides a definition of the term 'payments for current transactions':

> means payments which are not for the purpose of transferring capital, and includes, without limitation:

55 In the balance of payments position of a country the second element ('international payments system') is related to the 'current account' and third element ('international capital movements') is related to the 'capital account'. While 'current account' restrictions are prohibited (or the 'current account convertibility' is a mandatory condition) 'capital account' restrictions are permitted (or 'capital account convertibility' is not always a condition). See definition of 'balances of payments' above.

56 IMF, 'The Liberalization and Management of Capital Flows: An Institutional View' (2012) 29–30 <www.imf.org/external/np/pp/> accessed 21 October 2021.

57 ibid. Also see IMF, 'Modernizing the Legal Framework for Surveillance – An Integrated Surveillance Decision' (n 8).

(1) all payments due in connection with foreign trade, other current business, including services, and normal short term banking and credit facilities;
(2) payments due as interest on loans and as net income from other investments;
(3) payments of moderate amount for amortization of loans or for depreciation of direct investments; and
(4) moderate remittances for family living expenses.

This term includes transactions in goods and services and also some transfers for capital transactions.[58] The transactions must be 'international' as opposed to domestic transactions and the prohibition reaches only to the 'making' of international payments and transfers *outwards* and not to the 'reception' of international payments and transfers *inwards*. Notwithstanding the prohibition, the Articles of Agreement recognise some particular exceptions and allow for the introduction of restrictions.[59] The trend towards the liberalization of international payments is widely accepted and the events of the GFC did not enhance restrictive measures on international payments.[60]

On the other hand, Article VI, Section 3 of the Articles of Agreement expressly recognizes the right of the Fund's members to regulate capital flows: 'Members may exercise such controls as are necessary to regulate international capital movements, but no member may exercise these controls in a manner which will restrict payments for current transactions or which will unduly delay transfers of funds in settlement of commitments'.[61] This discretion provides the opportunity for the Fund's members to regulate international

58 For a detailed study of the scope of this term see Deborah Siegel, 'Legal Aspects of the IMF/WTO Relationship: The Fund's Articles of Agreement and the WTO Agreement' (2002) 96 AJIL 561, 600.

59 The Articles of Agreement consider four possible exceptions to the 'current account convertibility': Article XIV allows member states to a transitional period before committing under Article VIII; a specific Fund approval to impose the restriction based on a balance of payments purposes; for national or international security reasons; and when a currency is declared scarce by the IMF according to Article VII, Section 3(b). For a detailed explanation of the exceptions see chapter 6.

60 This tendency is exposed by the results of the 'Annual Report on Exchange Arrangements and Exchange Restrictions' issued by the IMF. See above at n 52.

61 According to these provisions the IMF's jurisdiction reaches 'current international transactions' and not 'international capital movements'. This differentiation has received much criticism but an extension of the IMF's jurisdiction on capital transactions will require an amendment to the Articles of Agreement, which does not seem feasible in the near future. On this issue see Lastra, *International Financial and Monetary Law* (n 6) 450.

capital movements both *outwards* and *inwards* as long as their measures do not affect current transactions.

The Articles of Agreement do not provide a definition for the term 'capital'. The Fund's interpretation is that capital transactions are those that fall outside the definition of 'payments for current transactions' provided expressly by Article XXX(d) of the Articles of Agreement. This right to regulate capital movements has been indirectly limited by the qualifications established under the new obligations for the Fund's members introduced by the Second Amendment under Article IV, Section 1 (relating to the stability of the exchange rates system). The longstanding debate about the liberalization of international capital movements and the benefits of capital controls have been revitalised since the start of the GFC. Viterbo considers that 'Governments resort to capital controls to regulate the volume, composition, or allocation of international capital flows and to restrict foreign investors' entrance or exit opportunities'.[62] She also mentions that these measures can have a precautionary purpose or an emergency nature and can target capital inflows and capital outflows.[63]

In this context and acknowledging both the risks and benefits of capital flows and in order to provide consistent advice to its members, the IMF approved the Institutional View in 2012.[64] This view states that 'Capital flow management measures (CFMs) are measures that are specifically designed to limit capital flows' and a differentiation is made between residence-based measures (capital controls) and others. This view does not alter the members' obligations under the Articles of Agreement and also states that the measures limiting international capital movements should be limited and temporary.

3.3 *Fourth Element – Monetary Reserves and Access to Liquidity*

The *fourth element* of the IMS ('monetary reserves and access to liquidity') is about the external reserve assets held by countries and the arrangements governing the management of and access to liquidity (the so-called global financial safety-net (GFSN)). The term 'reserve assets' is expressly defined in the IMF 'Balance of Payments Manual' as follows:

> Reserve assets are those *external assets* that are *readily available* to and controlled by *monetary authorities* for meeting balance of payments financing needs, for intervention in exchange markets to affect the currency exchange rate, and for other related purposes (such as maintaining

62 Viterbo (n 6) 155.

63 ibid, 157.

64 IMF, 'The Liberalization and Management of Capital Flows: An Institutional View' (n 56).

> confidence in the currency and the economy, and serving as a basis for foreign borrowing).[65]

In October 2015 the IMF Statistics Department published a note aiming to clarify the concept of reserve assets and reserve currency as defined in the 'Balance of Payments Manual'. In this note it is stated that the qualities of a *reserve asset* are, 'the asset should actually exist and it should be an external asset, be under effective control of monetary authorities, and be readily available'. To be *readily available* a reserve asset 'must be liquid and denominated in a convertible currency'. In this context it is also clarified that convertibility means 'exchangeability of that currency to other currencies'.[66]

As explained by Lastra, the management of monetary reserves (both gold and foreign reserve currencies) is part of the foreign exchange policy dictated by the government and implemented by the monetary authorities (usually a central bank). Lastra also mentioned that this role of the central bank as guardian of the monetary reserves has changed over time and depends on the country's choice of exchange regime.[67] Also, the Second Amendment has incorporated a new provision (Art VIII, Section 7) in relation to this element of the IMS that establishes a new obligation on the part of member states of the IMF and reads as follows:

> Each member undertakes to collaborate with the Fund and with other members in order to ensure that the policies of the member with respect to reserve assets shall be consistent with the objectives of promoting better international surveillance of international liquidity and making the special drawing right the principal reserve asset in the international monetary system.

When this provision was included the main purpose was to favour the role of special drawing right (SDR) and diminish the role of gold as reserve assets.[68]

---

65 IMF Statistics Department, 'Balance of Payments Manual', 6th edition (2009) 111 <www.imf.org/external/pubs/ft/bop/2007/pdf/bpm6.pdf> accessed 21 October 2021 (emphasis added).

66 IMF Statistics Department, 'Clarifying the Concept of Reserve Assets and Reserve Currency' (2015), 3 <www.imf.org/external/pubs/ft/bop/2015/pdf/15-14.pdf> accessed 21 October 2021.

67 Lastra, *International Financial and Monetary Law* (n 6) 51–52.

68 The SDRs are the IMF's unit of account and an international reserve asset. The value of the SDR was initially defined with a gold equivalent and since the collapse of the Bretton Woods system it was redefined as a basket of currencies. This basket consists of the US dollar, euro, Japanese yen, and pound sterling and more recently includes the Chinese

However, it can be stated that the course of history did not follow such purpose and that the reserve currencies, especially the US dollar, acquired a *de facto* central role for this element of the IMS.

Some 'national currencies' are used as 'international currencies' because they are the currencies that dominate the worldwide volume of international transactions (in both trade and finance) and there is confidence that they have a stable purchasing power. The US dollar acquired importance in the inter-war period and consolidated its *de facto* leading role as the principal 'reserve currency' in the aftermath of the Second World War.[69] Since then, the US dollar dominates as a unit of account, medium of exchange and store of value.[70] According to the Fund's quarterly data on the currency composition of official foreign exchange reserves, in the second quarter of 2021 the US dollar amounted to a total of 59.23 % of the world's allocated reserves by currency.[71] Other 'national currencies', for instance the euro and the Chinese renminbi, have a growing relevance both for international trade and finance and as reserve currencies.[72] However, as explained by Prasad these currencies cannot contest the dollar's dominant status that will remain preeminent for the foreseeable future. He states that:

> getting away from the dollar trap will require significant financial and institutional reforms in countries that aspire to have their currencies

renminbi, which was included in October 2016. See IMF, 'Special Drawing Right (SDR)' (2021) <http://www.imf.org/external/np/exr/facts/sdr.htm> accessed 21 October 2021.

69 Lastra explains that being a 'reserve currency' has both pros and cons. Lastra, *International Financial and Monetary Law* (n 6) 421–422.

70 'The U.S. dollar is preeminent as a unit of account and medium of exchange for international trade and financial transactions, denomination of international debt securities, commodity pricing, anchor for monetary regimes, and as a store of value'. See IMF, 'Strengthening the International Monetary System – A Stocktaking' (n 19).

71 The IMF releases quarterly data on the currency composition of official foreign exchange reserves (COFER). COFER is a database containing end-of-period quarterly data of reporting countries/jurisdictions. With the separate identification of reserves in Chinese renminbi since October 2016, eight currencies are now distinguished in COFER data (US dollar; euro; Chinese renminbi; Japanese yen; pound sterling; Australian dollar; Canadian dollar; and Swiss franc. All other currencies are included in the category "other currencies".). See COFER, <http://data.imf.org/?sk=E6A5F467-C14B-4AA8-9F6D-5A09EC4E6 2A4> accessed 21 October 2021.

72 Since the start of the GFC the emerging market countries have been increasingly engaging in bilateral and regional agreements aiming to use their own currencies for international trade and financial transactions and also as reserve currencies. Examples of this point are the European Stability Mechanism, the Asian Infrastructure Bank, the BRICs Contingent Reserve Agreement, among others.

> erode the dollar's dominance. And it will take major reforms to global governance to reduce official demand for safe assets by providing better financial safety nets for countries. Such reforms would eliminate the need for accumulation of foreign exchange reserves as self-insurance against currency and financial crises.[73]

The *fourth element* of the IMS is also about the 'access to international liquidity' as a main component of the GFSN. There is no international regulation on the supply of liquidity despite it being a core element for the smooth functioning of the IMS. It can be indicated that the GFSN is comprised of four classes of elements: foreign exchange reserves, bilateral currency swap lines, regional financing arrangements (RFAs), and financing through multilateral institutions.

A recent IMF Policy Paper detailed the strengths and weaknesses of each of the elements of the GFSN. It noted that: the official reserves are at the forefront of the GFSN resources but it is unclear as to the countries' intention or ability to draw down on the reserves; the bilateral central bank swaps are used to cover short term liquidity needs (most of the swaps lines created during the GFC have already expired); the RFAs have grown exponentially since the GFC but they are a heterogeneous group with limited resources and imprecise rules for the access to the funds; and the Fund financing – despite being at the centre of the GFSN with a new set of instruments in place since the GFC – is not widely used because of the time constraints and stigma associated with the use of its instruments.[74]

4 Conclusion

It can be stated that today's global monetary order is governed both by international regulations and domestic policies. These dominions are not static and interact with each other. However, the GFC demonstrated that in times of crisis domestic and regional concerns prevailed over global stability considerations.

---

73 Eswar Prasad, 'The Dollar Reigns Supreme by Default' (2014) 51(1) Finance & Development <http://www.imf.org/external/pubs/ft/fandd/2014/03/prasad.htm> accessed 21 October 2021.

74 For more detailed information about the GFSN see IMF, 'Adequacy of the Global Safety Net' (2016) <https://imf.org/external/np/pp/eng/2016/031016.pdf> accessed 21 October 2021.

The role of public international law in monetary affairs seems to have reached its limits and thus a reconsideration of the role of the states in the pursuit of international monetary stability, through their monetary authorities, is required.[75] In this sense, Mario Draghi, former president of the ECB, considers that:

> We have to think not just about the composition of policies within our jurisdictions, but about the global composition that can maximise the effects of monetary policy so that our respective mandates can best be delivered without overburdening further monetary policy, and so as to limit any destabilising spillovers. This is not a preference or a choice. It is simply the new reality we face.[76]

Consequently, the next chapter studies the relationship between the stability of the IMS and the attributes of the monetary sovereign powers of the states while also arguing that domestically and regionally oriented monetary policies have spillover effects beyond its jurisdictional borders.

75 Thomas Cottier and Lucía Satragno, 'The Potential of Law and Legal Methodology in Monetary Affairs' in Thomas Cottier and others (eds), *The Rule of Law in Monetary Affairs* (CUP 2014) 411 and Lucía Satragno, 'Responsibility for International Monetary Stability in the Post-Crisis Era' in Samantha Besson (ed), *International Responsibility: Essays in Law, History and Philosophy* (Schlthess 2017) 77.

76 Mario Draghi, 'The International Dimension of Monetary Policy' (ECB Forum on Central Banking, Sintra, 28 June 2016) <www.ecb.europa.eu/press/key/date/2016/html/sp160628.en.html> 21 October 2021.

Annex 1

Historical Overview of the International Monetary System

	Classic Gold Standard (1819–1914) Gold Exchange Standard (1925–31)	**Bretton Woods System (1944–73)**	**Post-Bretton Woods Period (1973 onwards)**
System Features			
Rules			
Exchange Rate	Parity between each country's currency and gold	USD pegged to gold and other currencies pegged to USD Exchange rates adjustable if "fundamental disequilibrium"	Different exchange rate regimes; increased prevalence of both flexible exchange rates and currency unions
Capital Controls	No capital account restrictions	Capital controls	Regulations on capital account openness differ across countries
Trade	Liberal trade policies	Free trade promoted (e.g., GATT)	Mixed trade policies
Reserve Asset	Gold as reserve asset	USD as reserve currency	Market determined, USD as predominant reserve currency
Institutions	Bank of England under Classic Gold Standard; No central institution under Gold Exchange Standard	IMF as central institution	IMF remains as central institution Emergence of international fora (G7/20) and regional financing arrangements Financial Stability Forum/Financial Stability Board

Historical Overview of the International Monetary System

Mechanisms			
External v. Internal Policy Priorities	Domestic policy goals subordinated to external stability	More domestic policy autonomy but attempt to contain exchange rate volatility and to discipline monetary policy	Focus on domestic policy, with countries choosing their preferred monetary regime
Liquidity	Global liquidity determined by stock of gold	Global liquidity determined by stock of gold and US BoP deficits SDRs created (1969); first SDR allocation	No regulation on supply of global liquidity SDR allocations in 1979–81 and 2009
Safety Net	None	IMF support to bridge temporary BoP difficulties; self-insurance	Evolution of IMF lending instruments, periodic efforts to boost Fund resources although not in line with economic and financial developments Self-insurance; emergence of RFAs (e.g., ESM, CMIM)
Structural Shifts	Shift of economic power to the US First wave of globalization Democratization; unionization; growing social spending	Rapid expansion of Europe, Japan and many developing countries leading to increased demand for reserves, surpluses against the US and overvalued USD (Triffin Dilemma) Trade liberalization/ Rapid growth of trade volumes Gradual relaxation of capital controls	Rise of EMs, including China Dissolution of the Soviet Union Globalization and financial integration Financial deregulation Dramatic escalation of economic and financial interconnectedness

Historical Overview of the International Monetary System

Cyclical Stresses of the System	WWI spending and associated widespread inflation Beggar-thy-neighbor policies (trade barriers, competitive devaluations) Soaring interwar unemployment Great Depression	US spending due to Vietnam war and President Johnson's "Great Society"	Global imbalances; volatility of capital flows Competitive devaluations Increasingly large financial crises (EMEs, Global Financial Crisis, Euro Area Crisis)
Breaking Point	Confluence of structural and cyclical factors meant that in practice, domestic policy concerns took primacy over external stability, undermining the credibility of the Gold Standard	US expansionary fiscal and monetary policies undermined credibility of system; US forced to terminate convertibility in 1971	

SOURCE: IMF POLICY PAPER, 'STRENGTHENING THE INTERNATIONAL MONETARY SYSTEM – A STOCKTAKING' (2016) <WWW.IMF.ORG/EXTERNAL/NP/PP/ENG/2016/022216B.PDF> [PAGE 8].

CHAPTER 2

Monetary Stability

Competing Policy Objectives and Trade-offs

The present chapter revisits the concept of monetary stability at the different levels of governance (domestic, regional and international). In doing so it argues that monetary stability, domestic and regional, is a clear policy objective entrusted by law or treaty to their corresponding monetary authorities on the premise of monetary sovereignty of states. This chapter thus explores the modern notion of monetary sovereignty and its main attributes for the issuance and regulation of money in a given jurisdiction. Based on these attributes of monetary sovereignty the states decide what is to be considered monetary stability within its territorial borders and how it is to be achieved and protected.

Notwithstanding the indisputable fact that monetary stability is a sovereignty issue, it also has an international dimension. This global dimension refers to the stability of the international monetary system (IMS) as a whole. Accordingly, this chapter considers the stability of the international monetary order with special emphasis on the roles of public international law and the central international monetary institution, International Monetary Fund (IMF or Fund). This chapter continues by pointing out that the different dimensions of monetary stability are not static and influence each other. Domestic and regional monetary systems are relevant parts of the international system and they have a direct influence on its stability or instability. Hence, this chapter argues that the main channel of influence is the collection of international spillovers of monetary policy. That is, in a world of highly interconnected financial and monetary systems, locally- and regionally-oriented policies have effects beyond their intended borders.

1 Monetary Sovereignty Today

International law recognises a state's sovereignty over its internal affairs within its territorial boundaries. Hence, sovereignty is usually defined as the supreme authority of a state within its own territory, only limited by the accepted rules of international public law. This means that 'a state that is not subject, within its territorial jurisdiction, to the governmental (executive, legislative, or judicial) jurisdiction of a foreign state or to foreign law other than public international law'.[1] Jackson remarks that this aspect of sovereignty – i.e. the supreme authority in a given territory – derives from the traditional 'westphalian' concept of sovereignty and it relates to the notion of 'equality of states' and the correlative 'duty of non-intervention' by any foreign or international powers (unless consented to by the respective state).[2] He argues in consequence that there is a 'logical connection between the sovereignty concepts and the very foundation and sources of international law', implying that 'no international law norm is valid unless the state has somehow "consented" to it'.[3]

The power to issue and regulate currency is one of the undeniable sovereign attributes of a state.[4] Notwithstanding that, the international community has not explicitly defined or recognised the concept of monetary sovereignty in any instrument of international law. In 1929 a judgment of the former permanent court of international justice acknowledged the principle of monetary sovereignty for the first time in modern international law (the *Serbian Loans Case*) by stating that 'it is indeed a generally accepted principle that a state is entitled to regulate its own currency'.[5] Consequently, states are obliged to recognize the attributes of monetary sovereignty of other states and also to accept such consequences of the exercise of monetary sovereignty.

According to Proctor the concept of monetary sovereignty presents both internal and external attributes. '"Internal" sovereignty includes the rights to define the monetary system, to devalue the currency, and to operate a

1 See Rosa M Lastra, *International Financial and Monetary Law* (2nd edn, OUP 2015) 5–6. For recent legal studies on the concept of sovereignty see John H Jackson 'Sovereignty Modern: A New Approach to an Outdated Concept' (2003) 97 AJIL 782; Anne-Marie Slaughter, *A New World Order* (Princeton: Princeton University Press 2004); Dan Sarooshi, 'The Essentially Contested Nature of the Concept of Sovereignty: Implications for the Exercise by International Organizations of Delegated Powers of Government' (2004) 25 Mich J Intl L 1107; Wenhua Shan, Penelope Simons and Dalvinder Singh (eds), *Redefining Sovereignty in International Economic Law – Studies in International Trade Law (No.7)* (Hart Publishing 2008).

2 The 'Treaty of Westphalia' is a peace treaty signed in 1648 among the Holy Roman Emperor and the King of France and their allies. The treaty does not contain an expressed notion of sovereignty but the interpretation of this treaty with the passing of the time contributed to the development of the concept of 'westphalian sovereignty' as we know today. See Jackson (n 1) 786–787.

3 Jackson (n 1) 782.

4 For an extended analysis of the notion of monetary sovereignty and its evolution please see, *inter alia*, François Gianviti, 'Current Legal Aspects of Monetary Sovereignty' in IMF (ed), *Current Developments in Monetary and Financial Law*, vol 4 (2005) 3–16; Lastra, *International Financial and Monetary Law* (n 1) 3–27; Claus D Zimmermann, *A Contemporary Concept of Monetary Sovereignty* (OUP 2013), ch 1.

5 *Serbian* and *Brazilian Loan Cases*, Judgment of 12 July 1929, Publications of the Court, Series A nos. 20–1, 44 and 122.

monetary policy; "external" sovereignty includes the right to impose a system of exchange control'.[6] Accordingly, he argues that while the exercise of the 'internal aspects' of monetary sovereignty cannot be challenged by other states and must be accepted and respected, the exercise and the scope of the 'external aspects' of monetary sovereignty may be questioned under the rules of public international law because of the extraterritorial impact that can affect other states.[7] Notwithstanding that, a proper exercise of the attributes of monetary sovereignty of the states cannot be disputed before any national or international tribunal.[8]

States exercise monetary sovereignty in the issuance and regulation of money according to the law of the currency (*lex monetae*), which defines what money is and the nominal value that money has in a particular jurisdiction. Economic theory provides a useful definition of money based on its core four functions. These are: money as a commonly accepted medium of exchange, money as a means of payment, money as a unit of account, and money as a store of value. The importance of each of the functions have varied over time and the medium of exchange function is regarded nowadays as the key function of money. In consequence, the law must reflect that monetary debts can be paid by that medium of exchange.[9] As remarked by Proctor, the *lex monetae* theory was developed by Mann on the premise of the universally accepted 'principle of nominalism'[10] which 'applies to contractual arrangements and involves an obligation to pay the nominal amount of the debt in the currency

---

6 Charles Proctor, *Mann on the Legal Aspect of Money* (7th edn, OUP 2012) 526–528.

7 On this point Proctor cited what the Court held in the *Case of Certain Norwegian Loans*, 'the question of conformity of national legislation with international law is a matter of international law'. See *Case of Certain Norwegian Loans* (*France v Norway*) [1957] ICJ Rep 9.

8 Proctor (n 6).

9 For an extended legal study on the concept of 'money' see Proctor (n 6), ch 1. For the economic definition of money see the definition provided in Steven N Durlauf and Lawrence E Blume (eds), *The New Palgrave Dictionary of Economics* (2nd edn Palgrave Macmillan, 2008) <https://link.springer.com/referenceworkentry/10.1057/978-1-349-95121-5_2742-1> accessed 21 October 2021.

10 The 'principle of nominalism' is usually defined as: A debt expressed in the currency of another country involves an obligation to pay the nominal amount of the debt in whatever is the legal tender at the time of payment according to the law of the country in whose currency the debt is expressed (*lex monetae*), irrespective of any fluctuations which may have occurred in the value of that currency in terms of sterling or any other currency, of gold, or of any commodities between the time when the debt was incurred at the time of payment.

Albert Venn Dicey, John H.C. Morris, Lawrence Collins (eds), *Dicey, Morris and Collins on the Conflict of Laws* (15th edn, Sweet & Maxwell 2012), rule 259.

in which it was expressed'.[11] Hence money, as a creation of the law, is territorial and must be studied within a legal system.

The 'state theory of money', adopted in most modern constitutions, claims that money is what the law of the states dictate it to be and as a result falls within the jurisdiction of the issuing state.[12] The 'state theory of money' was mainly developed by Mann who considered that:

> in law, the quality of money is to be attributed to all chattels that are:
> (a) issued under the authority of the law in force within the State of issue;
> (b) under the terms of that law, denominated by reference to a unit of account; and
> (c) under the terms of that law, to serve as the universal means of exchange in the State of issue.

Consequently, the 'state theory of money' can be considered as part of the law of the state.[13] The scope of this traditional theory was the subject of debate by legal literature and two new theories emerged – firstly the 'societary theory of money' and more recently the 'institutional theory of money'.

The 'societary theory of money' claims 'that it is the usage of commercial life or the confidence of the people which has the power to create or recognize "money"'.[14] Hence, according to this theory it is the attitude of the society and not the sovereign attribute of the state that recognizes what money is. The

11 Charles Proctor, 'Indexation and Value Clauses' in Mario Giovanoli and Diego Devos (eds), *International Monetary and Financial Law, The Global Crisis* (OUP 2010) 576; Proctor (n 6), ch 9.

12 For example, among others, the constitution of the United States of America states that 'The Congress shall have the power ... 5. To coin money, regulate the value thereof, and of foreign coin, and fix the standard of weights and measures'. (US Const Art 1, §8). The Federal Constitution of the Swiss Confederation establishes that 'The Confederation is responsible for money and currency; the Confederation has the exclusive right to issue coins and banknotes'. (Federal Constitution of the Swiss Confederation of 18 April 1999 Art 99, para 1). The Constitution of the Argentine Nation declares that 'Corresponds to the Congress ... 6. Establish and regulate a federal bank with the power to issue currency ... 11. To seal currency, fix its value and that of foreign companies; and adopt a uniform system of weights and measures for the whole nation'. (Constitución Argentina Art 75).

13 Proctor (n 6) 15, citing FA Mann, *The Legal Aspects of Money* (5th edn OUP, 1991) 8.

14 Proctor (n 6) 24. The 'societary theory of money' was established by legal literature among the nineteenth and twentieth centuries by Friedrich Carl von Savigny and Arthur Nussbaum. See Zimmermann (n 4) 13.

'institutional theory of money' developed recently by Sainz de Vicuña, former general counsel of the European Central Bank (ECB), considers that money 'is no longer a chattel, but a transferrable credit within an overall institutional legal framework'.[15] He advocates that the 'state theory of money' is outdated and that money is more than physical banknotes and coins but also 'scriptural money' (that is, demand deposits in credit institutions). This 'scriptural money' is widely accepted by society because it is based on a strong institutional framework – an independent central bank in control of the amount of money, both physical and scriptural, in a national economy.[16]

Notwithstanding the emergence of the new theories, a broad interpretation of the 'state theory of money' is still dominant. Lastra argues that:

> Though the societary theory of money provides an important complementary approach to the legal study of money, as long as we have a system in which the state keeps an important role in money creation (with regard to the issue of currency), control of the money supply through monetary policy (a function entrusted to a central bank, usually with independence from political instruction, yet a state function), and a certain degree of control over the banking and financial system through regulation and supervision and oversight of payment systems, the state theory of money – broadly understood as the public legal framework in which the economic institutions of money and central banking operate – remains valid in my opinion.[17]

Under the precepts of international law states are obliged to recognise the sovereign powers of other states in monetary affairs. However, this monopoly power of states in the monetary field is no longer absolute and has been subject to some limitations. As explained by Lastra, the limitations to monetary sovereignty are both consensual and *de facto*. 'Consensual limitations represent a voluntary surrender of monetary sovereignty. *De facto* limitations are the result of globalisation, the information revolution and of economic and financial developments during the last three decades of the twentieth century'.[18] Zimmermann argues that legal constraints to the monetary sovereignty

15 Antonio Sainz de Vicuña, 'An Institutional Theory of Money' in Giovanoli and Devos (eds), *International Monetary and Financial Law* (n 11) 517.

16 ibid.

17 Lastra (n 1) 18.

18 Rosa M Lastra, 'The Role of Central Banks in Monetary Affairs: A Comparative Perspective' in Thomas Cottier and others (eds), *The Rule of Law in Monetary Affairs* (CUP 2014) 98.

of states play a minor role in comparison to the *de facto* economic constraints that emerge from economic globalization and integration of financial markets.[19] The dominant role of global financial markets impacts *de facto* on some formal state competences in the realm of monetary and financial affairs. Also, the *de facto* use of a foreign currency, such as the USD or the euro, as a store of value, unit of account and/or medium of exchange by the residents of a certain country, in parallel or instead of the local currency represents a limitation to monetary sovereignty.[20]

The Articles of Agreement of the IMF (Articles of Agreement) – specifically Article IV (code of conduct) and VIII (general obligations) – contain the most prominent consensual limitation to the attributes of monetary sovereignty of the state members at the international level.[21] The creation of the Economic and Monetary Union (EMU) in 1999 in Europe is the most notable example of the consensual limitation of monetary sovereignty at the regional level. The member states of the EMU transfer to the regional level (ECB) the attribute of currency creation (euro). With respect to this transfer of monetary sovereign powers in Europe from the national level to the regional level, Lastra considers that 'the surrender of monetary sovereignty does not imply the erosion of national sovereignty in other respects. It is a limited surrender, a non-exclusive transfer of sovereign powers. The members of the Euro zone retain their national sovereignty in those domains where no other consensual limitation has been agreed'.[22]

Moreover, there were other attempts to regional monetary integration in Europe before the formation of the EMU. Sweden and Denmark fixed their currencies against each other by reference to a gold par value in 1873 and Norway joined in 1875. This Scandinavian union did not create either a common currency or a central monetary authority. The start of the first

19 Zimmermann (n 4) 17. Robert Howse provides an interesting analysis of the relation between globalization and sovereignty by considering that: In understanding the significance of globalisation … for sovereignty we must always bear in mind the fundamentally dual or ambiguous nature of the concept – that it remains both a statement of a normative ideal (connected to self-determination, cultural and national autonomy, democracy, and related concepts) and a judgment about the actual capacity of states and/or their governments to affect or determine outcomes.

See Robert Howse, 'Sovereignty, Lost and Found' in Wenhua Shan, Penelope Simons and Dalvinder Singh (eds), *Redefining Sovereignty in International Economic Law* (Hart Publishing 2008) 61–75.

20 Zimmermann (n 4) 188.

21 For a more extensive study of these IMF Articles see chapters 5 and 6 of this book.

22 Lastra (n 1) 22.

world war put an end to this monetary union. France, Belgium, Italy and Switzerland established the Latin Monetary Union in 1856 with Greece joining at a later date. In this union, the currency of each member state was accepted as legal tender through the union, and the central banks of the members accepted the coins of the other central banks at par without limitations. This monetary union was also dissolved with the outbreak of the first world war. Again, this union did not involve a common currency or supranational monetary institution. Belgium and Luxembourg created a monetary union in 1922 that was only ended with the advent of the EMU in 1999. In this long-lasting union the Belgian franc was legal tender in both countries but only the Belgian national central bank issued the currency. Beyond the monetary union examples in Europe, there are monetary unions in Africa and the Caribbean.[23]

In addition to the consensual limitations of monetary sovereignty, Proctor remarks that the conduct of monetary affairs is not only limited but also assisted by the rules of public international law through specific treaty provisions and also by rules of customary international law.[24] Article 38 of the Statute of the International Court of Justice states that the primary sources of international law are international treaties, customary international law and general principles of law accepted by all nations.[25] For the purposes of this study the primary sources of international law in international monetary affairs are the Articles of Agreement, the applicable customary international law and general principles of law.

Notwithstanding the consensual and *de facto* limitations to monetary sovereignty, states remain as key actors in the exercise of their own attributes of monetary sovereignty. This situation was emphasised by the remarkable return to national frontiers (or de-globalization) in financial and monetary affairs as evidenced during the 2007–2009 global financial crisis (GFC) and its aftermath. However, the sovereign power of states is no longer absolute. As remarked by Lastra, 'Centripetal and centrifugal forces have diffused the power of the nation state, and today a variety of actors, including international organizations, multinational corporations, regions, local communities, and the civil society also exercise power'.[26] It is in this context that Zimmermann argues that a contemporary concept of monetary sovereignty can be understood both in a direct manner by focusing only

23 Proctor (n 6) 671.

24 Proctor (n 6) 587.

25 Statute of the International Court of Justice, art 38.

26 Lastra (n 1) 21.

on the supreme authority of states and also in an indirect manner as form of 'cooperative sovereignty' that can be exercised at the different layers of governance. This is done by considering 'the various sovereign powers that originally all derive from the same source, namely the capacity of independent statehood'.[27]

Another timely example of the change of powers in monetary affairs is the emergence of local or regional currencies and of virtual or digital currencies. The local or regional currencies, also known as community currencies or parallel currencies, 'are currencies that are not legal tender and are intended to be used in parallel to the respective national currency and which trade only in a rather limited geographical area and usually not across borders'.[28] The most prominent examples today are the Brixton Pound and the Stroud Pound in the United Kingdom and the Chiemgauer in Germany. The virtual or digital currencies are 'digital representations of value, issued by private developers and denominated in their own unit of account'.[29] This concept is wide and encompasses internet and mobile coupons as well as cryptocurrencies like the widely known Bitcoin.[30] For an expanded analysis on virtual currencies see chapter 5 section 1.1.3 on this book.

---

27 Zimmermann (n 4) 18. He argues in favor of contemporary monetary sovereignty as cooperative sovereignty by stating that 'in light of the increasing integration of financial markets and the interdependence of "national" economies, the effective promotion of global monetary and financial stability requires cooperation among those exercising sovereign powers in the realm of money and finance'. Also, Zimmermann argues that: The concept of sovereignty has indeed always been deeply rooted in safeguarding peace, order and prosperity, in accordance with ultimate goals of international law. And in light of contemporary challenges, such as global climate change and the increasing integration of financial markets, these goals can best or exclusively be achieved by means of international cooperation. Cooperative, or shared, sovereignty is the therefore indeed the only realistic option at hand.

Claus D Zimmermann, closing statement in Thomas Cottier (ed) *The Prospects of Common Concern of Humankind in International Law* (CUP 2021).

28 Zimmermann (n 4) 14.

29 Dong He and others, 'Virtual Currencies and Beyond: Initial Considerations' (2016) IMF Staff Discussion Note 16/03, 7 <https://imf.org/external/pubs/ft/sdn/2016/sdn1603.pdf> accessed 21 October 2021. On virtual currencies also see European Central Bank, 'Virtual Currency Schemes' (2012) <https://www.ecb.europa.eu/pub/pdf/other/virtualcurrencyschemes201210en.pdf> accessed 21 October 2021; Zimmermann (n 4) 14–15.

30 For a critical legal study on Bitcoin see Jonathan Turpin, 'Bitcoin: The Economic Case for a Global, Virtual Currency Operating in an Unexplored Legal Framework' (2014) 21 Indiana Journal of Global Legal Studies 335.

2 A Revision of the Concept of Monetary Stability at the Different Levels of Governance

The concept of monetary stability is intrinsically linked with the sovereign power of states in the realm of money. As remarked by Lupo-Passini, 'The power to devise and implement economic policies or maintain domestic stability is legally structured as a sovereign prerogative'.[31] It is under the exercise of their attributes of monetary sovereignty that the states define what is to be considered monetary stability at the domestic level. According to Lastra, 'The "stability culture" is in itself a modern phenomenon, which has influenced legislative developments in recent decades'.[32]

Monetary stability was included in central bank laws and statutes as the core objective of its monetary policy since the late twentieth century. In the aftermath of the GFC some central banks also consider financial stability as the primary or concomitant objective of their monetary policy together with monetary stability. This stability phenomenon is not only confined to the domestic sphere. It also has a regional and an international dimension. These dimensions are not static and influence each other through spillover effects or cross-border externalities generated by policies and decisions aimed to achieve a desired level of stability in the domestic sphere. It can be argued that the main reason for the existence of those spillovers is the very nature of interconnectedness of the global financial and monetary systems. A study prepared by the IMF highlights that:

> The rapid financial globalization of the past three decades – reflected in the over six-fold increase in the external assets and liabilities of nations as a share of GDP … – has been accompanied by an increase in financial interconnectedness. Countries have become more and more interlinked with each other, particularly since the mid-1990's, as the asset and liability management (ALM) strategies of their sovereigns, financial institutions, and corporations have become increasingly global in nature.[33]

31 Federico Lupo-Pasini, 'Financial Stability in International Law' (2017) 18(1) MJIL 52.

32 Lastra (n 1) 55–56.

33 IMF, 'Understanding Financial Interconnectedness' (2010) <http://imf.org/en/Publications/Policy-Papers/Issues/2016/12/31/Understanding-Financial-Interconnectedness-PP4503> accessed 21 October 2021.

2.1 *Domestic Monetary Stability*

Monetary stability is both a fundamental economic goal and an essential monetary policy objective. Lastra provides a definition of monetary stability that considers both a positive and a negative perspective:

> In positive terms, monetary stability refers to the maintenance of the internal value of money (i.e., price stability) as well as of the external value of the currency (e.g., the stability of the currency vis-à-vis other currencies, which is, in turn, influenced by the choice of exchange rate regime). In negative terms, monetary stability refers broadly to the absence of instability.[34]

Gianviti, a former general counsel of the IMF, offers a positive notion, 'Monetary stability means that the value of the currency should be preserved, but this could be understood in terms of preserving its external value (that is, exchange rate), or its internal value (that is, domestic prices), or both'.[35] There is no universally accepted definition for monetary stability. Also, sometimes monetary stability is used as a synonym of price stability. However, as clarified in the previously mentioned definitions, price stability refers only to the internal aspect of monetary stability without considering the external dimension.

While 'internal monetary stability' refers to the stability of domestic prices and is generally measured by the consumer price index calculated by a public agency,[36] 'external monetary stability' is understood as the stability of the value of a specific currency vis-à-vis other currencies and the law refers to it in very ambiguous terms. On this point Lastra considers that the law is ambiguous about the external dimension of domestic monetary stability because 'the issue of which is the best exchange rate arrangement for a given country (fixed, floating, or some version of managed float) remain a matter of great controversy'.[37] The law follows the long standing debate on macro-economic

---

34 See Lastra (n 1) 56.

35 See François Gianviti, 'The Objectives of Central Banks', in Mario Giovanoli and Diego Devos (eds), *International Monetary and Financial Law* (n 11) 465.

36 The *Oxford Dictionary of Finance and Banking* states that the Consumer Price Index (CPI):

> 1. In the UK, ... a measure of price level introduced in 1997 to enable comparisons within the EU. ... 2. In the USA, the measure of price level calculated monthly by the Bureau of Labor Statistics. It is commonly known as the cost-of-living index and gives the cost of specific consumer items compared to the base year of 1967.

Jonathan Law and John Smullen (eds), *A Dictionary of Finance and Banking* (4 rev ed, OUP 2008).

37 Lastra (n 1) 60.

policy about stability or flexibility when it comes to monetary and exchange rate policies.[38]

Gianviti highlights that most central banking laws refer to monetary stability in its internal aspect as the main objective of monetary policy because 'a price stability objective may initially be compatible with an exchange rate objective, but in the medium or long term these two objectives are incompatible'.[39] For example, the ESCB's 'primary objective ... shall be to maintain price stability',[40] the Fed, to 'promote ... stable prices'[41] and the Bank of England, 'to maintain price stability'.[42]

The price stability target pursued by the central banks, through monetary policy as the single tool, follows the so called 'Tinbergen Rule'.[43] This rule relies on the assumption that each policy objective correlates to a policy instrument. Multiple policy objectives should be achieved with multiple instruments otherwise some of the targets will be missed or under achieved. That said, the rule applied to monetary affairs is: one goal – monetary stability, one instrument – monetary policy, performed by one institution – the central bank.

The Tinbergen Rule prevailed in central banking since the 1990's. However, it was challenged by the GFC because central banks now have to achieve several goals, in particular the rediscovered objective of financial stability, by resorting to a wider set of instruments.[44] According to Zimmermann, financial stability

---

38 It was Milton Friedman who made a strong case for flexible exchange rates in a seminal contribution in 1953. Milton Friedman, 'The Case for Flexible Exchange Rates', published in *Essays in Positive Economics* (University of Chicago Press, 1953).

39 Gianviti (n 35) 473. To illustrate the issue of conflicting monetary policy objectives Zimmermann provides the following example, 'a central bank that increases the monetary base in order to prevent its currency from appreciating in line with economic fundamentals, thereby aiming to maintain an unrealistic currency peg, will in the long run fuel inflation, thus endangering domestic price stability'. Zimmermann (n 4) 25 (footnote omitted).

40 Treaty on the Functioning of the European Union [2008] OJ C115/47 Art 127 and Protocol (No 4) on the Statute of the European System of Central Banks and of the ECB [2010] OJ C326/230 Art 2.

41 12 US Code 226 Federal Reserve Act, Section 2 A.

42 Bank of England Act 1998, Section 11.

43 Jan Tinbergen, *On the Theory of Economic Policy* (North Holland Pub Co 1952).

44 In US, the Dodd Frank Act 2010 reinforced the mandate of financial stability of the Federal Reserve System. In UK, the law governing the Bank of England was changed to include financial stability together with monetary stability as dual mandate. In the EU, despite monetary stability remaining as the primary objective in the Treaty, the mandate of the ECB has been expanded through secondary law during the GFC and a new 'banking union' is underway. For a detailed explanation of these regulatory changes and the rediscovered objective of financial stability see Lastra (n 1) 29–110; Rosa M Lastra and Charles A E Goodhart, 'Interaction Between Monetary Policy and Bank Regulation' (2015)

is not a target of monetary policy but central banks have no choice and should achieve both objectives together.[45] Financial stability refers to the stability of the financial system as a whole. Consequently, authorities have turned to macro-prudential instruments to deal with financial stability considerations. Macro-prudential tools are at the centre of monetary policy and micro-prudential instruments, thus adding a new layer of complexity to central bank operations, institutional design and responsibilities.[46]

2.2 *International Monetary Stability*

International or global monetary stability refers to the stability of the whole IMS. Domestic and regional monetary systems are relevant parts of this international dimension and they have a direct influence on its stability or instability. According to the Fund's view,[47] the stability of the IMS refers to the stability of the overall system of exchange rates in accordance with the purpose of the Fund as stated in the Article I, (iii) of the Articles of Agreement, that is, 'To promote exchange stability, to maintain orderly exchange arrangements among members, and to avoid competitive exchange depreciation'.

However, as stated in the previous chapter the stability of the IMS goes beyond stability of exchange rate agreements and also depends on the stability of the other key elements of the system. These are the international payments system, international capital movements, and monetary reserves and access to liquidity. The stability of the IMS relies on the smooth operation of each of these core elements or, in other words, the stability of the countries' balance of payments position.

The role of the IMF as the central international monetary institution has evolved since its conception, but its primary purpose to 'ensure the stability of the international monetary system – the system of exchange rates and international payments that enables countries (and their citizens) to transact

Monetary Dialogue Papers – European Parliament <www.europarl.europa.eu/committees/en/econ/monetary-dialogue.html?id=20150914CPU05481> accessed 21 October 2021.

45 Claus D Zimmermann, 'Global Benchmark Interest Rates: conflicting objectives and increasing hybridisation' in Cottier and others (eds), *The Rule of Law in Monetary Affairs* (n 18).

46 As pointed by Lastra, 'The trend after the global financial crisis is to give the central bank responsibility for financial stability (macro-prudential supervision) and for micro-prudential supervision (directly as in the case of the ECB or indirectly as in the case of the Bank of England)'. See Lastra (n 1) 111–146.

47 IMF, 'Modernizing the Legal Framework for Surveillance – An Integrated Surveillance Decision' (2012) <http://imf.org/external/np/pp/eng/2012/071712.pdf> accessed 21 October 2021.

with each other'[48] remains unchanged. With the entry into force of the Second Amendment the Fund shifted the centre of its activities from a rule-based system monitoring the 'par value' regime to a surveillance-based function[49] (that, coupled with the other key IMF functions, namely conditional financial assistance, provides the post Second Amendment *raison d'etre* of the IMF).[50]

According to new 'jargon' incorporated by the IMF in its *2007 Decision on Bilateral Surveillance over Member's Policies*[51] and the subsequent *2012 IMF Decision on Bilateral and Multilateral Surveillance*[52] the term that covers stability of the overall IMS is 'systemic stability'. These decisions also clarify that the Fund considers that 'systemic stability' is achieved by a combination of both 'balance of payment stability' and 'domestic stability' of each of its members. The concept of 'balance of payments stability' is defined as 'a balance of payments position that does not, and is not likely to, give rise to disruptive exchange rate movements'[53] and the concept of 'domestic stability' refers to the 'policies that are consistent with members' obligations under Article IV, Section 1 and, in particular, the specific obligations set forth in Article IV, Section 1, (i) through (iv).[54]

While recognizing the relevance of the new concepts introduced by the Fund's 'jargon', the concept of 'systemic stability' does not fully encapsulate the concept of 'international monetary stability' that this book aims to cover. The main reason for this is that the Fund's 'systemic stability' term only

48 IMF, *The IMF at a Glance* (2021) <http://imf.org/About/Factsheets/IMF-at-a-Glance?pdf=1> accessed 21 October 2021. Article I of the Articles of Agreement enumerates the objectives of the IMF in a detailed manner.

49 According to Guitián this surveillance-based function of the IMF is discretionary and thus judgement is of the essence. However, he also remarks that the discretion is limited by the code of conduct enshrined in the Articles of Agreement. Manuel Guitián, 'The Unique Nature of the Responsibilities of the International Monetary Fund' (1992) Pamphlet Series No 46 <https://imf.org/external/pubs/ft/pam/pam46/pam46con.htm> accessed 21 October 2021.

50 IMF, The Fund's Role and Mandate – An Overview (2010) <http://www.imf.org/external/np/pp/eng/2010/012210a.pdf> accessed 21 October 2021; IMF, The Fund's Mandate – The Legal Framework (2010) <http://imf.org/external/np/pp/eng/2010/022210.pdf> accessed 21 October 2021.

51 IMF, 'IMF Executive Board Adopts New Decision on Bilateral Surveillance over Members' Policies' (Public Information Notice, PIN 07/69, 15 June 2007) <https://imf.org/external/np/sec/pn/2007/pn0769.htm#decision> archived at <https://perma.cc/3C3A-MQ6P> accessed 21 October 2021.

52 IMF, 'Modernizing the Legal Framework for Surveillance' (n 47).

53 ibid 16. This term was previously known as 'external stability' and it was changed for clarification purposes to 'balance of payment stability'.

54 ibid 16.

considers the cross-border or spillover effects of the domestic policies to the extent which they affect the exchange rate system of Article IV of the Articles of Agreement. This book deals with a broader notion of 'international monetary stability' that covers the cross-border or spillover effects of domestic policies when they have a negative or destabilizing impact on any of the elements of the IMS and is not limited to exchange rates. Consequently, the use of the term 'international monetary stability' through this book refers to the smooth functioning of the core elements of the IMS in an integrated global economy and in absence of cross-border negative spillovers generated by domestic monetary policies.[55]

There are also other international actors that play a fundamental role in the functioning of the IMS:

> the World Trade Organization focuses on the regulation of international trade. The Bank for International Settlements (BIS), aims to foster international monetary and financial stability, acting as a forum for "cooperation among central banks and the financial community". The Financial Stability Board (FSB) focuses on promoting international financial stability. And the World Bank's overarching goal is poverty reduction through inclusive and sustainable globalization.[56]

Besides these actors and since the onset of the GFC, the Group of Twenty (G20) assumed a fundamental role as an informal political forum for the coordination and promotion of reforms to the international financial and monetary system.[57]

---

55 Financial and fiscal policies are at the core of the economic policies of the state together with monetary policy. They interact among each other and in some scenarios, especially during crises times, the frontiers between those polices become blurred. Hence, while recognizing that it is impossible to exclude financial and fiscal policies entirely from a comprehensive study of monetary stability, the proposed definition for 'international monetary stability' in this book does not cover the financial or fiscal policies that can have a cross-border impact on the countries and it is limited to monetary related policies. Lupo-Pasini, on the contrary, in his very interesting study about financial stability in international law provides a definition of global stability 'as the absence of global systemic risk or negative cross-border spillovers in an integrated economic system' clarifying that, 'Global stability is … the situation in which each state is not affected in its domestic stability by external spillovers from partner countries' monetary, financial, or fiscal policies'. Lupo-Pasini (n 31) 53.

56 IMF, 'Strengthening the International Monetary System: Taking Stock and Looking Ahead' (2011) < https://www.imf.org/external/np/pp/eng/2011/032311.pdf> 21 October 2021.

57 Zimmermann (n 4) 192.

3 International Spillovers of Monetary Policy and Their Impact on Monetary Stability

As argued before, international monetary stability depends on a delicate balance between the stability of domestic systems and the stability of the overall monetary system. Domestic monetary stability is an essential regulatory objective based on the monetary sovereign attributes of the states. As a consequence of globalisation and financial integration, the borders separating the different levels of governance have become blurred. Consequently, monetary policies and actions taken by one participant of the system (domestically or regionally) aimed at fulfilling domestic objectives within the scope of specific mandates may have a cross-border impact with spillover effects on other participants and also on the monetary system as a whole.[58]

As expressly recognized by the Fund in the preamble of the Integrated Surveillance Decision, 'there have been significant developments in the global economy that have highlighted the extent of trade and financial interconnections and integration and the potential benefits and risks of spillovers across national borders'.[59] The term preferred by the Fund's terminology to refer to the cross-border effect of domestic and regional monetary policies is 'spillovers' and it is the term that I chose to use throughout my book because it better reflects these positive or negative cross-border effects of monetary policy and it distinguishes from the term 'externalities' used mostly by economists.[60]

Central banks and monetary authorities worldwide reacted to events of the GFC not only by using conventional monetary policy tools (like changes in the interest rate policies) but also unconventional monetary policy instruments. These unconventional tools comprise 'credit support, credit easing, interventions in foreign exchange and securities markets, provision of liquidity in foreign currency and quantitative easing (QE)'.[61] It can be

58 Palais-Royal Initiative, 'Reform of the International Monetary System: A Cooperative Approach for the Twenty First Century' (2011) <http://global-currencies.org/smi/gb/telechar/news/Rapport_Camdessus-integral.pdf> accessed 21 October 2021.

59 IMF (n 47) 4.

60 Most central bank press releases and legal and economic literature refer to monetary policy 'spillovers'. The economic concept of 'externalities', firstly laid out by Alfred Marshall and later refined by Arthur Pigou, consider both 'the beneficial or negative effects on third parties arising out of the behaviour of agents that are not internalised by the agents. Third parties, therefore, either enjoy the beneficial effects of another party's behaviour without paying for them, or they suffer the costs of those behaviours without remedy'. See Lupo-Pasini (n 31) 59.

61 Lastra (n 1) 41–42. For an extended analysis of the unconventional monetary policies taken since the GFC see Claudio Borio and P Disyatat, 'Unconventional Monetary Policies: An

inferred that the main reasons for turning to unconventional tools were the expansion of the objectives of central banks (financial stability, growth, employment) and the lack of effectiveness of the existing instruments to tackle the problems that arose during such a crisis (e.g. in a world of zero lower bound, changes in the interest rate policy are no longer effective).[62] These unconventional tools are meant to be exceptional and temporary: exceptional measures for exceptional times. These measures have also raised the debate about the interaction between monetary and fiscal policy and remain controversial.[63]

After a decade of experience with unconventional monetary policy tools (UMPTs) the Committee on the Global Financial System of the BIS published in October 2019 a report entitled 'Unconventional monetary policy tools: a cross-country analysis' (the Report on UMPTs).[64] The Report on UMPTs studied four sets of UMPTs: negative interest rate policies, new central bank lending operations, asset purchase programmes, and forward guidance. It offers a summary of central banks' common understanding of the efficacy of these instruments across countries and discusses how they were structured and coordinated from the onset of the GFC until the release of the report. According to the report, the use of UMPTs aims at:

> broadly pursuing two main objectives: (i) addressing disruptions in the monetary policy transmission chain (DTC events); and (ii) providing additional monetary stimulus once the main conventional instrument (the policy rate) was constrained by the effective lower bound (ELB).

Appraisal' (2009) BIS Working Paper No 292 <www.bis.org/publ/work292.pdf> accessed 21 October 2021.

62 Proctor pointed out that 'The limitations on the ability of interest rates to influence economic activity have, however, become apparent as a result of the recent economic crisis'. Proctor (n 6), 95. Also see Zimmermann (n 4) 86–87.

63 In a recent note prepared by the IMF Legal Department the authors consider that the unconventional measures adopted by central banks to address crises 'could be considered to take place in the "twilight zone" between monetary policy and quasi-fiscal operations'. See IMF, 'Central Bank Exceptional Measures in the COVID-19 Crisis: Key Legal Design Issues' (2021) 6 <www.imf.org/en/Publications/SPROLLs/covid19-special-notes#Legal> accessed 21 October 2021.

64 BIS, 'Unconventional monetary policy tools: a cross-country analysis' (October 2019) <www.bis.org/publ/cgfs63.htm> accessed 21 October 2021. Report prepared by a Working Group chaired by Simon M Potter (Federal Reserve Bank of New York) and Frank Smets (European Central Bank).

> The assessment of central banks is that UMPT s were effective in terms of both these objectives but that they also have their limits.[65]

The Report on UMPTs provides a brief overview of the types of UMPTs and the main examples are summarised as follows:[66]

Negative interest rate policy (NIRP): Before the GFC there was a perception that interest rates should be positive. Thus, the adoption of negative interest rates was new and they were considered unconventional because they imply a cost for the owner of excess reserves while placing them with the central bank and their implementation required some modification of the policy framework. The first central bank to introduce negative rates was the Riksbank in July 2009. The European Central Bank (ECB), the Danmarks Nationalbank (DN), the Swiss National Bank (SNB) and the Bank of Japan (BoJ) also announced negative rates between 2014 and 2016. NIRPs were adopted in some cases to address currency appreciation pressures (e.g. in Switzerland) and in other cases to further ease monetary policy to ensure the anchoring of long-term inflation expectations (e.g. in the European Union).

Expanded lending operations (LOs): At the beginning of the GFC the liquidity in money markets was scarce and central banks responded by taking measures to facilitate the financial institutions' access to liquidity. Hence, the second group of UMPTs entailed expanded lending operations to financial intermediaries. The main reason behind this was that in many jurisdictions, lending is an integral part of the central bank's toolkit. Hence, while the new LOs were not always new from a qualitative perspective, their scope, duration and size were unprecedented. The main objective was to provide ample liquidity to a broader group of financial institutions at the same time, under considerably looser conditions, for longer periods, and probably at a lower cost. LOs helped stressed financial intermediaries to provide credit to the economy, overcoming blockages in policy transmission.

The Report on UMPTs mentions as examples of LOs the backstop facilities established by central banks to facilitate access to liquidity in the event financial intermediaries were unable to fund themselves in the market at sufficiently low rates. The Term Securities Lending Facility Options Programme was launched by the Federal Reserve (the Fed) in July 2008. The Bank of Canada (BoC) created in 2008 the Term Loan Facility and the Term Purchase and Resale Agreement for Private Sector Instruments as backstop facilities.

---

65 ibid 1.

66 ibid 9. The summary on the four types of UMPTs and their corresponding examples are adapted from the Report on UMPTs.

Asset purchase programmes (*APPs*)*:* While open market purchase of domestic sovereign debt is a common feature in central banking, large-scale purchases of longer-term and private sector assets during the GFC were new and controversial. As discussed in chapter 5 of this book, purchasing private assets usually goes beyond the scope of central banks' mandates and such activities have given rise to several criticisms. The Report on UMPTS explains that:

> The typical rationale for central banks' use of large-scale asset purchases was their impact on asset prices. Purchases of government and private sector debt reduce relevant interest rates and associated risk premia, and thus potentially bypass impaired links in the transmission chain, lowering borrowing costs for the real economy. Purchases that remove safe assets from investors' portfolios can, through a substitution effect, stimulate demand for riskier assets, relaxing financial conditions, with the expectation that this will stimulate aggregate spending.[67]

The Report on UMPTS mention that seven central banks reported the use of large-scale APPS: the Bank of Mexico, the Bank of England (BoE), the BoJ, ECB, the Fed, Riksbank and SNB between 2008–17. The APPS have different characteristics and pursue different objectives. These programmes aimed to address disruptions in the transmission of monetary policy or to provide additional monetary stimulus, or both. The QE programmes undertaken by the BoE, BoJ, ECB, and the Fed are considered as APPS.

Forward guidance (*FG*)*:* The fourth group of UMPTS is forward guidance. Forward guidance entails communication by central banks to the public about their intentions concerning future policy actions to influence policy expectations. While communication about the future setting of short-term policy rates is not new, the use of FG to inform of future UMPTS such as LOS and APPS was introduced during the GFC. According to the report, 'The success of FG depends critically on the ability of central banks to effectively communicate their intentions and to support the credibility of their announcements'.[68] The Fed and the BoC introduced FG early on, in December 2008 and April 2009 respectively. The ECB and the BoE followed in July and August 2013 respectively. For Riksbank, methods for providing FG regarding the repo rate were unchanged from before the GFC, but new FG was added for asset purchases

67 ibid 12.
68 ibid 12.

and foreign exchange interventions. Since 1999, the BoJ has used FG mostly on occasions that it eased policy.

The Report on UMPTs concludes that UMPTs have helped the central banks that used them to address and mitigate crisis circumstances. However, it also identifies some collateral effects, such as disincentives to private sector deleveraging and spillovers to other countries. The Report on UMPTs also debates whether and how these instruments could be useful in the future, since they are already part of the central bank's monetary policy toolbox. On this issue the Report on UMPTs pointed out that the use of UMPTs should be accompanied by measures that mitigate their potential side-effects and also that countries should consider using a wider set of policies on top of UMPTs so as to avoid overburdening the central bank.

These changes in the monetary policy stance (mostly from advanced economies in control of the leading currencies) have had and continue to have spillover effects on other countries (commonly to emerging market countries).[69] In this regard, an International Finance Discussion Papers (IFDP) Note published on the Fed's website in February 2016 provides a short but comprehensive analysis on the basic issues connected to the international spillovers of monetary policy.[70] In this note the authors highlighted that the discussions on the topic are not new but started in the early interwar period and recovered relevance in the aftermath of the GFC due to the use of conventional and unconventional monetary policies by central banks in order to provoke monetary stimulus.

The authors of the IFDP Note recognized that international spillovers can be positive or negative, mainly subject to the strength of the channels of transmission.[71] However, they acknowledged that beyond the cost/benefit analysis

69 It is not only the policy change but also the discontinuity of the policies that brings associated spillovers. To illustrate this point Lastra provides the example of QE in the US and the effects of the so-called 'tapering'. See Lastra (n 1) 39–40.

70 John Ammer and others, 'International Spillovers of Monetary Policy' (2016) IFDP Notes <https://federalreserve.gov/econresdata/notes/ifdp-notes/2016/international-spillovers-of-monetary-policy-20160208.html> accessed 21 October 2021.

71 On this point Janet Yellen, former chair of the Fed, recognises the international linkages of domestic monetary policy by stating that: monetary policy actions in one country spill over to other economies through three main channels: changes in exchange rates; changes in domestic demand, which alter the economy's imports; and changes in domestic financial conditions – such as interest rates and asset prices – that, through portfolio balance and other channels, affect financial conditions abroad.

Janet L Yellen, 'Speech' The Elusive 'Great' Recovery: Causes and Implications for Future Business Cycle Dynamics, Boston, 14 October 2016 <https://federalreserve.gov/newsevents/speech/yellen20161014a.htm> accessed 21 October 2021. For further detail on the channels of transmission see chapter 6 of this book.

of the impact of the spillovers, the key issue relates to the impact of monetary spillovers on the stability of the global economy. On this issue the authors pointed out that:

> In response to common adverse shocks such as the GFC, the positive spillovers of easing actions by the Federal Reserve and other central banks proved stabilizing for the global economy. Conversely, some years afterwards, these positive spillovers from ongoing policy accommodation were not welcomed by emerging market economies (EMES) whose cyclical positions had much improved.[72]

Consequently, the authors conclude on this issue that international monetary policy spillovers can have both stabilizing and destabilizing effects on the global economy depending on the business-cycle[73] situation of states globally.[74]

It can be argued that the particular business-cycle of states also influences the course of monetary policy directions opted by central banks worldwide. For that reason, Benoît Cœuré, a member of the executive board of the ECB, considers that 'the global economy is currently characterised by an environment of diverging monetary policy cycles'[75] and as an illustration on the point

---

72 John Ammer and others (n 70).

73 ibid. The Oxford Dictionary of Finance and Banking provides a definition of 'business cycle' that reads as follows: The process by which investment, output, and employment in an economy tend to move through a recurrent cycle of upturn, prosperity, downturn, and recession. The cycle does not describe a regular pattern in either length or amplitude. Cycles in the immediate postwar period were of historically low amplitude, while those of the late 1970's and 1980's had greater amplitude and involved much deeper recessions. The reasons for the business cycle remain little understood.

Law and Smullen (eds) (n 36).

74 Accordingly, Albagli and others remarked that: While increased financial integration has multiple benefits, it also presents important challenges. In particular, it raises the question of whether the cost of funds in non-core economies can remain independent from developments in major financial centers, possibly undermining the ability of central banks in setting appropriate monetary conditions given each country's macroeconomic stance.

Elias Albagli and others, 'Channels of US Monetary Policy Spillovers into International Bond Markets' <https://bis.org/events/ccaconf2017/ccaconf2017_12.pdf> accessed 3 December 2019.

75 Benoît Cœuré, 'Domestic and Cross-Border Spillovers of Unconventional Monetary Policies' (SNB-IMF Conference 'Monetary Policy Challenges in a Changing World', Zurich, May 2015) <https://ecb.europa.eu/press/key/date/2015/html/sp150513.en.html> accessed 21 October 2021.

he presents the example of interest rate level disparities among the euro area and the United States of America.[76] Similarly, a special report issued by The Economist in 2018 remarked that:

> This divergence between America and the rest means divergent monetary policies, too. The Federal Reserve has raised interest rates eight times since December 2015. The European Central Bank (ECB) is still a long way from its first increase. In Japan rates are negative. China, the principal target of Mr Trump's trade war, relaxed monetary policy this week in response to a weakening economy. When interest rates rise in America but nowhere else, the dollar strengthens. That makes it harder for emerging markets to repay their dollar debts. A rising greenback has already helped propel Argentina and Turkey into trouble; this week Pakistan asked the IMF for a bail-out.[77]

Cœuré also remarks that this pattern of 'global monetary policy divergence' also brought with it the debate on the loss of monetary policy independence. On this point he argues that:

> central banks in large advanced economies can free themselves from the global financial cycle and regain monetary independence, provided that they show clarity in purpose and resolve in implementation. ... For emerging markets and smaller advanced economies, there is also evidence that while the global financial cycle has indeed been a dominant factor for the last two decades, the arrangement of open macro policies such as the exchange rate regime and financial openness still have direct influence on sensitivity to the financial cycle.[78]

Accordingly, Lastra argues that 'the ability to have a truly independent monetary policy diminishes with the growth of cross-border capital flow'.[79] The matters of monetary policy independence and the global business-cycle are intrinsically related to the so called 'monetary trilemma' identified almost 60 years ago by the economists Mundell (1963) and Fleming (1962).[80] This trilemma

---

76 ibid. While the Fed reacted to the GFC by implementing a series of interest rate cuts, the ECB maintained the interest rate unchanged for much longer.

77 The Economist, *The Next Recession* (11 October 2018).

78 Benoît Cœuré (n 75).

79 Lastra (n 1) 24–25.

80 Robert A Mundell, 'Capital Mobility and Stabilization Policy under Fixed and Flexible Exchange Rates' (1963) 29(4) The Canadian Journal of Economics and Political Science

considers that there is a policy trade-off among three objectives that cannot be achieved at the same time so governments must give up one of them. The conflicting objectives are: a fixed exchange rate, free capital movements and an independent monetary policy. A recent and influential study on this policy trade-off made by Hélène Rey considers that it is not a trilemma, but a dilemma between free capital movements and the control of local financial conditions.[81]

Mark Carney, former governor of the Bank of England, has argued in 2019 that those players at the center of the IMS, like the Fed, need to incorporate spillovers and spill backs. He also considers that

> central banks need to develop a better shared understanding of the scale of global risks and a recognition that concerted, cooperative action may sometimes be necessary … That doesn't mean that monetary policy makers in advanced economies must internalise fully spillovers from their actions on emerging market economies, given their mandates are to achieve domestic objectives. They must, however, increasingly take account of effects that spill back on their economy as well as shifts in the global equilibrium interest rate that their actions can spur.[82]

While recognizing the value of the studies performed by economic literature on the trade-offs connected to the issues associated with the so-called monetary trilemma or dilemma, the trade-offs that I want to highlight and discuss throughout this book are related but different. The economist monetary trilemma debates the trade-off among three competing policy objectives at the same level of governance (monetary policy, exchange rate policy and capital movements). That level of governance is the domestic level or, in the case of

---

475; Marcus J Fleming, 'Domestic Financial Policies under Fixed and under Floating Exchange Rates' (1962) 9(3) Staff Papers International Monetary Fund, 369.

81 Rey argues that: For the past few decades, international macroeconomics has postulated the 'trilemma': with free capital mobility, independent monetary policies are feasible if and only if exchange rates are floating. The global financial cycle transforms the trilemma into a 'dilemma' or an 'irreconcilable duo': independent monetary policies are possible if and only if the capital account is managed.

Hélène Rey, 'Dilemma not Trilemma: The Global Financial Cycle and Monetary Policy Independence' (2013) Proceedings – Economic Policy Symposium – Jackson Hole, Federal Reserve of Kansas City Economic Symposium, 285–333.

82 Mark Carney, 'Speech' (The Growing Challenges for Monetary Policy in the current International Monetary and Financial System, London, 23 August 2019) 11 <www.bis.org/review/r190827b.htm> accessed 21 October 2021.

the euro zone, the regional level. However, this study is interested in the trade-off among different levels of governance. Specifically, the trade-off among policies aimed at domestic and regional monetary stability and the stability of the overall IMS. This trade-off reached its peak during the GFC, triggered by the international spillovers of monetary policy. Consequently, I analyse in further detail this trade-off in the following chapters as it is a regulatory gap which I want to raise awareness to in legal doctrine.

4 Conclusion

This chapter claims that the term 'international monetary stability' encompasses the smooth functioning of the core elements of the IMS in an integrated global economy and the absence of cross-border negative spillovers generated by domestic monetary policies. Also, this chapter argues that there is a clear trade-off among the stability objectives at the different levels of governance of the international monetary order. It also contends that this trade-off benefits the stability of the domestic and regional orders over the stability of the whole international monetary order.

Accordingly, the Rapport Camdessus remarks that:

> There is no unified global governance structure to help ensure that major economic and financial policy decisions made nationally, including exchange rate policies, are mutually consistent and contribute to global stability. In a world so deeply inter-connected, economic outcomes in each country depend significantly on developments and policy decisions made in others. In such a world, there is a strong case for rules and processes to be developed to help ensure that major economic and financial policy decisions made nationally are mutually consistent and contribute to global stability.[83]

Consistent with the observations made by the Rapport Camdessus in the aftermath of the GFC, the next chapter introduces the emerging doctrine of Common Concern of Humankind as a valid methodological approach to issues that require a collective action response from the international community, like the stability of the IMS.

83 Rapport Camdessus (n 58) 4.

CHAPTER 3

A Common Concern of Humankind Approach to Monetary Stability

Monetary stability is indisputably a public good at the domestic level and an essential global public good (GPG) for the international community. Therefore, there are overlapping jurisdictions dealing with monetary stability at the different levels of governance.[1] Notwithstanding that, since the collapse of the rule-based system of 'Bretton Woods' in the 1970's, policies on national and regional levels have prevailed over multilateral and international solutions. As discussed in the previous chapter, this situation raised a trade-off between domestically-oriented policies and the stability of the global monetary order.[2]

Consequently, it is contended that the main causes of this imbalance are attributable to the current design of the international monetary order, a system mainly based on monetary sovereignty attributes of the states and soft international governance.[3] This state of affairs makes the case for the application of the emerging doctrine of common concern of humankind (Common Concern)[4] as an adequate methodological approach to cope with the underprovision of the

1 On the overlapping jurisdictions dealing with public goods Petersmann remarks that: As international public goods (like transnational rule of law, international financial, and energy security) are composed of, and dependent on, national public goods, prioritization of national public goods is morally justifiable and democratically inevitable. Yet, protection of national public goods often remains incomplete without simultaneous protection of international public goods (e.g. providing for reciprocal elimination of border discrimination and transnational pollution undermining national public goods).

E U Petersmann, 'International Economic Law, 'Public Reason', and Multilevel Governance of Interdependent Public Goods' (2011) 14(1) JIEL 30.

2 See chapter 2 of this book.

3 Drahos pointed out that: Increasingly the regulation of public goods takes place by means of global standards. When, for example, the Basel Committee on Banking Supervision issues guidelines on capital adequacy standards that are adopted by the world's central banks, the stability that these and other guidelines bring to the world's financial system is a global public good.

Peter Drahos, 'The Regulation of Public Goods' (2004) 7(2) JIEL 321.

4 Hereafter, the term 'Common Concern' or 'Common Concern of Humankind' in capital letters will be used to describe the doctrine and emerging principle as proposed to be applied in this book and the term 'common concern of humankind' or 'common concern' in small letters will be used to describe the general principle as used in international instruments and most of literature. Cottier develops the emerging doctrine and principle in Thomas Cottier,

GPG of international monetary stability and the debate about global cooperation and unilateral measures in monetary affairs.

To address the main issues associated with this trade-off, this chapter starts by exploring the concept of monetary stability as a local and also a global public good. It is followed by a description of the emerging doctrine and eventual principle of Common Concern as a valuable method to deal with collective action problems. It continues with a preliminary consideration of the three-dimensional approach proposed by the doctrine starting with the duty to cooperate in monetary affairs both from a *top-down* approach (international level of governance) and a *bottom-up* approach (central banking cooperation). The section continues by examining domestic obligations concerning monetary stability with an emphasis on the special role of central banks and also by examining some cases of unilateral actions and issues of extraterritoriality in the pursuit of monetary stability. Lastly, it offers some remarks on securing compliance with obligations that may emerge from an accepted Common Concern of international monetary stability. This chapter concludes with a description of the complexities that the Common Concern preliminary analysis exposes in the pursuit of monetary stability and offers some guidelines for the following chapters.

1 Monetary Stability as a Global Public Good

The term 'public good' is a key concept in economics introduced by Paul Samuelson in the 1950's and is mainly applied at the local or national level.[5] A public good has two essential characteristics: 'non-rivalry' in consumption and 'non-excludability' of benefits.[6] The first characteristic implies that the use of the public good by one person will not diminish its availability to others. The second characteristic denotes that the public good is available to everybody, whether they contribute to its production or not.

It was only in the 1990's that the theory of public goods was first applied at the global or international level with the expression 'global public goods'

'The Principle of Common Concern of Humankind' in Thomas Cottier (ed) '*The Prospects of Common Concern of Humankind in International Law*' (CUP 2021).

5 Paul Samuelson, 'The Pure Theory of Public Expenditure' (1954) 36 Rev Econ Stat 387.

6 Samuelson's study focused on the first characteristic of 'non-rivalry' while the second characteristic of 'non-excludability' was introduced by Musgrave. See Richard A Musgrave, 'Public Goods' in Brown E Cary and Robert M Solow (eds), *Paul Samuelson and Modern Economic Theory* (McGraw Hill 1983).

gaining interest among the works of the United Nations Development Programme (UNDP).[7] In 2003 the International Task Force on Global Public Goods was created and in 2006 it issued its final report defining the concept of 'global public goods' as 'issues that are broadly conceived as important to the international community, that for the most part cannot or will not be adequately addressed by individual countries acting alone and that are defined through a broad international consensus or a legitimate process of decision-making'.[8] Consequently, from this definition it is argued that 'Global public goods are those whose benefits could in principle be consumed by the governments and peoples of all states' and therefore 'consumption of the good by one state or its people in no way reduces its availability to others'.[9] This approach is in line with the qualities of 'non-rivalry' in consumption and 'non-excludability' of benefits of public goods as developed in the applicable theory from an economic perspective.[10]

While the provision of public goods at the national level requires the action of a single state, the provision of GPGs demands collective action at the international level. Both national public goods and GPGs create positive externalities (attributable to their characteristic of non-excludability of benefits). Whereas in the former case the externalities are intended to reach the population of a nation state within its geographical borders, in the latter case the externalities reach every country and the world wide population regardless of geographical and political borders. Therefore, in the absence of adequate international governance, there is a need for collective action and international cooperation among states for the production of GPGs. As remarked by Kaul, 'GPGs are public in the sense that they affect us all, and they are public in provision. It would be difficult for any nation to improve the availability of

---

7 The research on global public goods performed by the UNDP resulted in three publications. See Inge Kaul, Isabelle Grunberg and Marc Stern (eds), *Global Public Goods: International Cooperation in the 21st Century* (OUP 1999); Inge Kaul and others (eds), *Providing Global Public Goods: Managing Globalization* (OUP 2003); Inge Kaul and Pedro Conceiçao, *The New Public Finance: Responding to Global Challenges* (OUP 2006).

8 International Task Force on Global Public Goods, *Meeting Global Challenges: International Cooperation in the National Interest* (Final Report, Stockholm, 2006) 13 <https://ycsg.yale.edu/sites/default/files/files/meeting_global_challenges_global_public_goods.pdf> accessed 21 October 2021.

9 ibid.

10 For an excellent description on the evolution of the theory of global public goods see Annamaria Viterbo, *International Economic Law and Monetary Measures* (EE 2012) ch 1.

a GPG … through domestic policy initiatives alone. Most GPGs call for cross-border cooperation'.[11]

The main problems associated with the provision or underprovision of GPGs are threefold – the 'free-riding' or 'easy riders' issue, market failures, and government failures. The first problem is associated with the 'non-excludable' quality of the GPGs. This appears when some states rely on the provision of the GPG by some other states, letting themselves enjoy the benefits of the GPG for free and thus taking a 'free' or 'easy ride'. The second and third problems are the results of two types of failures. Market failure occurs when a market fails to provide the GPG or it provides the GPG in an inadequate manner. A government failure in the provision of GPGs is a failure of global governance. As explained by Kaul, 'GPGs tend to involve policy interdependence among countries, because in most instances no nation, however powerful, can self-provide these goods. They require international cooperation based on a blend of fairness and power politics …'.[12] This failure is exacerbated by the interference of national self-interests in the production of GPGs, which happens when states put their national interests above the global interest and therefore do not make appropriate commitments at the international level. This is identified in literature as a 'jurisdictional gap', that is, the gap among nation-states in charge of making policies within their territories and GPGs with transboundary benefits.[13]

Consequently, an effective international cooperation within the multilevel governance structure is needed.[14] This requires active participation by the authorities at the different levels of governance (local, national, regional and international) in the production of GPGs.[15] In the absence of an adequate

---

11 See Inge Kaul, 'Global Public Goods and Responsible Sovereignty' (*The Broker*, 1 July 2010) <https://www.thebrokeronline.eu/special-report-collective-self-interest/> accessed 21 October 2021.

12 Inge Kaul, 'Global Public Goods: Explaining their Underprovision' (2012) 15(3) JIEL 729.

13 See Inge Kaul, Isabelle Grunberg and Marc Stern (eds), *Global Public Goods: International Cooperation in the 21st Century* (n 6).

14 On the topic of multi-layered or multilevel governance see Thomas Cottier, 'Challenges Ahead in International Economic Law' (1999) 12(1) JIEL 3, 15; Thomas Cottier and Maya Hertig, 'The Prospects of 21st Century Constitutionalism' (2003) 7 *Max Planck Yearbook of United Nations Law* 261; Thomas Cottier, 'Multilayered Governance, Pluralism and Moral Conflict' (2009) 16(2) IJGLS 647; Thomas Cottier, 'Towards a Five Storey House' in C Joerges and E U Petersmann (eds), *Constitutionalism, Multilevel Trade Governance and International Economic Law* (Hart Publishing 2011); E U Petersmann, 'Framework of Analysis: Multilevel Governance' in Thomas Cottier and others (eds), *The Rule of Law in Monetary Affairs* (CUP 2014).

15 Petersmann justifies the application of the multilevel governance theory to the provision of GPGs by stating that: Multilevel governance is a normative necessity for the collective supply of most international public goods. The inadequate regulation of international

international regulatory framework for the provision of GPGs, the role of states as the main providers of such goods becomes more relevant in a multilevel governance context. Therefore, legal doctrine suggests that a state should have an 'intermediary state' role between the national and international interests to address the challenges posed by the underprovision of GPGs.[16] In doing so, some literature suggest that a state should exercise its sovereignty in a responsible manner considering not only the responsibility owed to its own citizens but also assuming the responsibility towards the international community for the external effects of their actions.[17]

Monetary stability, an indisputable national 'public good', has become increasingly globalized and also developed as a GPG for the international community. Michel Camdessus, former managing director of the International Monetary Fund (IMF), argued in 1999 that both the international monetary system and the international financial system should be considered GPGs on the premise that:

> It is essentially the same system for everyone. If it works well, all countries have the opportunity to benefit; if it works badly, all are likely to suffer. Hence, all have an interest in reforms that will improve the system for the global public benefit. And, as is so frequently true for public goods, not many people care for, and even fewer are prepared to pay for, its improvement even if many comment about it.[18]

---

financial markets confirms that collective supply of most international 'aggregate public goods' – like the international monetary system aimed at protecting monetary stability, liberal trade and international freedom of payments – requires going beyond 'realist', 'liberal', 'functional' and 'public choice' strategies by 'embedding' multilevel governance into 'multilevel constitutionalism' protecting rights of citizens, general consumer welfare and transnational rule of law 'bottom up' and justifying international public goods regimes in terms of human rights and domestic constitutional law. Transnational rule of law is essential for the democratic legitimacy, effectiveness and overall coherence of interdependent 'aggregate public goods'.

ibid E U Petersmann, 'Framework of Analysis: Multilevel Governance' 458 (footnote omitted).

16 The 'intermediary state' is a legal doctrine that promotes debate about the role of the states' sovereignty in the new globalized order. See John H Jackson, 'Sovereignty – Modern: A New Approach to an Outdated Concept' (2003) 97(4) AJIL782.

17 See Kaul, 'Global Public Goods and Responsible Sovereignty' (n 11).

18 See Michel Camdessus, 'International Financial and Monetary Stability: A Global Public Good? – Remarks by Michel Camdessus' (IMF/Research Conference, May 28 1999) <https://www.imf.org/en/News/Articles/2015/09/28/04/53/sp052899> accessed 21 October 2021. On monetary and financial stability as global public goods see, *inter alia*, Barry Eichengreen, 'Hegemonic Stability Theories of the International Monetary System' (March 1987) NBER Working Papers No 2193; Ettore Dorrucci and Julie McKay,

Accordingly, it can be argued that international monetary stability has the public good qualities of being non-rivalrous in its enjoyment and providing non-excludable benefits. This consideration was reinforced by events that occurred during the Global Financial Crisis (GFC) – 'The 2007–2010 crisis demonstrated that a coordinated global response was necessary to minimize free riding and negative spillovers and that global institutions should be strengthened and supported'.[19]

The increase in the spillover effects, which originated from decisions taken by the domestic monetary authorities since the beginning of the GFC, is the main example on this point. As remarked by Dorrucci and McKay, 'this neglect of the longer-term impact of domestic policies was one of the root causes of the global financial crisis'.[20] This situation highlighted both market and government failures and the consequent underprovision of the GPG of monetary stability.

As Lastra reminds us, 'It is the existence of market failures and deficiencies that provides the economic rationale for banking regulation'. She also states 'that is why a key aim of regulation is to internalize such externalities'.[21] Hence, it can be argued that the GFC revealed not only the market imperfections with an inadequate domestic regulatory framework to internalize negative externalities but also the absence of an appropriate international regulatory framework to ensure the provision and protection of the GPG of international monetary stability. On this point, Viterbo argues that the consideration of both international financial and monetary stability as GPGs provides 'a powerful way to explain why we need more global regulation and international cooperation to avoid the future occurrence of economic meltdowns and to reap the benefits of globalization'.[22]

'The International Monetary System After the Financial Crisis' (February 2011) 123 ECB Occasional Paper Series and Christian Tietje, 'The Role of Law in Monetary Affairs: Taking Stock' in Thomas Cottier and others (eds), *The Rule of Law in Monetary Affairs* (CUP 2014).

19 Viterbo, *International Economic Law* (n 10) 33.

20 These authors consider that monetary stability as a GPG includes two goods – international currency and external stability. See E Dorrucci and J McKay, 'The International Monetary System After the Financial Crisis' (n 18).

21 Rosa M Lastra, *International Financial and Monetary Law* (2nd edn, OUP 2015) 113.

22 Viterbo, *International Economic Law* (n 10) 10.

2 Common Concern of Humankind – Review of Literature and Evolution of the Principle

Common Concern refers to 'an important shared problem and shared responsibility, and for an issue which reaches beyond the bounds of a single community and state as a subject of international law'.[23] This incipient doctrine promotes Common Concern as a new principle in international law that redefines the responsibilities of states concerning the promotion and protection of GPGs by adding an extra layer of responsibility beyond their jurisdictional domains. Common Concerns and public goods correlate with each other at the different levels of governance but they are not the same. As stated by Cottier:

> The scope of public goods therefore is broader and different from Common Concerns of Humankind, properly speaking. The latter, as a concern, focuses on a number of serious problems threating peace, stability and welfare in the long run where public goods need to be created and protected while appropriate structures to this effect are not yet properly in place.[24]

The nature of problems associated with Common Concerns calls for a collective action response and demands cooperation among states. Under this doctrine, international cooperation among states is the preferred approach to solve the problems associated with Common Concerns, and unilateral lawful action stands as the second best approach.

2.1 *Expression in Treaties and Scholarly Work*

The emerging doctrine of common concern of humankind has its roots in the concept of common interests in the context of the nineteenth century discussions on global commons and the protection of the high seas.[25] Cottier also

23 In this section I rely extensively on Cottier's recent work on the emerging doctrine of Common Concern of Humankind. Cottier, 'The Principle of Common Concern of Humankind' (n 4).

24 Cottier, 'The Principle of Common Concern of Humankind' (n 4) 44.

25 Brunnée considers common concern as part of the doctrine of common interest, Jutta Brunnée 'Common Interest – Echoes from an Empty Shell?' (1989) 49 Heidelberg Journal of International Law 791. Also see, Arvid Pardo and Carl Q Christol, 'The Common Interest: Tension Between the Whole and the Parts' in R Macdonald and D Johnston (eds), *The Structure and Process of International Law* (Martinus Nijhoff Publishers 1993). Others connect the origins of common concern of humankind to the public trust doctrine. Ved P Nanda and William K Ris, Jr, 'The Public Trust Doctrine: a Viable Approach to International Environmental Protection', (1976) 5(2) *Ecology Law Quarterly* 291.

highlights that the notion of common concern of humankind was initially discussed as a response to the concept of common heritage of mankind[26] – avoiding property allocations.[27] While common heritage of mankind proposes to constrain national sovereignty common concern of humankind respects the principle of permanent sovereignty.[28] Common Concern of Humankind as an emerging doctrine and eventually a legal principle does not challenge existing foundations of public international law and aims to fit into the Westphalian system of nation states that is characterised by sovereign equality, the prohibition of use and threat of force and of occupation and appropriation of territory.

The international law discourse referred to this principle generally in connection with the field of environmental law[29] and has recently moved the discussion to the field of international human rights protection in general.[30] Nakavukaren Schefer and Cottier developed the relationship to the emerging responsibility to protect (R2P) in international humanitarian law and suggested that R2P amounts to perhaps the most advanced area of Common Concern, as it not only entails a right, but also an obligation, to act abroad.[31] Cottier considers that *jus cogens* could be conceptualised in terms of a principle of Common Concern of Humankind.[32] Kontolemis presents it as suitable for the case of

26 Kemal Baslar, *The Concept of Common Heritage of Mankind in International Law* (Martinus Nijhoff Publishers 1998); Rüdiger Wolfrum, 'The Principle of Common Heritage of Mankind', (19983) 43 Heidelberg Journal of International Law 312. Judge Cançado Trindade contemplates that common concern of humankind as a derivative concept of common heritage of mankind, A A Conçado Trindade, *International Law for Humankind: Towards a New Jus Gentium* (2nd ed, Martinus Nijhoff Publishers 2013) 344, 348 and 352.

27 Mostafa Tolba, 'The Implications of the "Common Concern of Mankind" Concept on Global Environmental Issues' (1991) 13 Revista Instituto Interamericano de Derechos Humanos 237, 240; Jutta Brunnée, 'Common Areas, Common Heritage and Common Concern' in Daniel Bodansky, Jutta Brunnée and Ellen Hey (eds), *The Oxford Handbook of International Environmental Law* (OUP 2007).

28 Cottier, 'The Principle of Common Concern of Humankind' (n 4) 51.

29 See Laura Horn, 'The Implications of the Concept of Common Concern of a Human Kind on a Human Right to a Healthy Environment' (2004) 1 Macquarie Journal of International and Comparative Environmental Law 233; Thomas Cottier and others, 'The Principle of Common Concern and Climate Change' (2014) 52(3) Archiv des Volkerretchts 293.

30 Charles R Beitz, 'Human Rights as a Common Concern' (2001) 95(2) American Political Science Review 269.

31 Krista Nakavukaren Schefer and Thomas Cottier, 'Responsibility to Protect (R2P) and the Emerging Principle of Common Concern' in Peter Hilpold (ed), *The Responsibility to Protect; A New Paradigm of International Law?* (Brill Nijhoff 2014).

32 Thomas Cottier, 'Improving Compliance: Jus Cogens and International Economic Law' (2015) 46 *Netherlands Yearbook of International Law* 329.

exchange rate policies.[33] Moreover, Cottier and Matteotti explored the limitations imposed on the principle of Common Concern by the disciplines of the law of the World Trade Organisation.[34]

There are references to common concern in international treaty language in relation to climate change (1992 UN Framework Convention on Climate Change and The 2015 Paris Agreement), biodiversity protection (1992 Biodiversity Convention), plant genetic resources (2001 International Treaty on Plant Genetic Resources for Food and Agriculture) and cultural goods in a broad sense (Preamble of the 2003 UNESCO Convention for Safeguarding of the Intangible Cultural Heritage).[35]

The 1992 UN Framework Convention on Climate Change (UNFCCC) states that 'change in the earth's climate and its adverse effects are a common concern of humankind'.[36] The preamble of the 2015 Paris Agreement related the common concern of humankind to human rights and intergenerational equity:[37]

> Acknowledging that climate change is a common concern of humankind, Parties should, when taking action to address climate change, respect, promote and consider their respective obligations on human rights, the right to health, the rights of indigenous peoples, local communities, migrants, children, persons with disabilities and people in vulnerable situations and the right to development, as well as gender equality, empowerment of women and intergenerational equity, …

The 2017 Declaration of Ethical Principles reaffirms climate change as a common concern and recognises the need for a multilevel governance effort:[38]

---

33 Zenon Kontolemis, 'Exchange rates are a matter of common concern: policies in the run-up to the euro?' (No 191 Economic Papers, Directorate-General for Economic and Financial Affairs Publications 2003).

34 Thomas Cottier and Sofya Matteotti, 'International Environmental Law and the Evolving Concept of "Common Concern of Mankind" ' in Thomas Cottier, Olga Nartova and Sadeq Z Bigdeli (eds), *International Trade Regulation and the Mitigation of Climate Change* (CUP 2009) 21.

35 See respectively, United Nations Framework Convention on Climate Change (1992) 31 ILM 849, 851; Adoption of the Paris Agreement (2015) FCCC/CP/2015/L.9/Rev.1, 21; Convention on Biological Diversity (1992) 31 ILM 818, 822; International Treaty on Plant Genetic Resources for Food and Agriculture (2001) 2400 UNTS 303, 379; Convention for the Safeguarding of the Intangible Cultural Heritage (2003) 2368 UNTS 3, 35.

36 United Nations Framework Convention on Climate Change (n 35).

37 Adoption of the Paris Agreement (n 35).

38 Declaration of Ethical Principles in relation to Climate Change (13 November 2017) <http://portal.unesco.org/en/ev.php-URL_ID=49457&URL_DO=DO_TOPIC&URL_SECTION=201.html> accessed 21 October 2021.

> *Also recognizing* that climate change is a common concern for all humankind, and convinced that the global and local challenges of climate change cannot be met without the participation of all people at all levels of society including States, international organizations, sub-national entities, local authorities, indigenous peoples, local communities, the private sector, civil society organizations, and individuals, …

The 1992 Biodiversity Convention also states that 'conservation of biological diversity is a common concern of humankind'.[39] The International Treaty on Plant Genetic Resources for Food and Agriculture affirms 'that plant genetic resources for food and agriculture are a common concern of all countries, in that all countries depend very largely on plant genetic resources for food and agriculture that originated elsewhere'.[40] The term is also used for the preservation of intangible cultural heritage in a broad sense. The preamble of the UNESCO Convention for the Safeguarding of the Intangible Cultural Heritage considers 'the universal will and the common concern to safeguard the intangible cultural heritage of humanity'.[41]

The International Law Commission (ILC) of the United Nations considered common concern of humankind in its debate about the legal protection of the atmosphere. In his second report, rapporteur Shinya Murase described in detail the emerging concept of common concern of humankind and recommended to recognise that the degradation of the atmosphere amounts to a common concern of humankind:

> **Draft Guideline 3: Common concern of humankind**
> The atmosphere is a natural resource essential for sustaining life on Earth, human health and welfare, and aquatic and terrestrial ecosystems, and hence the degradation of atmospheric conditions is a common concern of humankind. [42]

The second report on the protection of the atmosphere is the most extensive official document on common concern within the United Nations, as of today. The rapporteur reviewed extensively the references to common concern of humankind in existing treaties and literature, its connections to common

39 Convention on Biological Diversity (n 35).

40 International Treaty on Plant Genetic Resources for Food and Agriculture (n 35).

41 Convention for the Safeguarding of the Intangible Cultural Heritage (n 35).

42 Shinya Murase, 'Second report on the protection of the atmosphere' (A/CN.4/681, International Law Commission, 67th session, Geneva, 2 March 2015) 25, 49.

heritage, duties to cooperate and community obligations *erga omnes*. He acknowledges the emerging but still undefined status of common concern of humankind and he suggests including degradation of the atmosphere as a common concern of humankind to be promoted and protected.[43]

The suggestion to consider the degradation of the atmosphere as a common concern of humankind was ultimately opposed to by the Commission on the grounds that the concept is not known in the context of degradation of atmospheric conditions and that there is no evidence in state practice and, thus, should not be used.[44] In consequence, reference to common concern of humankind was removed in subsequent discourse on the protection of the atmosphere. On these objections made by the ILC of the UN, Cottier comments that:

> The renewed recognition of common concern of humankind in the 2015 Paris Agreement renders some of the objections made in the ILC obsolete. The problem of lacking precision and undefined and vagueness remains and needs to be addressed. Yet, rejecting common concern as a potential principle for such reasons reflects a strong positivist tradition which ignores the function of the ILC to contribute to the evolution of international law in addressing real life problems of the international community. (…) While some restraint may be justified in terms of a narrowly understood mandate of the ILC, rejecting the concept regrettably is an opportunity missed.[45]

In line with Cottier, this chapter considers that the emerging doctrine of Common Concern bears the potential to develop into a principle of law applicable in a multilevel governance structure and beyond the field of natural resources and environmental law. As stated by French, the emerging doctrine must 'provide normative coherence as to why certain issues are of common concern and some are not' because if not 'there is a real risk that the discussion descends into little more than retrospective realpolitik'.[46]

---

43 ibid 17–25.

44 International Law Commission, 'Provisional summary record of the 3246th meeting' (A/CN.4/SR.3246, 67th Session (first part), 11 January 2016) 4–5.

45 Cottier, 'The Principle of Common Concern of Humankind' (n 4).

46 Duncan French, 'Common concern, common heritage and other global(-ising) concepts: rhetorical devices, legal principles or a fundamental challenge?' in Michael Bowman, Peter Davies and Edward Goodwin (eds), *Research Handbook on Biodiversity and Law*, 344 (EE 2016).

2.2 *Foundations and Evolution of the Principle*

According to the Oxford Dictionary the term *common* not only refers to the ordinary, but also something 'Shared by, coming from, or done by two or more people, groups, or things', or 'Belonging to or involving the whole of a community or the public at large'.[47] The noun *concern* contains a proposition of 'anxiety, worry', but also 'a matter of interest or importance to someone'.[48] As suggested by literature and treaty language, the expression 'common concern of humankind' comprises a shared problem and a shared responsibility for the international community as a subject of international law.

The International Court of Justice (ICJ) in the *Barcelona Traction* case recognised that international law comprises obligations owed to the international community of states as a whole rather than to particular states. In this decision the ICJ consider that the obligations owed to the international community, 'by their very nature … are the concern of all States'.[49] Therefore, the issues categorised as Common Concerns require a 'collective action' response and demand 'international cooperation' among states.[50] In this line Bodansky considers that 'One way of conceptualizing these obligations *erga omnes* is in terms of global public goods: if an obligation primarily relates to the provision of a global public good or the prohibition of a global public bad, then the obligation protects a 'collective' or 'common' interest and should be owed to the international community of states as a whole'.[51]

Common Concern as an emerging principle in international law aims to redefine the responsibilities of the states concerning the promotion and protection of GPGs. Bodansky remarks that 'Although international law does not recognise the category of "global public goods", several international law concepts bear a close relationship to it'.[52] Common Concern is one of the concepts that relates intrinsically to GPGs, but they are not the same. Basically, while

47 'Meaning of common in English' (Lexico) <www.lexico.com/definition/common> accessed 21 October 2021.

48 'Meaning of concern in English' (Lexico) <www.lexico.com/definition/concern> accessed 21 October 2021.

49 *Barcelona Traction, Light and Power Company, Limited,* ICJ Reports 1970, 3, 32.

50 According to Cottier and others, 'The term "collective action problem" describes a situation in which multiple individuals would all benefit from a certain action, which, however, has an associated cost that makes it implausible that any one individual can or will undertake and solve it alone'. See Cottier and others, 'The Principle of Common Concern and Climate Change' (n 29).

51 Daniel Bodansky, 'What's in a Concept? Global Public Goods, International Law, and Legitimacy', (2012) 23(3) EJIL 651.

52 ibid.

Common Concern refers to an unresolved international issue, public goods are non-rivalrous and non-excludable goods. Hence, Common Concern intervenes when there is an underprovision or deficiency of a GPG. Common Concerns are global but also exist at the local and regional levels of governance and correlates with the public goods appropriate at each level. On this point Cottier and others consider that 'Local common concerns call for different answers from global common concerns. What they share is that a problem exceeds a single community and it should ideally be addressed with a cooperative effort. In both cases the law needs to answer the question of what to do if such cooperation fails to materialise'.[53]

The literature on both GPGs and Common Concern recognise that the underprovision of GPGs justifies and triggers the need for international cooperation among states to provide and promote GPGs for the benefit of humanity. However, while recognising that international cooperation among states remains the best outcome to solve the problems associated with Common Concerns, this emerging principle proposes the use of unilateral lawful action as the second best approach in case of failure or absence of cooperation. In this regard, Cottier and others state that 'The principle of Common Concern, understood beyond co-operation, seeks then to delineate obligations to act, and rights to act beyond the scope of territorial application of laws of the nation states. The understanding is informed by the experience gained in trade policy, where unilateral action, or the threat of it, triggered co-operation …'.[54]

Beyond economic and political considerations, it can be stated that the main reason for failure of cooperation at the global level is rooted in the current legal and institutional design of the multilevel system of governance. That is, as mentioned before, powerful sovereign states driven by domestic interests, and soft-law arrangements and weak institutions at the international level. In this context, Common Concern aims to work as a foundation to strengthen international cooperation and also to define and legitimize unilateral domestic measures in the absence of adequate cooperation. On this issue it has been

53 Cottier and others, 'The Principle of Common Concern and Climate Change' (n 29) 293.

54 ibid 321. Kiss sustained that common concern, as a concept provides the basis for the international community to act. However, he pointed out that such right and duty of the international community should be balanced with national sovereignty. Alexandre Kiss, 'The Common Concern of Mankind' (1997) 27 Environmental Policy and Law 244, 246–247. Later on, Shelton argues in the same position as Kiss, Dinah Shelton, 'Common Concern of Humanity' (2009) 5 Iustum Aequum Salutare 33, 38.

argued that states should 'take domestic action as a matter of international law'.[55]

It is in this context that international cooperation within the multilevel governance structure is needed. Common concerns are not restricted to the international level but can also be found at the domestic and regional levels of governance. Hence, the process of claims and responses will determine the level of governance at which the Common Concern in question is better addressed, and the theories relating to multilevel governance provide valuable assistance for such considerations.

These multilevel or multilayered governance doctrines encompass diverse constitutional theories, a human rights based approach, sovereignty concerns and global administrative law considerations.[56] These doctrines aim to contribute to an optimal promotion and protection of public goods at the different levels of governance, which are informed not only by states and international organisations but also non-state actors.[57] Within these doctrines, the 'five storey house' doctrine in particular argues that all levels of governance are of equal relevance but recognises that the international level has a key role to play in the pursuit of GPGs, which include Common Concerns.[58] To complement these multilevel governance doctrines Cottier argues that:

> Common Concern will help refining jurisdiction in matters, which no longer can be dealt with on the basis of strict territorial application of domestic law; it will explore channels of mobilising non-state actor action to resolve Common Concern issues through participation and deliberation in the broader and more transformative sense of reinvention of

---

55 ibid. On this point, Ahmad raised the debate about the co-existence of the duty to cooperate and the unilateral domestic measures. See Zaker Ahmad, 'State Responsibility Aspects of a Common Concern Based Approach to Collective Action' in Samantha Besson (ed), *International Responsibility Essays in Law, History and Philosophy* (Schulthess 2017) 107.

56 For multilevel governance doctrines see: on constitutional theories, Neil Walker, 'The Idea of Constitutional Pluralism' (2002) 65 Modern Law Review 317; Anne Peters 'Compensatory Constitutionalism: The Function and Potential of Fundamental International Norms and Structures' (2006) 19 Leiden Journal of International Law 579; on human rights considerations, Ernst-Ulrich Petersmann, *International Economic Law in the 21st Century: Constitutional Pluralism and Multilevel Governance of Interdependent Public Goods* (Hart Publishing 2012); for the administrative law-based approach, Benedict Kingsbury and others (eds), 'The Emergence of Global Administrative Law' (2005) 68 Law and Contemporary Problems 1.

57 E U Petersmann, 'Framework of Analysis: Multilevel Governance' in Thomas Cottier and others (eds), *The Rule of Law in Monetary Affairs* (n 14).

58 Cottier, 'Towards a Five Storey House' (n 14).

> governance. Yet, states and government continue to play a key role. The multitude of actors does not undermine the structure of multi-layered governance.[59]

It is in this context that the notion of 'cooperative sovereignty', as explained in chapter 2 of this book, also applies. Besson's findings on general sovereignty in correlation to the multilevel governance approach argue that:

> gradually the exercise of sovereignty has turned from an individual exercise into a cooperative enterprise … sovereign political entities can no longer exercise their traditional competences and functions alone … This form of sovereignty triggers duties of cooperation on the part of the entities which cannot ensure the protection of all the values they should protect, as much as on the part of the entities which can help the former to protect those values they share. They should all be seen as working towards the same end: their realization of their shared sovereign values and principles.[60]

These considerations on general sovereignty also apply to monetary sovereignty as there is a correlation among the public good of monetary stability at the different levels of governance that must be protected and promoted on a cooperative manner.

Despite the aforementioned references to Common Concern in treaty language, the normative concept and implications of the emerging doctrine are not yet specified. Cottier, in what can be considered the most extensive and comprehensive work on the concept and emerging doctrine of Common Concern of Humankind acknowledges that:

> Common concern of humankind, so far, has mainly been a source of inspiration. It encourages and stimulates taking up responsibilities and to reflect and to develop appropriate policy instruments in addressing a challenge of magnitude. As a source of inspiration, it assists in developing new forms of cooperation, funding and interaction emerging in state practice and treaty-making. It thus is able to influence, as a powerful message, the evolution of development of international law in the age of globalization facing new types of challenges beyond longstanding threats

59 Cottier, 'The Principle of Common Concern of Humankind' (n 4) 46.

60 Samantha Besson, 'Sovereignty in Conflict' (2004) 8 European Integration Online Papers 13 <https://papers.ssrn.com/abstract=594942> accessed 21 October 2021.

> to international peace and security addressed in the United Nations Charter.[61]

At the same time, Cottier recognises the main objections that may arise in response to the emerging doctrine:

> the notion is devoid of a normative concept and thus part of hortatory treaty language of no legal consequence. It may deploy symbolic and psychological effects. It may stimulate debate and action, emphasizing the seriousness of a problem. Indeed, the description of common concern in the 2015 Paris Agreement encompasses all kinds of inflationary aspirations which render meaning difficult beyond existing normative concepts in public international law. Moreover, it can be easily objected that the scope is limited to specific declarations and treaties calling upon common concern in specific areas of environmental law; it therefore cannot be applied in terms of a general principle. Finally, it may be argued that common concern does, and cannot, not amount to a general principle if law.[62]

This book, while acknowledging the objections to the emerging doctrine of Common Concern, aims to test the value and feasibility of the application of this doctrine to the case of international monetary stability using the special approach proposed by Cottier, detailed below.

Cottier argues that Common Concern may evolve as a legal principle within a process of claims and responses that will determine its contours and normative contents.[63] The differentiation between principles and rules acquires relevance in this process.[64] While rules are specific and apply in a particular context, legal principles aim to provide guidance and directions.[65] Cottier also asserts that the development of Common Concern as an emerging principle may follow the footsteps of the established principles of international law such

---

61 Cottier, 'The Principle of Common Concern of Humankind' (n 4) 26.

62 ibid.

63 ibid 26.

64 Ronald M Dworkin, 'The Model of Rules' (1967) 35(1) The University of Chicago Law Review 14.

65 Robert Kolb, 'Principles as Sources of International Law (With Special Reference to Good Faith)' (2006) 53(1) Netherlands International Law Review; Jan Wouters, Dominic Coppens and Dylan Geraets, 'The Influence of General Principles of Law' in Sanford E Gaines and others (eds), *Liberalising Trade in the EU and the WTO – A Legal Comparison* (Cambridge University Press 2012).

as sovereignty, non-interference and self-determination and that the emerging doctrine can build upon existing legal disciplines and theories such as the traditions of equity, the doctrine of public trust, the doctrine of community interests and the essential function of law and legal principles to preserve peace and stability in society.[66]

International law recognises a state's sovereignty over its internal affairs within its territorial boundaries. Hence, sovereignty is usually defined as the supreme authority of a state within its own territory, only limited by the accepted rules of international public law. This aspect of sovereignty – i.e. the supreme authority in a given territory – derives from the traditional Westphalian concept of sovereignty and it relates to the notion of *equality of states* and the correlative *duty of non-intervention* by any foreign or international powers (unless consented to by the respective state). Hence, Jackson argued that there is an intrinsic connection between the concept of sovereignty and the very foundations and sources of international law. That is to say, that 'no international law norm is valid unless the state has somehow "consented" to it'.[67]

Should Common Concern of Humankind develop as a principle of international law, it would inevitably affect or restrict a state's sovereignty over its affairs in connection to the common concern in question. These limitations to the state's sovereignty may attract some criticisms to the emerging doctrine of Common Concern on the grounds of national sovereignty, self-determination and liberty. However, Cottier remarks that the limitations that the principle of Common Concern may impose on the sovereignty of states will be done on a legal and consensual basis and thus he cannot see the basis for contention on these grounds.[68]

The emerging doctrine of Common Concern of Humankind aims to extend its applicability beyond the field of natural resources and environmental law by laying down the foundations and guidance to be applied across the board for public international law. The most recent studies encompass the application of the emerging doctrine to shared problems in income inequality, the realisation of the core and undeniable essence of human rights, the duty to

66 Cottier, 'The Principle of Common Concern of Humankind' (n 4) 26.

67 John H Jackson 'Sovereignty Modern: A New Approach to an Outdated Concept' (2003) 97 AJIL 786.

68 On this point Cottier considers that: As states need to agree to an emerging principle in treaty law and in the formation of customary law, these principles are respected. It is subject to consent and thus not different from other principles of international law. States are not obliged to sign and ratify treaties relating to Common Concern. They may persistently object to legal recognition in customary law.

Cottier, 'The Principle of Common Concern of Humankind' (n 4) 54.

protect (R2P), the problem of migration, transfer of technology and problems relating to pollution of the high seas.[69]

3 Common Concern of Humankind – Process of Claims and Responses

It is argued that the process of claims and responses in order for an issue to amount to a Common Concern can be initiated both by states and non-state actors in the context of an international forum or organisation that deals with that specific area. Cottier considered that while the role of the Security Council of the United Nations is limited in this process (because it only deals with short term crises), the Group of 20 (G20) should take the lead in the consideration of potential Common Concerns of horizontal nature and, in particular, when they involve economic issues.[70]

The benchmark or threshold for an issue to be considered a Common Concern is a *threat to peace, stability and welfare*. The main reason for having a threshold lies in the reality that not all collective action problems can be considered common concerns. The emerging doctrine aims to contemplate only those problems that, because of their seriousness and magnitude, cannot be solved by states in isolation and demand transboundary cooperation.[71] The recognition of climate change and the loss of biological diversity as common concerns of humankind illustrate the level of seriousness of the issues to be contemplated under this emerging doctrine.

The considerations of peace, stability and welfare derive from the foundations of public international law – that some situations legitimise limitations to the traditional notions of state sovereignty, independence and self-determination. Hence, only problems in the various fields of public international law which potentially threaten peace, stability and welfare can act as the trigger to start the process of claims and responses in order for an issue to be considered a Common Concern of Humankind. Such threats are not limited to classic threats of warfare and aggression but also involve those with potential and disastrous implications such as climate change and loss of biodiversity. Hence, Cottier proposes that 'the threshold should be comparable to, and

69 Cottier, 'The Principle of Common Concern of Humankind' (n 4). This book deals with new collective action problems that may amount to novel common concerns of humankind in different fields of international public law and calls for further work to be done.

70 ibid 42.

71 ibid 39.

commensurate with, the one recognised in international law for threats to peace and security as defined by the UN Security Council and state practice'.[72]

The threat to international peace, stability and welfare does not provide specific criteria. Consequently, the benchmark will act as a trigger to start the process of claims and responses to determine whether a collective action problem is to be considered a Common Concern. The process of claims and responses should be analysed from a three-dimensional perspective. Firstly, enhancing the *duty to cooperate*, consult and negotiate (international cooperation among states). Secondly, providing the basis for *obligations at home* (responsibilities at the state level – homework) delineating not only the rights but also the duties of the states to act beyond the scope of the territorial application of laws in order to comply with international commitments made (extraterritoriality). Thirdly, *securing compliance* with the obligations that emerge from Common Concerns.[73] These three elements are the essence of the potential legal principle of Common Concern of Humankind and go beyond existing rights and obligations under international law.

3.1 *The Duty to Cooperate*

The duty to cooperate, one of the key elements of the emerging doctrine of Common Concern, entails an improved transparency in information sharing and the timely and accurate publication of laws and regulations. This is aimed to increase mutual trust among the actors and intervene in the process of claims and responses. Hence, a principle of Common Concern would entail minimal standards to grant access to information upon request, and to publish relevant information, legislation, practices and precedents. Cooperation to address Common Concerns also involves the duty to consult and to negotiate in order to arrive at an agreement. Inherently, by acknowledging that a matter is a common concern, countries and authorities imply their willingness

72 ibid 39. International peace and security is dealt with by the states and the powers of the Security Council of the United Nations. United Nations, 'Peace and Security' <https://www.un.org/en/our-work/maintain-international-peace-and-security> accessed 21 October 2021.

73 Cottier and others argued that while testing the emerging doctrine of Common Concern to climate change: The concept of Common Concern is intended to cover situations that fall outside the traditional categorization of state responsibility … The concept covers situations of multiple state responsibilities, such as those in which states engage in concerted efforts or those in which states engage in independent actions, whether in breach of an international obligation or not, that cause damage to the environment.

Cottier and others, 'The Principle of Common Concern and Climate Change' (n 29) 315.

and readiness to consult and to negotiate in addressing the transboundary problem.

Cottier recognises that under current international law there is no general duty to cooperate, consult and negotiate but when one of such obligations exists it is usually enshrined in a treaty or based on customary international law. Thus, the emerging principle aims to enhance the duty to cooperate in matters that are considered as Common Concerns of Humankind. Duties to cooperate, consult and negotiate were firstly dealt with in the emerging field of natural resources and international environmental law[74] and recognised specifically by the International Court of Justice in the 1974 *Fisheries Jurisdiction Case* in order to clarify the allocation of marine resources to competing interests.[75] These duties can also be found within the multilateral trading system of the WTO. For example, WTO members are obliged to negotiate within trade rounds under good faith efforts to seek results and agreement. Another example is the obligation for member states, under the universal standards of UN law and the Friendly Relations Declaration, to settle their disputes by peaceful means in line with the prohibition to use or threaten to use force.[76]

Consultation and negotiation will involve discussions on the sharing of burdens and allocation of responsibilities among the actors involved in the specific subject matter to be considered as a Common Concern. On this point Cottier remarks that:

> the recognition of a problem as a Common Concern always entails the basic obligation to make contributions by States commensurate with historical performance in creating the problem at hand, existing levels of GDP and other accepted indices, such as the Global Development Index (GDI), or specific indicators applicable to a particular policy area falling under the principle Common Concern. It strongly depends upon the subject matter.[77]

74 Frederic L Kirgis, *Prior Consultation in International Law* (University Press of Virginia 1983).

75 *Fisheries Jurisdiction (United Kingdom v Iceland)* Merits, Judgement, ICJ Reports 1974 p 3.

76 '2625 (XXV) Declaration on Principles of International Law concerning Friendly Relations and Co-operation Among States in Accordance with the Charter of the United Nations', (United Nations General Assembly, 25th Session, Resolutions Adopted on the Reports of the Sixth Committee,24 October 1970) 121; see Helen Keller, 'Friendly Relations Declaration (1970)', *Max Planck Encyclopedias of Public International Law IV* (2012) 250.

77 Cottier, 'The Principle of Common Concern of Humankind' (n 4) 61. Also, Ahmad elaborates on burden-sharing and differentiated responsibility on issues considered as common concerns of humankind in his case study on the implications of Common Concern on transfer of technology in renewable energy. Zaker Ahmad, 'Trade-Related Measures

He also recalls the principle of shared and differentiated responsibility in climate change adaption and mitigation under the 1992 Framework Convention and the 2015 Paris Agreement as an example of this point.[78]

In addition, Common Concern demands cooperation in the implementation of, and compliance with, international commitments through domestic law and policy. Cottier considers that in doing so:

> Regulatory agencies assigned to comparable tasks in different countries shall exchange information, consult and work together with a view to prepare the ground for regulatory convergence and cooperation and implementation relating to the problem recognised as a Common Concern of Humankind. These activities also prepare the ground to foster co-operation in law enforcement, requiring specific rules to define jurisdiction and powers of authorities and courts of law in engaging in transboundary law-enforcement and recognition of foreign legal acts and judgments.[79]

Consequently, the recognition of a Common Concern in a specified area of international law should come with an advanced level of cooperation entailing mutual assistance by administrative bodies and judicial assistance by legal authorities, and thus eventually achieving legal integration.

3.2 *Obligation to Do Homework*

The emerging doctrine of Common Concern grants a special place to the *obligations at the domestic level* or *obligations to do homework*. The term 'homework' was introduced by the emerging doctrine as a legal denomination to encompass all the obligations that are attached to the principle of Common Concern of Humankind. With recourse to the doctrines of multilevel governance, the issues considered as common concern would engage the appropriate level of governance. Hence, this element encompasses not only the duty to promote and protect the Common Concern at the local level but also the duty to implement international commitments assumed in international agreements and in customary law. Construing international law in accordance with the principles

---

to Spread Low Carbon Technologies: A Common Concern Based Approach', in Thomas Cottier (ed) '*The Prospects of Common Concern of Humankind in International Law*' (n 4).

78 ibid. On shared responsibility see André Nollkaemper, 'Issues of Shared Responsibility before the International Court of Justice' in Eva Rieter and Henri de Waele (eds), *Evolving Principles of International Law; Studies in Honour of Karel C. Wellens* (Martinus Nijhoff Publishers 2012).

79 Cottier, 'The Principle of Common Concern of Humankind' (n 4) 61.

set out in Article 31 of the Vienna Convention on the Law of Treaties, Cottier remarks that the doctrine is not meant to affect the existing obligations under international law but to confer them with the foundations of the emerging principle of Common Concern. That is, encouraging the timely and effective implementation of international commitments and promoting bottom-up initiatives to address the global challenges presented by the Common Concerns.

Beyond the implementation of international commitments, the emerging doctrine aims to inspire autonomous domestic policymaking to address the issues underlying the Common Concerns. As in international law, Common Concern may also influence the interpretation and implementation of domestic law. For example, when international cooperation to safeguard a specific Common Concern is limited, lawful domestic unilateral measures with international effects are encouraged.

As stated in the 1927 Lotus rule[80] and mostly developed in international criminal law and in competition law and policy, extraterritorial jurisdiction of states requires sufficient attachment to the territory of the state. However, it may be difficult to respect such jurisdictional attachment in the case of common concerns. The nature of the problems considered as Common Concerns are in their nature shared, transboundary problems, often of global reach. Hence, as clarified by Cottier:

> Measures adopted in implementing international law obligations or of domestic measures may often deploy effects beyond the boundaries of the particular jurisdiction. International law does not exclude such effects, but seeks a careful balance between the interests of different jurisdiction. States are free to adopt measures having extraterritorial effect unless prohibited by international law.[81]

Common Concern as a principle of international law would not require such territorial linkages but would examine whether the measures and actions are able to support the classification of an issue as a Common Concern, as achieved by the international community during the process of claims and responses.

3.3 *Securing Compliance*

Last but not least, Cottier remarks that the most controversial aspect of the emerging doctrine and principle of Common Concern relates to *securing*

80 *The Case of the S. S. Lotus (France v Turkey)* (1927) PCIJ Series A, No 10. Also see Cedric Ryngaert, *Jurisdiction in International Law* (OUP 2008).

81 Cottier, 'The Principle of Common Concern of Humankind' (n 4).

compliance with the obligations that emerge from Common Concerns.[82] He argues that there is a fundamental difference between the discretionary right of states to act under the existing mechanism of international law of sanctions and countermeasures, and the new obligation to act as suggested by Common Concern. This new obligation to act will apply only to identify Common Concerns within the process of claims and responses and will be subject to the principles of proportionality and accountability.

International law is characterised by voluntary compliance with international obligations. Most of the states comply voluntarily with international obligations as a matter of self-interest.[83] As reciprocal interests are in place, compliance with international law usually does not rely on enforcement mechanisms. However, some areas of international law do not involve reciprocity and, thus, call upon additional disciplines to secure compliance with the obligations in place. It is here that the principle of Common Concern can play a role.

In the absence of reciprocity and mutual benefits, states may opt out and let others assume main responsibilities to produce global public goods. Other than in international trade and investment, which depend on immediate mutual benefits, such reciprocity is lacking in areas such as the issues of climate change, protection of biodiversity and migration. It is also the case in the field of human rights.[84] In order to avoid free-riding, the emerging doctrine of Common Concern calls for the lawful implementation of instruments and incentives supporting international compliance and securing that a recognised Common Concern of Humankind is dealt with in priority in domestic and international processes.

Cottier recalls that these instruments are mainly found in the disciplines of state responsibility in international law. States are entitled to the use of countermeasures, subject to the prerogatives of the UN Security Council under Chapter VII of the UN Charter in response to threats on peace, and to

82 ibid 73.

83 Edith Brown Weiss, 'Rethinking compliance with international law' in Eyal Benvenisti and Moshe Hirsch (eds), *The Impact of International Law on International Cooperation* (CUP 2004); Moshe Hirsch, 'Compliance with international norms in the age of globalization' in Eyal Benvenisti and Moshe Hirsch (eds), *The Impact of International Law on International Cooperation* (CUP 2004).

84 Bogdanova demonstrates that failures to comply with international obligations in the field of international human rights are endemic. Iryna Bogdonava, 'Reshaping the Law of Economic Sanctions for Human Rights Violations: The Potential of Common Concern of Humankind' in Thomas Cottier (ed) '*The Prospects of Common Concern of Humankind in International Law*' (n 4).

mandatory obligations of dispute settlement in the field of international trade regulation. States are entitled to the reestablishment of lawful conditions (*restitutio in integrum*), but usually opt for sanctions or countermeasures (in trade, the withdrawal of market access concessions) in order to remedy the violation and injury suffered.

In order to avoid free-riding and non-compliance, a matter recognised as a Common Concern may require all states involved to take countermeasures. Consequently, the emerging doctrine calls for a multilateral system and appropriate international institutions to secure compliance. On the eventual implications of an accepted principle of Common Concern, Cottier calls for a reform of the United Nations sanction system and a review of the task of the Security Council to collectively address failing states in areas recognised as a Common Concern of Humankind, unless the matter is assigned to specialised international organisation empowered to act against violations of the principle. However, he also recognises that, 'Given the difficulties to achieve such a goal, it remains imperative that individual states, and groups of states, for the time being, remain free to take recourse to unilateral economic measures on behalf of the international community in areas governed by the principle of Common Concern of Humankind'.[85]

In the absence of multilateralism, Common Concern provides the foundations of the *right to act*. That is, the right to act equally on behalf of the international community and the affected states as stated in the still-controversial Article 54 of the ILC draft articles on States' Responsibility.[86] State responsibility is usually invoked to address and remedy harm and injury done by violating international obligations. However, violations of norms relating to Common Concerns may not entail direct injury to other states but rather to the international community at large. Hence, the emerging doctrine reinforces calling upon state responsibility in the case of violation of community norms and call for cessation or assurances of non-repetition in accordance with Article 48(2) of the ILC draft articles on States' Responsibility.[87] Thus, injury and harm are not prerequisites to invoking state responsibility any longer. Therefore, Cottier claims that, 'Enforcing compliance will require large markets with bargaining powers to take action and exert pressures to comply. Smaller countries often

85 Cottier, 'The Principle of Common Concern of Humankind' (n 4) 68.

86 International Law Commission, 'Draft articles on responsibility of States for internationally wrongful acts' (2001) 2(2) *Yearbook of the International Law Commission* 26.

87 ibid. Also see James Crawford, 'State Responsibility', *Max Planck Encyclopedias of Public International Law* <https://opil.ouplaw.com/view/10.1093/law:epil/9780199231690/law-9780199231690-e1093> accessed 21 October 2021.

do not have the leverage, unless measures are taken jointly or within an international organization. Economic and trade sanctions are of utmost importance'.[88] On this point he also recalls that 'actors taking unilateral measures are subject to the rule of law and to the principle of proportionality in shaping countermeasures'.[89]

Beyond the *right to act* under the auspices of the principle of Common Concern of Humankind, the *duty to act* is more controversial. While the right to act is discretional, the duty to act entails an obligation. Hence, it can be acknowledged that despite the notions of state responsibility, *jus cogens* and obligations *erga omnes,* States usually refrain from acting if they are not directly affected by the underprovision of a global public good and, eventually, a Common Concern. Hence, States tend not to assume responsibilities where there is a lack of reciprocity.

In this scenario Cottier reflects on whether the principle of Common Concern should entail a basic *duty to act* in order to promote and protect the areas recognised as a Common Concerns. He considers that the principle should contemplate such obligations to act in light of the existing structural weaknesses of international law. It is suggested that the principle will not trigger automatic action but must consider the principles of proportionality and accountability. If accepted, this principle of Common Concern with its duty to act 'adds a new dimension in general international law calling for a reasoned response to violations of community rights. In many instances, action will not be suitable and possible. But the mere fact that such action needs to considered and options examined renders states accountable towards the principle of Common Concern and thus enhanced compliance with international law'.[90]

Once the normative dimensions that an eventual principle of Common Concern of Humankind may entail (with its three-dimensional elements) are clarified, it is important to consider the role that the principle will play in applying and interpreting law. In this regard, Cottier considers that once the principle is recognised in customary international law and treaty law it offers valuable guidance and informs the interpretation and application of rules on a case-by-case basis. Furthermore, he reflects that the principle informs the decisions of domestic courts in applying international law. Also, if established as a general principle of law, it may be directly applied as a matter of domestic constitutional law, informing the interpretation of legislation and regulations in various and often complex technical fields. This latter function is expected

88 Cottier, 'The Principle of Common Concern of Humankind' (n 4) 70.

89 ibid.

90 ibid 73.

to be important, as domestic courts are likely to play a relevant role in redressing the lack of reciprocity of interests identified, jointly with the influence and impact of non-state actors in the realm of domestic fora in addressing common concerns.[91]

Cottier also emphasises the role of non-state actors in the process of recognition of potential common concerns. The main reason for this is that states are generally reluctant to engage with issues that transcend their jurisdictions or where there is lack of reciprocity among the participants or possible free riders. For non-state actors, he refers in particular not only to political parties and non-governmental organisations, but also to business associations, multinational corporations and the media. All of these actors may have a voice and play an important role in introducing to the public whether or not an issue should be considered as a common concern and thus be dealt with within the process of claims and responses stipulated under the principle of Common Concern of Humankind.[92] Also, Cottier argues that non-state actors can play a role in monitoring whether governments implement and comply with international obligations and, eventually, being entitled to file law suits in domestic courts to assess whether the homework is properly undertaken and whether the basic duty to act and to take appropriate and reasonable measures against failing states is being honoured.[93]

3.4 *Arguments in Support of the Principle of Common Concern of Humankind*

Finally, Cottier considers that a fully-fledged doctrine, and eventually principle, of Common Concern of Humankind will deploy long-term structural effects on international law. It will apply as a legal principle equally within all the layers of governance in order to address shared relevant problems. Cottier also recognises the objections to this doctrine based upon claims of national sovereignty and self-determination. He replies to these claims by providing six arguments that addresses main weaknesses of the doctrine and support the possible recognition of Common Concern of Humankind as a general principle of law:[94]

> ***First***, the principle of Common Concern of Mankind and its obligations and effects is limited to shared, serious problems. It does not apply across

---

91 ibid 78.

92 See Anne Peters and others (eds), *Non-State Actors as Standard Setters* (CUP 2009).

93 Cottier, 'The Principle of Common Concern of Humankind' (n 4) 78.

94 ibid (n 4) 87.

the board. States face enhanced rights and obligations only in areas structurally perilous to peace, stability and welfare. The acceptance of the principle and its extension to particular collective action problems is subject to claims and responses and thus acceptance in treaty law or customary international law. In cannot be unilaterally imposed but is achieved due to persuasion in addressing pressing needs.

Second, the principle of Common Concern of Humankind with its obligations to cooperate, homework, compliance and duties to act addresses the lack of reciprocal interests and free-riding inherent to many collective action problems. It introduces appropriate carrots and sticks to foster mutual interests of states and communities to take up a problem, framing also the roles of non-state actors and courts of law. The costs of abstaining and free-riding exceed the benefits of cooperation.

Third, the principle of Common Concern of Humankind domestically supports governments in taking appropriate measures and in convincing electorates and overcoming populist resistance and nationalism vis-à-vis collective action problems at stake. Recourse to international law obligations to act and accountability structures the debate and facilitates positive outcomes.

Fourth, the principle of Common Concern of Humankind facilitates and supports the adoption of appropriate domestic policy measures. This is of great importance for large markets and powerful states and entities. The extension of extraterritorial application of domestic law pertaining to areas falling under the principle of Common Concern facilitates the adoption of measures and policies which otherwise are opposed due to impending losses of comparative advantage and competitiveness. Such incentives are of paramount importance as the resolution of main collective action problems, in particular climate change, loss of biological diversity, monetary stability, migration, human rights compliance, corporate taxation and benefit shifting (BEPS), essentially depends upon homework undertaken in large markets and how they treat imported products (goods and services) and immigration. Medium and smaller markets and countries tend to follow these policies in securing access to larger markets. It is therefore essential that the principle of Common Concern of Mankind primarily facilitates action by large markets and powerful states in addressing collective action problems.

Fifth, the principle of Common Concern of Humankind does not leave medium and small states powerless once they have agreed to treat a problem under its umbrella. They can form flexible coalitions in supporting the principle and its application of severe problems. They can develop initiatives on the international level at cooperation and harmonization of standards and rules. They can shape appropriate procedures of participation and decision-making in international organizations by adopting majority rulings. They can offset passivity and even resistance by large markets and powers and develop joint leadership under the principle of Common Concern of Humankind.

Sixth, the principle of Common Concern of Humankind is subject to judicial control in international courts and arbitration. Measures taken and having extraterritorial effect, as well as countermeasures and sanctions imposed are subject to the principle of proportionality. They need to pass a necessity test. Should countries, in particular large markets, adopt measures not suitable to address the collective action problem in a conducive manner, such measures can be challenged in court and are subject to single or collective countermeasures.

4 Monetary Stability as a Common Concern of Humankind – A Preliminary Assessment

The current state of affairs of the international monetary system (IMS) together with the problems highlighted by the GFC make a strong case for the consideration of international monetary stability as a Common Concern. As highlighted in chapter 1, the GFC evidenced two central loopholes in the current structure of the IMS: the lack of appropriate global institutions and the lack of adequate international cooperation. Despite the efforts of the international community to tackle these global issues, as the chapter pointed out, the role of public international law in monetary affairs has reached its limits and thus a reconsideration of the role of the states in the pursuit of international monetary stability, through their monetary authorities, is required. In this context, chapter 2 acknowledged that monetary stability, while being an indisputable sovereignty issue, also has an international dimension. Therefore, it is claimed that there is a clear trade-off among the stability objectives at the different levels of governance of the international monetary order. The outcome of this trade-off is the preference of the stability of the domestic and regional orders to the stability of the whole international monetary order.

On this imbalance among international stability, globalisation (or global governance) and national sovereignty, Dani Rodrik in his influential work proposes a return to nation states and national sovereignty as a strong critique on the failures of global governance. Rodrik considers that there is a 'political trilemma of the world economy' by arguing that it is impossible to have at the same time: hyper-globalization (deep economic integration), nation state (national sovereignty) and democratic politics. He considers that we can have at most two out of three. Hence, since democracy cannot be conceded, Rodrik proposes a return to nation states.[95] He reflects that 'global standards and regulations are not just impractical; they are undesirable. The democratic legitimacy constraint ensures that global governance will result in the lowest common denominator, a regime of weak and ineffectual rules'.[96] On the contrary, this book argues elsewhere that the answer to the dichotomy among national laws and global markets is more international laws and international institutions to govern global markets. Indeed, underprovided GPGs, such as international monetary stability, demand enhanced international rules.

Consequently, it can be argued that the process of claims and responses for an issue to amount to a Common Concern, as proposed by the Common Concern doctrine, is a valuable methodological approach to evaluate the problems associated with the provision of monetary stability from a multilevel governance perspective. In order to start the process of claims and responses the threshold of threat to peace, stability and welfare must be fulfilled. In the context of this book, an unstable international monetary system can lead to unrest and breakdowns. This is illustrated by the historical example of the inter-war period, during which the economic breakdown in the Great Depression contributed to the breakdown of international peace and stability. As very clearly remarked by Lastra, the maintenance and promotion of peace, stability and welfare is enshrined in the very foundations of the IMF:

> Drawing on the lessons of history, it was in the context of World War II that countries were ready to make the sacrifices needed in terms of sovereignty by signing a number of international treaties that gave rise to international organizations such as the United Nations, the International Monetary Fund (IMF), and the World Bank. John Maynard Keynes had wisely stated that in order to win the war we needed to 'win the peace'. It was this understanding that also inspired Henry Morgenthau (then US

95 Dani Rodrik, *The Globalization Paradox: Democracy and the Future of the World Economy* (W W Norton & Company 2011) 200.

96 ibid, 204.

> Treasury Secretary) to proclaim in the opening remarks of the Bretton Woods conference in New Hampshire in July 1944 that 'prosperity like peace is indivisible'. Neither Keynes nor Morgenthau were thinking only in territorial/national terms: they were thinking in international terms.[97]

Having reached the threshold for the consideration of international monetary stability as a matter of Common Concern the process of claims and responses should be analysed from a three-dimensional perspective. As described above, it starts with the *duty to cooperate*, consult and negotiate, continuing with the basis for *obligations at home* and ending with *securing compliance* with the obligations that may emerge from the Common Concern of monetary stability. The following three chapters of this book are devoted to the study and analysis of these three dimensions in order to provide an assessment on whether international monetary stability amounts to a Common Concern of Humankind.

Firstly, the emerging doctrine of Common Concern aims to enhance and strengthen the *duty to cooperate* internationally as the best solution to solve the problems associated with Common Concerns. As remarked elsewhere in this book, international cooperation for the pursuit of monetary stability has experienced different periods, from a rule-based and multilateral system during the Bretton Woods period to the bilateral, regional and soft-law based system that we have at present. The powers conferred on the IMF concerning the pursuit of global stability have been limited since the Second Amendment to the Articles of Agreement of the IMF (the Second Amendment). The GFC showed that central banking cooperation works well in a crisis, but its efficacy diminishes when the crisis starts to calm down and independent and uncoordinated responses flourish everywhere.

Consequently, Common Concern, if established as a principle, aims to enhance the duty to cooperate in monetary affairs both from a *top-down approach* and a *bottom-up approach*. While the *top-down approach* relates to the duty to cooperate at the international level of governance with the IMF as the central international monetary institution, the *bottom-up approach* considers cross-border cooperation among countries with a special emphasis on monetary policy coordination among central banks. This first dimension is examined in detail in chapter 4. The chapter starts by providing an analysis of the *top-down approach* with a focus on the key role played by the IMF at the international level of governance and an examination of the core elements of

97 Lastra, 'Do We Need a World Financial Organization?' (2014) 17 JIEL 787.

the IMS. It continues with a study of the *bottom-up approach* giving emphasis to the cases of central banking cooperation.

Secondly, the emerging doctrine of Common Concern promotes the *obligations to do homework* with two levels of commitment: the duty to promote and protect the Common Concern at the local level and the duty to implement international commitments assumed in international agreements and in customary law. For the *first level of commitment*, the pursuit and maintenance of monetary stability as a domestic public good and a local Common Concern is a clear sovereignty attribute and a state defines what is to be considered as monetary stability locally. The pursuit of monetary stability is usually entrusted to an independent central bank or the relevant monetary authority. For the *second level of commitment*, states shall comply with international commitments assumed in international agreements and in customary law.

As detailed elsewhere in this book, since the modifications introduced by the Second Amendment the limits set by international public law on the monetary sovereignty powers of the states are general, non-specific and of a soft-law nature. In consequence, the emerging doctrine aims to encourage autonomous domestic policymaking to cope with the underlying issues related to the Common Concern. That is, to reinforce the role of states as main providers of GPGs not only locally but also globally. In monetary affairs, unilateral actions with extraterritorial effects have proved useful in the pursuit of monetary stability but are limited and temporary in nature. This second dimension of the doctrine is studied in deep in chapters 5 and 6. While chapter 5 deals with the special role of central banks (or relevant monetary authority) as the guardians of monetary stability locally, chapter 6 considers domestic unilateral actions with extraterritorial effects regarding monetary affairs.

Thirdly, the last element of the emerging doctrine of Common Concern relates to *securing compliance* with the obligations that may emerge from the doctrine and eventually principle of Common Concern. These obligations, as laid out in the doctrine of Common Concern, entail an enhanced duty to cooperate globally and the obligations to do homework both within the local jurisdiction and across borders when needed through unilateral lawful measures. As presented elsewhere in this book, the lack of effectiveness of the existing mechanisms of international law to secure compliance with the obligations concerning global monetary stability bring back to the debate the trade-off among the different levels of governance in monetary affairs. This delicate debate about compliance is studied in chapter 6 of this book.

5 Conclusion

The most recent global financial crisis, the GFC, exposed both market and governance failures in the provision and protection of GPGs such as global financial and monetary stability. The market imperfections uncovered the governance failures at the different levels of governance with inadequate domestic regulatory frameworks to internalise negative externalities and also the absence of an appropriate international regulatory framework. As remarked by Shaffer, 'Globalization pressures transform issues that formerly were national in scope into global ones. With globalization, national decision-making increasingly has externalities on outsiders, and it is increasingly insufficient to attain national goals. International law and institutions thus rise in importance'.[98]

This chapter argues that the underprovision of GPGs, in particular international monetary stability, demands a collective action response with increased international cooperation among the different levels in the multilevel governance structure. It also contends that international public law and institutions are fundamental to overcoming collective action problems. However, formal and enforceable international public law in monetary affairs seems to have reached its limits.[99] Consequently, this chapter claims that the emerging doctrine of Common Concern of Humankind offers some valuable guidance and directions for the issues pointed out in this specific case study on global monetary stability. As defined by Cottier:

> Common Concern of Humankind, as a source of inspiration, direction and eventually a legal principle of international law recognised by the international community deploys significant long-term structural effect on international law. It will move it from co-existence and cooperation to integration in the long run. In reality, this blueprint is likely to materialise piece-meal in a gradual process of claims and responses, trial and error. In the long run, it will develop and foster a new understanding of sovereignty of states and the realization of multi-level governance with

---

98 Gregory Shaffer, 'International Law and Global Public Goods in a Legal Pluralist World' (2012) 23(3) EJIL 692.

99 Petersmann argues that 'ineffective protection of public goods is mainly due to a lack of adequate theories, rules, and institutions for overcoming the collective action problems in multilevel governance of interdependent public goods'. Petersmann, 'International Economic Law, "Public Reason", and Multilevel Governance of Interdependent Public Goods' (n 1) 23.

> a view to produce appropriate public goods on appropriate levels of governance.[100]

Accordingly and despite the fact that, at the moment, a reform of the legal and institutional arrangements concerning monetary affairs at the international level with the new obligation to act proposed by Common Concern seems unrealistic, this book aims to be a source of debate and inspiration for academics and policymakers alike in the path to achieve a more prosperous and stable international monetary system with the guidance of the emerging doctrine of Common Concern of Humankind.

100 Cottier, 'The Principle of Common Concern of Humankind' (n 4) 84.

CHAPTER 4

The Duty to Cooperate

The Fund's Role and Cooperation among States

This chapter examines the duty to cooperate internationally as the best solution to solve the problems associated with Common Concerns. Recognising that there is no general duty to cooperate, consult and negotiate under current international law, this duty would apply only to matters that are considered Common Concerns of Humankind. This proposed duty to cooperate under the emerging doctrine of Common Concern would entail an improved transparency in information sharing and the timely and accurate publication of laws and regulations. It would also involve the duty to consult and negotiate to reach a consensus. The discussions will surround the issue of the burden-sharing among parties and the shared but differentiated responsibilities of the actors involved in the specific subject matter.[1]

Concerning monetary affairs and as presented elsewhere in this book, since the collapse of the 'Bretton Woods System'[2] in the 1970's the role of international public law and international institutions is limited. Thus, international cooperation for the pursuit of monetary stability lacks an appropriate international regulatory framework and instead rests on soft governance arrangements and mostly on the good-will of the states to promote monetary policy coordination among the central banks. Consequently, Common Concern if established as a principle, aims to enhance the duty to cooperate in monetary affairs both from a *top-down approach* and a *bottom-up approach.* While the *top-down approach* relates to the duty to cooperate at the international level of governance with the International Monetary Fund (IMF or the Fund) as the central international monetary institution, the *bottom-up approach* considers the cross-border cooperation among countries with a special emphasis on monetary policy coordination among central banks.

1 Thomas Cottier, 'The Principle of Common Concern of Humankind' in Thomas Cottier (ed) '*The Prospects of Common Concern of Humankind in International Law*' (CUP 2021).

2 As described in chapter 1, section 3 of this book.

1 Top-down Approach – International Level of Governance

Notwithstanding the indisputable fact that monetary stability is a sovereignty issue, it also has an international dimension. This global dimension refers to the stability of the international monetary system (IMS) as a whole. According to the Fund's view,[3] the stability of the IMS refers to the stability of the overall system of exchange rates in accordance with the purpose of the Fund as stated in the Article I(iii) of the Articles of Agreement of the International Monetary Fund (Articles of Agreement), that is, 'To promote exchange stability, to maintain orderly exchange arrangements among members, and to avoid competitive exchange depreciation'.[4]

However, the stability of the IMS goes beyond stability of exchange rate agreements. It also depends on the stability of the other key elements of the system. These are, as explained in detail in chapter 1 of this book, the four core elements of the IMS: exchange rates, international payments system, international capital movements, and monetary reserves and access to liquidity. Moreover, the stability of the IMS is intrinsically related to the stability of the international financial system despite them being two different systems.[5] Hence, the international level of governance from a *top-down approach* considers the IMS as being an integral part of the so-called global or international financial architecture (IFA).[6]

---

3 IMF, 'Modernizing the Legal Framework for Surveillance – An Integrated Surveillance Decision' (July 2012) <www.imf.org/external/np/pp/eng/2012/071712.pdf> accessed 21 October 2021.

4 The Articles of Agreement of the International Monetary Fund (Articles of Agreement) were adopted as a result of the United Nations Monetary and Financial Conference, Bretton Woods, held in New Hampshire, United States of America, on 22 July 1944 and were entered into force on 27 December 1945. They were amended on six occasions. IMF, 'Articles of Agreement of the International Monetary Fund' <www.imf.org/external/pubs/ft/aa/> accessed 21 October 2021.

5 Janet Yellen, former chair of the Fed, provides a definition that distinguishes the two systems: The international monetary system is the set of rules, conventions, and institutions associated with monetary policy, official capital flows, and exchange rates. It also includes mechanisms to provide official sector support to countries facing funding pressures. The international financial system is much broader, encompassing both private and official participants in global financial markets.

Janet Yellen, 'Improving the International Monetary and Financial System' (Banque de France International Symposium, Paris, 4 March 2011) <https://www.federalreserve.gov/newsevents/speech/files/yellen20110304a.pdf> accessed 21 October 2021.

6 Christian Tietje, 'The International Financial Architecture as a Legal Order' (2011) 54 German Yearbook of International Law (2011).

Since the breakdown of the 'Bretton Woods' system in the 1970's and the consequent end of the par-value system, the international financial markets experienced a significant expansion. This development was triggered mostly by the liberalisation of finance brought by the elimination of exchange restrictions, the introduction of convertible currencies and the expansion of private capital flows. In this context, between the 1970's and the 1980's, the IFA started to develop with central banks playing a crucial role in the management of the international monetary and financial systems, intergovernmental groups of countries, such as the Group of Ten (G10), taking the lead on political processes and other international bodies issuing international standards to cover the absence of international financial regulation.[7] Most notably, the Basel Committee on Banking Supervision (BCBS) was established after the collapse of several important banks in 1974 (Herstatt Bank in Germany, British-Israel Bank in Tel Aviv and London and Franklin National Bank in New York and London) as one of the leading international financial standard-setting bodies.[8]

Despite the lack of consensus on the notion of IFA, most of the definitions provided by the literature on IFA involve normative and institutional aspects. A first attempt at definition was provided by Mario Giovanoli in 2000: 'This concept is generally understood as encompassing the rules, guidelines, and other arrangements governing international financial relations as well as the various institutions, entities and bodies through which rules, guidelines and other arrangements are developed, monitored and enforced'.[9] Later on, Andrew Crockett reflects in 2010 that the IFA comprise of three interrelated elements: 'first, the basic economic model that governs cross-border monetary and financial relations; second, the institutional structure that exists to

7 For an extended description of the evolution of the IFA see Annamaria Viterbo, *International Economic Law and Monetary Measures: Limitations to States' Sovereignty and Dispute Settlement* (EE 2012) ch 3; Claus D Zimmermann, *A Contemporary Concept of Monetary Sovereignty* (OUP 2013) ch 5; Rosa M Lastra, *International Financial and Monetary Law* (2nd edn, OUP 2015) ch 14.

8 The BCBS, with headquarters at the Bank for International Settlements (BIS) in Basel, Switzerland was established to enhance financial stability by improving the quality of banking supervision worldwide and to serve as a forum for regular cooperation between its member countries on banking supervisory matters. Detailed information on the BCBS is available at its official website <www.bis.org>. On the history and development of the BCBS see Gianni Toniolo, *Central Bank Cooperation at the Bank for International Settlements 1930–1973* (CUP 2005); Charles Goodhart, *The Basel Committee on Banking Supervision: A History of the Early Years 1974–1997* (CUP 2011).

9 Mario Giovanoli, 'A New Architecture for the Global Financial Markets: Legal Aspects of International Financial Standard Setting' in Mario Giovanoli (ed), *International Monetary Law: Issues for the New Millennium* (OUP 2000) 9.

manage and, where necessary, adapt these relations; and third, the distribution of decision making authority in international institutions'.[10] In this chapter I consider both the institutional aspect of the IFA that relates to the governance structure and the main actors that are involved with it and the normative aspect of the IFA that is based on a system of international standard-setting (mostly soft-law).

1.1 *The International Financial Architecture – Governance Aspects*

As noted by Giovanoli, the term international financial architecture or IFA appeared in 1999 as a result of the financial crises experienced during the 1990's.[11] In particular, Giovanoli remarks that the Asian crisis provoked the formation of the Group of 20 (G20)[12] and the Financial Stability Forum (FSF)[13] succeeded later by the Financial Stability Board (FSB) with the aim to coordinate the diverse standard-setting bodies and reduce regulatory and supervisory gaps at domestic levels that may threaten systemic stability. Notwithstanding the international community's efforts to coordinate and harmonise global financial standards within the IFA framework, the global financial crisis of 2007–2009 (GFC)[14] uncovered some serious deficiencies.

As also observed by Giovanoli, these shortcomings revealed by the GFC were not only related to the design and functioning of the international financial system but also to flaws in domestic regulation and supervision.[15] Consequently, a profound restructuring of the IFA was called upon together with a regulatory reform agenda under the purview of the G20. The G20, which was mostly inactive since its creation in 1999 until the onset of the GFC (with the exception of the annual meetings of central bank governors and finance ministers), assumed a key role as the leading forum for international economic

10 Andrew Crockett, 'What Have We Learned in the Past 50 Years about the International Financial Architecture?' (Reserve Bank of Australia 50th Anniversary Symposium, Sydney, February 2010) <www.rba.gov.au/publications/confs/2010/pdf/crockett.pdf> accessed 21 October 2021.

11 Mario Giovanoli, 'The International Financial Architecture and its Reform After the Global Financial Crisis' in Mario Giovanoli and Diego Devos (eds), *International Monetary and Financial Law: The Global Crisis* (OUP 2010) 3.

12 For more information about the G20 visit the official website at <https://g20.org/en/summit/about/> accessed 21 October 2021.

13 Visit the FSB website for comprehensive details of the history and functioning of the body <www.fsb.org/about/> accessed 21 October 2021.

14 See Rosa M Lastra and Geoffrey Wood, 'The Crisis of 2007–2009: Nature, Causes, and Reactions' (2012) 13 JIEL 531.

15 Giovanoli, 'The International Financial Architecture' (n 11).

cooperation, directed by the decisions taken during the 'Leaders' Summits' held in November 2008 (Washington Summit) and April 2009 (London Summit).

At the Washington Summit of November 2008 the G20 Leaders designed an action plan with the view to implement the five agreed principles for the reform of the IFA. Those principles are: strengthening transparency and accountability, enhancing sound regulation, promoting integrity in financial markets, reinforcing international cooperation and reforming international financial institutions.[16] The London Summit of April 2009 gave a boost to the IFA reform by strengthening the international financial institutions, particularly by increasing the resources available to the IMF and establishing a new FSB with a strengthened mandate, as a successor to the FSF.[17] These 'Leaders' Summits' continue to be held on an annual basis (with two meetings held during 2009 and 2010). Most of the financial regulatory and supervisory reforms endorsed by the G20 at its various Leaders' Summits have been extensively analysed and covered by the existing literature.[18] Hence, this chapter does not observe those initiatives and only examines the governance and normative aspects of the IFA.

The main actors in the reformed IFA have been categorised by Lastra in two big groups.[19] On the one hand 'formal' international organisations and on the other hand 'informal' international groupings. Under the first category there are international financial institutions formally recognised by treaty, including both multilateral organisations and regional institutions and also international forums that meet under the aegis of any of these formal organisations (like the FSB and the BCBS under the auspices of the BIS in Switzerland). The key multilateral organisations under the IFA are: the IMF, the World Bank Group, the BIS, the Organisation for Economic Co-operation and Development

16 Group of 20, 'Declaration Summit on Financial Markets and the World Economy' (15 November 2008) <www.mofa.go.jp/policy/economy/g20_summit/2008/declaration.pdf#action> accessed 21 October 2021. Viterbo observed that 'Many of the measures identified by the G20 as necessary to overcome the crisis – and prevent contagion – were implemented at national level and financed by government budgets'. Viterbo, *International Economic Law* (n 7) 113–114.

17 Group of 20, 'London Summit – Leaders' Statement' (2 April 2009) <www.mofa.go.jp/policy/economy/g20_summit/2009-1/communique.pdf> accessed 21 October 2021.

18 Charles Goodhart, *The Regulatory Response to the Financial Crisis* (EE 2009); Mario Giovanoli and Diego Devos (eds) *International Monetary and Financial Law: The Global Crisis* (OUP 2010); Thomas Cottier, John H Jackson and Rosa M Lastra (eds), *International Law in Financial Regulation and Monetary Affairs* (OUP 2010); Dirk Schoenmaker, *Governance of International Banking: The Financial Trilemma* (OUP 2013); Thomas Cottier and others (eds), *The Rule of Law in Monetary Affairs* (CUP 2014).

19 Rosa M Lastra, *International Financial and Monetary Law* (n 7) 543–544.

(OECD) and the World Trade Organization (WTO). The regional institutions comprise an array of diverse institutions such as the regional development banks (European Bank for Reconstruction and Development, Inter-American Development Bank, African Development Bank, Asian Development Bank) and other supranational institutions at the European and worldwide level. In the second category of 'informal' international groupings dealing with global financial and economic matters there are de facto groupings created by governments (like the Group of 7, Group of 10, G20), national central banks, finance ministers or treasuries meeting through their representatives in diverse formal or informal groupings and private financial institutions performing at a global level.

Adopting the comprehensive categorisation provided by Lastra, it can be stated, in line with Giovanoli's view, that the current IFA is led by three predominant and distinct entities: the IMF, the G20 and the FSB, as illustrated by the graphic attached as Annex 1 to this chapter.[20] These three entities are different in their membership, mission and legal status.

The IMF, created in 1945, is an international organisation with almost universal membership (190 countries as of March 2021). The Fund's main purpose is to ensure the stability of the international monetary system and since 2012, when its mandate was updated, it also considers macroeconomic and financial sector issues that bear on global stability. The key functions of the Fund are surveillance, conditional financial assistance and technical assistance. It's based on a system of quotas and the resources are mainly provided by its members.[21]

The G20, launched in 1999, is an informal political forum composed of 19 member states and the European Union. The purpose of the forum is to strengthen international economic cooperation among members while overseeing the overall functioning of the IFA. The G20 is supported by international organisations, including the FSB, the IMF, the International Labour Organisation, the OECD, the United Nations, the World Bank and the WTO.[22]

20 Brummer makes a differentiation among agenda-setters (G20 and FSB), sectoral and specialist standard-setters (BCS, IOSCO and OECD, among others) and the entities that monitor the system and compliance with the standards (IMF and the World Bank). Chris Brummer, *Soft Law and the Global Financial System – Rule Making in the 21st Century* (CUP 2015) 69.

21 For detailed information about the Fund see 'About the IMF' <www.imf.org/en/About> accessed 21 October 2021.

22 For more information about the G20 see 'What is the G20 Summit?' <https://g20.org/en/summit/about/> accessed 21 October 2021.

The G20 Finance Ministers and Central Bank Governors created in April 2017 the G20 Eminent Persons Group on Global Financial Governance (the 'EPG').[23] The work of the EPG is centered around the following tasks: (1) to review current and possible future challenges and opportunities facing the international financial and monetary systems, and the current state of the global financial architecture and governance; (2) to consider the optimal role of the IFIs; and (3) to recommend practical reforms to improve the functioning of the global financial architecture and governance so as to promote economic stability and sustainable growth. The EPG will provide its findings and recommendations to G20 Finance Ministers and Central Bank Governors for their deliberation.

The FSB, established in 2009 as the successor to the FSF, is an international body that monitors and makes recommendations about the global financial system. Its membership comprises 24 countries, the European Union, international financial institutions (IFIs) and standard-setting bodies. The FSB promotes international financial stability; it does so by coordinating national financial authorities and international standard-setting bodies as they work toward developing strong regulatory, supervisory and other financial sector policies.[24]

The improvements in the governance aspects of the IFA since the GFC have no doubt enhanced the institutional foundations.[25] Notwithstanding that, it can be argued that the present IFA is based on the 'horizontal' cooperation of domestic regulators under the guidance of the G20, as opposed to the institutional 'vertical' process of treaty-based international organisations. As pointed out by Viterbo, 'As the time was not ripe for a new multilateral agreement or for a swift reform leading to a greater role of the IMF in the financial sector, the strategy adopted was the reinforcement of the GFA, building on the existing structure'.[26] Consequently, some major challenges concerning the institutional legitimacy of the entities involved in the process of international

23 The EPG comprises eminent persons with deep knowledge and experience in the area of the global financial architecture and governance. For more information on the EPG see, <https://www.globalfinancialgovernance.org/about-g20-epg/> accessed 21 October 2021.

24 For more details about the FSB see 'About the FSB' <www.fsb.org/about/> accessed 21 October 2021. See also the recent paper by de Stefano who argues in favour of a further institutionalisation of the FSB Carlo de Stefano, 'Reforming the Governance of International Financial Law in the Era of Post-Globalization' (2017) 20(3) JIEL 509.

25 For a description about the improvements in the institutional aspects of the IFA in the aftermath of the GFC see Zimmermann, *Monetary Sovereignty* (n 7) 191.

26 Viterbo, *International Economic Law* (n 7) 112.

financial standard setting (IFSs) and the limits of the soft-law approach in IFSs remained unsolved.[27]

1.2 *The Fund's Role*

The regulatory function in global monetary affairs is shared by a number of formal and informal international standard-setters, including most notably the FSB and BIS as detailed in the previous section. However, this chapter asserts that the IMF maintains its lead as the central international monetary institution and is also at the centre of the IFA.[28] The role of the IMF has changed since its origin, as pointed out by Lastra, 'Over the last few decades, the IMF's mandate has been broadened: from being primarily an international monetary institution to becoming an international financial institution, encompassing not only monetary issues but also other financial issues (capital markets, payment systems, etc)'.[29]

As part of the IFA reforms prompted by the GFC, the IMF members introduced two ambitious packages on the Fund's existing quotas and governance in 2008 and 2010.[30] The IMF is a quota-based institution where each member is assigned a quota representing its position on the world economy and such quota determines the members' voting power, financial commitment to the Fund and access to IMF financing.[31] The quotas are denominated in Special Drawing Rights (SDRs) as the unit of account. These far-reaching reforms aimed at enhancing the Fund's role in the promotion of global financial stability gave more influence to emerging and developing economies while also

---

27 Mario Giovanoli, 'The International Monetary and Financial Architecture – Some Institutional Aspects' in Thomas Cottier and others (eds), *The Rule of Law in Monetary Affairs* (CUP 2014) 45.

28 As remarked by Zimmermann, 'Under the impact of the Global Financial Crisis, the Fund has finally come to realize that it is not possible to durably secure the stability of the international monetary system without also looking after the stability of the international financial system more broadly'. Zimmermann, *Monetary Sovereignty* (n 7) 217.

29 Lastra, *International Financial and Monetary Law* (n 7) 497.

30 The 2008 quota and voice reforms were approved on 28 April 2008 by the IMF Board of Governors and entered into force on March 2011. The 2010 reform package resulted from the 14th General Review of Quotas and was approved by the IMF Board of Governors on 15 December 2010. For detailed and updated information on these reforms see 'IMF Quota and Governance Publications' <www.imf.org/external/np/fin/quotas/pubs/index.htm> accessed 21 October 2021.

31 The current quota formula is a weighted average of GDP (weight of 50 percent), openness (30 percent), economic variability (15 percent) and international reserves (5 percent). 'IMF Quotas' (4 March 2021) <www.imf.org/en/About/Factsheets/Sheets/2016/07/14/12/21/IMF-Quotas> accessed 21 October 2021.

preserving and enhancing the voice and participation of low-income countries. As remarked by Zimmermann, 'the major overhaul of IMF governance aimed at increasing the organization's credibility, legitimacy and effectiveness'.[32]

The entry into force of the Second Amendment to the Articles of Agreement in 1978 (Second Amendment)[33] represents an inflection point from a rule-based system monitoring the 'par value' regime to a surveillance-based function.[34] The Fund's main functions in relation to its members are established in the Articles of Agreement as surveillance (Article IV), financial assistance (Article V, Section 3) and technical assistance (Article V, Section 2(b)). While obligations relating to IMF's surveillance function are of a mandatory nature for all IMF members, obligations relating to financial assistance and technical assistance have a voluntary nature and are performed by the Fund only upon the member's request.[35]

The *surveillance function* is at the centre of the Fund's operations and provides the post Second Amendment *raison d'etre* of the IMF.[36] This function enables the IMF to monitor compliance with standards and rules and to provide incentives for member states to comply with such standards and rules (through the design of conditionality policies).[37] The legal basis of surveillance set forth in Article IV, sections 1 and 3 provides both obligations upon members and specific powers to the Fund to oversee and monitor the member's compliance with its obligations. In order to provide clear guidance on the surveillance

---

32 Zimmermann, *Monetary Sovereignty* (n 7) 227.

33 The Second Amendment to the Articles of Agreement came into effect on 1 April 1978, by the modifications approved by the Board of Governors in Resolution No. 31–4.

34 According to Guitián this surveillance-based function of the IMF is discretionary and thus judgement is of the essence. However, he also remarks that the discretion is limited by the code of conduct enshrined in the Articles of Agreement. Manuel Guitián, 'The Unique Nature of the Responsibilities of the International Monetary Fund' (1992) Pamphlet Series No 46 <https://imf.org/external/pubs/ft/pam/pam46/pam46con.htm> accessed 21 October 2021.

35 Moreover, as argued in chapter 6 of this book, the main obligations of the IMF member states under the amended Articles of Agreement are considered of 'soft' nature and would only require the 'best efforts' of the members with the exception of Article IV, Section 1(iii) regarding exchange rate manipulation.

36 IMF, The Fund's Mandate – An Overview (22 January 2010) <http://www.imf.org/external/np/pp/eng/2010/012210a.pdf> accessed 21 October 2021; IMF, The Fund's Mandate – The Legal Framework (22 February 2010) <http://imf.org/external/np/pp/eng/2010/022210.pdf> accessed 21 October 2021.

37 Conditionality only applies to IMF member states that request for financial assistance from the Fund. 'IMF Conditionality' (2021) <www.imf.org/en/About/Factsheets/Sheets/2016/08/02/21/28/IMF-Conditionality> accessed 21 October 2021.

policies the Fund adopted specific principles of surveillance in a decision of April 1977, as replaced by a new decision of June 2007.[38]

Also, beyond bilateral surveillance performed by individual countries, the IMF performs multilateral surveillance of the global economy, thus helping to identify the impact domestic policies may have on other countries and the global economy.[39] Consequently, a new decision on bilateral and multilateral surveillance was adopted in July 2012.[40] This new decision maintains the key principles of the 2007 decision on bilateral surveillance and adopts new principles for multilateral surveillance. As stated by Viterbo 'As monetary and financial stability are inextricably intertwined, the IMF is perfectly equipped to monitor "holistically" its members' macroeconomic and macrofinancial policies, as well as their linkages and implications for global stability'.[41]

The surveillance of rules and standards is done via consultations in accordance with Article IV of the Articles of Agreement, the Financial Sector Assessment Program (FSAP) and the Reports on the Observance of Standards and Codes (ROSCs).[42] The FSAP comprises a profound analysis of a country's financial sector and is the joint responsibility of the IMF and World Bank in developing economies and emerging markets and the sole responsibility of IMF in advanced economies.[43] ROSCs are a crucial part of the FSAP because they summarise the extent to which countries observe certain internationally-recognised standards and codes.[44] As pointed out by Lastra, both FSAP and

38 Decision of the Executive Board No 5392-(77/63) of 29 April 1977 as replaced by the Decision of the Executive Board of 15 June 2007. See 'Bilateral Surveillance over Members' Policies' (21 June 2007) <www.imf.org/en/News/Articles/2015/09/28/04/53/pn0769#decision> accessed 21 October 2021.

39 'IMF Surveillance' (2021) <www.imf.org/en/About/Factsheets/IMF-Surveillance> accessed 21 October 2021.

40 IMF, 'Modernizing the Legal Framework for Surveillance' (n 3). The 2012 Integrated Surveillance Decision has been reviewed and further developed as part of the 2014 Triennial Surveillance Review (TSR) and the 2018 Interim Surveillance Review (ISR), and will be again comprehensively assessed in 2020 as part of the Comprehensive Surveillance Review (CSR). 'IMF Surveillance' (2021) <www.imf.org/en/About/Factsheets/IMF-Surveillance> accessed 21 October 2021.

41 Viterbo, *International Economic Law* (n 7) 112.

42 For a detailed study on IMF surveillance see Nadia Rendak, 'Monitoring and Surveillance of the International Monetary System: What can be learnt from the trade field?' in Thomas Cottier and others (eds), *The Rule of Law in Monetary Affairs* (CUP 2014) 204.

43 'Financial Sector Assessment Program (FSAP)' (2021) <www.imf.org/en/About/Factsheets/Sheets/2016/08/01/16/14/Financial-Sector-Assessment-Program> accessed 21 October 2021.

44 The IMF has recognised 12 areas and associated standards as useful for the operational work of the Fund and the World Bank. These comprise accounting; auditing; anti-money laundering and countering the financing of terrorism (AML/CFT); banking supervision;

ROSCs are performed as part of the technical assistance functions of the Fund with the purpose of informing its surveillance function.[45] These activities are voluntary with the exception of those jurisdictions considered systemically important based on the size and interconnectedness of their financial sectors.[46] According to the latest annual report to the G20 on the implementation and effects of reforms issued by the FSB in November 2018, all of FSB's jurisdictions have now published their financial system stability assessment reports and the results of their standards compliance assessments in FSAPs.[47]

The second main function of the Fund, *financial assistance*, is performed through the provision of financing to countries with balance of payments difficulties upon their request.[48] The aim is to provide temporary financing and to support policies aimed at correcting underlying problems. The IMF's various lending instruments are custom-made to different types of balance of payments problems as well as the specific conditions of its different members. The Fund's lending usually requires a country's commitment to undertake certain policy actions, known as policy conditionality. Lending to low-income countries are particularly directed at poverty reduction.[49]

The third key function performed by the Fund is the provision of *technical assistance* to its members upon their request. The aim is for the Fund to work jointly with the members in order to fortify their economic institutions by offering technical assistance and training on crucial economic issues, such as public financial management, tax policy and administration, banking supervision, monetary and exchange rate policy, official statistics and legal issues.

---

corporate governance; data dissemination; fiscal transparency; insolvency and creditor rights; insurance supervision; monetary and financial policy transparency; payments systems; and securities regulation. 'Reports on the Observance of Standards and Codes (ROSCs)' (21 June 2019) <https://www.imf.org/external/NP/rosc/rosc.aspx> accessed 21 October 2021.

45 Lastra, *International Financial and Monetary Law* (n 7) 462.

46 In December 2013, the IMF's Executive Board revised the methodology for determining jurisdictions with systemically important financial sectors and its application led to an increase in the number of systemically important jurisdictions to 29. 'Financial Sector Assessment Programme', n (43).

47 FSB, 'Implementation and Effects of the G20 Financial Regulatory Reforms: Fourth Annual Report' (28 November 2018) <www.fsb.org/2018/11/implementation-and-effects-of-the-g20-financial-regulatory-reforms-fourth-annual-report/> accessed 21 October 2021.

48 'IMF Lending' (2021) <www.imf.org/en/About/Factsheets/IMF-Lending> accessed 21 October 2021.

49 For a detailed description on the Fund's conditional financial assistance see Lastra, *International Financial and Monetary Law* (n 7) 463–482.

The Fund's recommendations in these aspects are contained in technical assistance reports at the request of the members.[50]

1.3 *International Standard-Setting and Soft Law*

As stated above, the normative aspect of the IFA is based on a system of IFSs that is mostly based on soft-law arrangements. The so-called 'soft law' are rules or standards characterised as informal, voluntary and non-enforceable. Soft law usually emerges to fill regulatory 'gaps' but it cannot replace the named 'hard law' or formal law. Hard law, as opposed to soft law, is characterised as being formal, externally imposed and enforceable.[51] In an interesting and detailed article written by Shaffer and Pollack the authors explored how hard and soft law interact under different conditions and observed that existing literature on the topic can be sorted by the three main theories: legal positivist, rationalist and constructivist.[52] They remarked that:

> Legal positivists tend to favor hard law and view hard and soft law in binary terms. For them, hard law refers to legal obligations of a formally binding nature, while soft law refers to those that are not formally binding but may nonetheless lead to binding hard law. Rationalists, in contrast, contend that hard and soft law have distinct attributes that states choose for different contexts. They also find that hard and soft law, in light of these different attributes, can build upon each other. Constructivists maintain that state interests are formed through socialization processes of interstate interaction which hard and soft law can facilitate. Constructivists often favor soft-law instruments for their capacity to generate shared norms and a sense of common purpose and identity, without the constraints raised by concerns over potential litigation.[53]

---

50 'IMF Capacity Development' (2021) <www.imf.org/en/About/Factsheets/imf-capacity-development> accessed 21 October 2021.

51 Eilis Ferran and Kern Alexander, 'Can Soft Law Bodies be Effective? The Special Case of the European Systemic Risk Board' (2010) 35(6) European Law Review 751; Chris Brummer, 'Why Soft Law Dominates International Finance – and not Trade' in Thomas Cottier and others (eds), *International Law in Financial Regulation and Monetary Affairs* (OUP 2010); Chris Bummer, *Soft Law and the Global Financial System – Rule Making in the 21st Century* (CUP 2011).

52 Gregory C Shaffer and Mark A Pollack, 'Hard vs. Soft Law: Alternatives, Complements, and Antagonists in International Governance' (2010) 94 Minn L Rev 706.

53 ibid 707.

According to this categorisation it can be argued that the emerging principle of Common Concern favours a rationalist approach to the interaction between hard law and soft law, with the view to complement each other in the development of international law. The authors also highlight that the rationalist scholars acknowledge the main advantages and disadvantages of the use of hard and soft law as alternatives from an institutional view point.[54] Briefly, they argued that hard-law instruments make state commitments more credible because they can have direct legal effects in national jurisdictions or they can require domestic legal action. Also, hard law instruments allow states to monitor and enforce their commitments, including through the use of dispute-settlement bodies such as courts. However, rationalists also recognise that hard law agreements involve significant costs and are less flexible to adapt to changing circumstances. Moreover, they noted that hard law formal commitments may restrict the behaviour of states and infringe on their sovereignty in sensitive areas such as money and finance. In respect of soft law instruments, rationalists consider that they are easier and less costly to negotiate and impose less sovereignty costs on states in sensitive areas. Also, these instruments provide greater flexibility and allow states to engage in enhanced cooperation without worrying about enforcement.

Notwithstanding the above-mentioned advantages of the institutional use of soft law instruments, it is still a contended subject for legal and international relations scholars. Consequently, in this specific case study there are still some major challenges concerning the institutional legitimacy of the entities involved in the process of IFSs and the limits of the soft-law approach in IFSs that remain unsolved.[55] As remarked by Brummer, 'Yet perhaps the most difficult challenge derives from the fact that the production of international financial law departs from the classical model of public diplomacy embodied by formal "international organizations" '.[56] That is, international financial standards are issued mostly by informal international groupings created under informal by-laws, agreements or declarations. These arrangements provide efficiency and flexibility but they are unable to create international commitments or formal legal obligations in the traditional sense unless they are incorporated into domestic legislation and turned into legally binding rules. The implementation of the IFSs are actively promoted both by market incentives and official incentives (e.g. peer pressure, ROSCs, FSAPs).[57]

54 ibid 717.

55 Mario Giovanoli, 'The International Monetary and Financial Architecture' (n 27) 45.

56 Brummer, *Soft Law and the Global Financial System* (n 20) 63.

57 Mario Giovanoli, 'The International Monetary and Financial Architecture' (n 27) 65.

Brummer classifies these soft-law instruments in three categories: best practices, regulatory reports and observations, information sharing and enforcement cooperation agreements.[58] He considers that best practices usually acquire the form of 'core principles' or 'codes of conduct' in order to provide the minimum standards to be achieved on specific financial issues considering the diversity of markets and regulatory authorities involved. Main examples of soft-law instruments in this category are the core principles issued by the International Organisation of Securities Commissions (IOSCO) on securities regulation and the BCBS for banking. On regulatory reports and observations Brummer points out that they are used by local and global regulators to collect data and produce assessments that may influence the course of policy making in financial and monetary law. Key examples are the reports produced by international organisations and relevant global experts during the GFC, such as the IMF report issued in February 2009 concerning financial sector regulation and supervision and central bank liquidity management titled 'Lessons of the Financial Crisis for Future Regulation of Financial Institutions and Markets and for Liquidity Management'[59] and the so-called 'Rapport Camdessus'[60] issued in February 2011 by a group of worldwide leading economists focused on international monetary stability. On information sharing agreements Brummer highlights that they mostly take the form of memoranda of understanding to promote better international coordination among domestic regulators to improve the surveillance of globally active domestic institutions. Concerning enforcement cooperation agreements he notes that they are also usually with the form of memoranda of understanding to address the terms under which countries assist each other while enforcing domestic obligations overseas. Main examples of this category of soft-law instruments are linked to banking and securities regulatory issues.

Giovanoli provides an analysis of the issues concerning the legitimacy or representativity of the IFA institutions on a case by case basis.[61] He pointed out that while both the IMF and the World Bank have almost universal

58 Brummer, *Soft Law and the Global Financial System* (n 20) 121.

59 IMF, 'Lessons of the Financial Crisis for Future Regulation of Financial Institutions and Markets and for Liquidity Management' (4 February 2009) <www.imf.org/en/Publications/Policy-Papers/Issues/2016/12/31/Lessons-of-the-Financial-Crisis-for-Future-Regulation-of-Financial-Institutions-and-Markets-PP4316> accessed 21 October 2021.

60 Palais-Royal Initiative, 'Reform of the International Monetary System: A Cooperative Approach for the Twenty First Century' (8 February 2011) <http://global-currencies.org/smi/gb/telechar/news/Rapport_Camdessus-integral.pdf> accessed 21 October 2021 (the 'Rapport Camdessus').

61 ibid 55.

membership, it is not in the case of the BIS, which has a membership of 45 members from 28 jurisdictions (consisting of central banks and authorities with formal responsibility for the supervision of banking business), the G20, which comprises of 19 individual countries plus the European Union, and the FSB, which consists of 68 member institutions from 25 jurisdictions (comprising ministries of finance, central banks, and supervisory and regulatory authorities) and also 10 international organisations and standard-setting bodies and 6 regional consultative groups.

As a result, Giovanoli considers that there is no legitimacy problem for the BIS because its role in the standard-setting process is limited to initiating, hosting and financing some of the standard-setting bodies such as BCBS and the FSB and is not involved in the process itself. The issue is more complex for the G20 because of its informal nature as a political steering group without a legal mandate. However, Giovanoli invokes the argument that the G20 represents around 85 percent of the world gross domestic product and involves over two-thirds of the global population which gives it a powerful informal role in the conduct of the IFA. Concerning the FSB, the membership was expanded in 2009 and as a result it includes more emerging economies. Yet, it can be argued that for both the G20 and the FSB there is still an issue of selective and restrictive membership.

The decision-making in the standard-setting process of IFSs is usually based on general consensus which has been highly successful because it lends credibility to the decision and ensures acceptance of the standards.[62] Notwithstanding that, Giovanoli remarks that this successful decision-making approach has also raised an issue of transparency because the arrival at such consensus outcome involves a degree of confidentiality that prevents an open debate. That said, he also points out that this issue has been mitigated with the implementation of wide consultation process.[63]

To sum up, the soft law instruments in the form of IFSs have been a key success in the development of a more robust and resilient international order in monetary and financial law. However, the above-mentioned shortcomings on legitimacy and transparency surrounding the standard-setting process are not fully addressed yet. In concordance, Giovanoli affirms that:

62 The decision-making process, both at the IMF and the World Bank, follows the principle of weighted voting power. That is, an objective system of quotas based on the economic power of each member. ibid 55.

63 ibid 58.

without minimising the contribution of IFSs to international financial stability, it is important to recognise their limits: they are not a talisman warding off international financial crises and are certainly not a substitute for the prudent behaviour of all stakeholders, including not only financial institutions and their regulators, but also monetary authorities and politicians, acting with a view to preventing excessive credits or over-indebtedness leading to dangerous bubbles.[64]

2 Bottom-up Approach – Central Banking Cooperation

This section studies cross-border cooperation among countries from a *bottom-up approach* with a special emphasis on monetary policy coordination and cooperation among central banks. Cross-border central banking cooperation is not a new phenomenon and it relates back to the late nineteenth and early twentieth centuries.[65] Hence, this section starts by examining the evolution of central banking cooperation through history. Then it continues with a description of the main examples of effective central bank involvement in international coordination since the collapse of the Bretton Woods system and ends with an analysis of the responses provided by central banks during and after the GFC up to date.

2.1 *The Evolution of Central Banking Cooperation*

The evolution of this type of international cooperation has been intrinsically linked with the development of the international monetary and financial systems and the recurrent economic and financial crises throughout history that have acted as catalysts for change. Also, central banking cooperation has been strongly influenced by the evolving notion or conception of monetary stability and financial stability both domestically and globally. That is, monetary stability and financial stability are not only considered as key domestic public goods but also as desired global public goods as discussed in chapter 3 of this book.

In this regard, Borio and Toniolo remarked in 2006 that:

64 Mario Giovanoli, 'The International Monetary and Financial Architecture' (n 11) 70.

65 For an excellent description on the history of monetary cooperation, see Lastra, *International Financial and Monetary Law* (n 7) ch 12. Also see Douglas W Arner, Michael A Panton and Paul Lejot, 'Central Banks and Central Bank Cooperation in the Global Financial System' (2010) 23(1) Pacific McGeorge Global Business & Development Law Journal 1, 31.

> Central bank cooperation through history has ultimately been directed to ensuring monetary and financial stability. However, the conception of these objectives, the relationship between the two, the balance in their pursuit, and the strategies followed have evolved over time, reflecting changes in the monetary and financial environment as well as in the political and intellectual climate. Accordingly, depending on the circumstances and the intellectual perspective of the time, we think of monetary stability as covering either stability in an aggregate price level (index) or in the relative price of two units of account, i.e. the exchange rate between national currencies or between a given currency and gold. We think of financial stability, narrowly defined, as being impaired whenever widespread defaults threaten to take place, due to either a banking or a sovereign debt crisis.[66]

Broadly speaking, central banking cooperation can be divided into three historical periods: the 'Gold Standard Period', the 'Bretton Woods Period' and the 'Post-Bretton Woods Period'.[67] Each of these periods have experienced different levels of intensity of cross-border banking cooperation. According to Caruana, former general manager of the BIS, in a speech given in July 2012 the main factors that have determined and continue to determine the level of cooperation in each of these periods are 'the challenges presented by the evolution of the international monetary and financial environment, changes in institutional frameworks and advances in economic thought'.[68]

66 Claudio Borio and Gianni Toniolo, 'One hundred and thirty years of central bank cooperation: a BIS perspective' (2006) BIS Working Papers No 197 <www.bis.org/publ/work197.htm> 27 March 2019, 2.

67 These periods coincide with the historical evolution of the International Monetary System as explained in chapter 1 of this book: starting with the period of the Gold Standard (1819–1914) and the Gold Exchange Standard (1925–31), continued by the Bretton Woods System (1944–73) and closing with the ongoing Post-Bretton Woods period (1973-present). For a more detailed explanation of these historical periods see Annex I to chapter 1 in this book.

68 Jaime Caruana, 'Central bank cooperation: reflections on the experience of the last eight decades' (CEMLA's 60th Anniversary Commemorative Conference on 'Central bank cooperation at the beginning of the 21st century', 20 July 2012) <www.bis.org/speeches/sp120724.htm> accessed 21 October 2021. Borio and Toniolo added the following factors on top of the factors highlighted by Caruana: (i) the overall conditions in international relations; (ii) the prestige enjoyed by central banks with the public at large, which also affects their institutional relationship with the political authorities (i.e. the allocation of tasks in monetary policymaking, including provisions for central bank independence); and (iii) the technical nature of the problems requiring cooperation.

Borio and Toniolo, 'One hundred and thirty years of central bank cooperation' (n 66) 3.

With these factors in mind, Caruana provides in his 2012 speech a clear detail of the level of international cooperation experienced during the abovementioned three periods that can be summarised as follows:

'Gold Standard Period' (1819 – 1931): This period includes both the Classic Gold Standard (1819–1914) and the Gold Exchange Standard (1925–31). Under the Classic Gold Standard, gold convertibility was believed to achieve both stable prices (monetary stability) and financial stability. Hence, central bank cooperation was limited to the maintenance of gold convertibility mostly on a bilateral basis and through emergency liquidity lending to central banks with low level of gold reserves. The First World War marked the abandonment of the Classic Gold Standard and the imposition of exchange controls. International efforts to restore the standard were made in the interwar period with an increase in central bank cooperation that led to the creation of the BIS in 1930 as an institutionalised vehicle for multilateral cooperation.[69] However, with the onset of the Great Depression in the 1930's central bank cooperation reduced and the BIS acted as a forum for research and exchange of information among central banks.

'Bretton Woods Period' (1944 – 1973): This second period was characterised by the establishment of fixed but adjustable exchange rate regimes, with gold initially acting only as a soft limit on the system, but which *de facto* evolved to the dollar standard or 'par value' regime (each currency had a par value with gold or with the US gold dollar standard). A newly established international organisation, the IMF, was entrusted with the management of the exchange rates. Consequently, during this period international central banking cooperation was focused on re-establishing the conditions for current account convertibility and sustaining fixed exchange rates through the provision of emergency liquidity lending and the so-called 'gold pool'.[70]

69 Wartime reparations and debts provided the rationale for the creation of the BIS, as remarked by Borio and Toniolo: The main driving force behind the creation of an 'international bank', as part of a treaty on reparations, was the so-called 'commercialisation' of the reparation payments, whereby part of the German debt would be issued in the form of long-term bonds to be subscribed by international private banks and financial houses. (…) Given that obligations of sovereign states are notoriously difficult to enforce, the creation of an international organisation such as the BIS was seen as potentially useful in improving the chances of future payments enforcement.

Borio and Toniolo, 'One hundred and thirty years of central bank cooperation' (n 66) 9.

70 ibid 3. According to Borio and Toniolo the 1960's saw a peak in central bank cooperation. In particular, decisions on the gold pool, the sterling group agreements, the IMF General Agreement to Borrow (GAB) and the G-10 multilateral surveillance were held under the auspices of the BIS. ibid 14.

'Post-Bretton Woods Period' (1973 onwards): With the collapse of the Bretton Woods system at the beginning of the 1970's, international central banking cooperation on monetary affairs became limited. Floating exchange rate regimes emerged and domestic price stability turned out to be the main task of central banks. Hence, global cooperation for monetary stability considerations was restricted and domestic affairs prevailed over international solutions.[71] On the contrary during this same period, the scope for global cooperation in financial affairs gained place. Financial openness with quick expansion of international banking and international capital mobility gave rise to more recurrent banking crises that prompted an increase in central banking cooperation in the pursuit of international financial stability.

The collapse of the Herstatt Bank in Germany and the Franklin National Bank in the United States of America (US) at the beginning of 1974 gave momentum to the creation of the BCBS and other committees hosted by the BIS. As explained in the previous section of this chapter, these committees were and are still aimed at developing common standards and policies in the field of international monetary and financial cooperation. Consequently, according to Borio and Tonniolo, the evolution of the elements of cooperation both in monetary and financial matters was based mainly on standards and codes through soft law provisions and arrangements, thus shaping the so-called new 'international financial architecture' as detailed in the previous section of this chapter.[72]

2.2 *Diplomacy and Coordination*

As stated before, central bank cooperation has evolved over time and adapted to the new economic and financial landscapes. Simmons remarks that 'central bank cooperation has adapted remarkably well to the demands of the times. (…) Cooperation among them has been shaped by the economic conditions they have encountered, the theoretical lenses through which they view the world, and even the political context in which they operate'.[73] These central bank interactions through history have been analysed from different angles by legal, economic and political scientist scholars and an interesting classification

---

71 Europe marked the exception to the general trend towards limited global cooperation on monetary policy affairs during this period, because it was then when it started to design the regional monetary union with the so-called currency snake and the European monetary system. Caruana, 'Central Bank Cooperation' (n 68) 2.

72 Borio and Toniolo, 'One hundred and thirty years of central bank cooperation' (n 66) 16.

73 Beth A Simmons, 'The future of central bank cooperation' (2006) BIS Working Papers No 200 <www.bis.org/publ/work200.htm> accessed 21 October 2021.

for these interactions was made by Kahn and Meade in 2018.[74] They divide central bank interactions into two main categories named 'diplomacy' and 'coordination'. *Diplomacy* refers to the relationship-building initiatives among central banks including all forms of public and non-public information exchange usually taking place in the context of international forums aiming to create knowledge and professional relationships and to enhance trust. *Coordination* encompasses joint actions performed by central banks such as, standard or rule setting, foreign exchange market intervention and liquidity provision.[75] Kahn and Meade relate both categories by stating that, 'Although coordination does not necessarily occur only in times of crisis, relationships built through diplomacy lay the ground work for coordination when a crisis occurs'.[76]

Under *diplomacy* Kahn and Meade highlight the role of main international forums and organisations in which central banks participate. As detailed in the previous section of this chapter, these interactions among central banks are mainly held at diverse working groups and meetings within IMF, BIS, FSB and G20. As to how central banks move from *diplomacy* to effective *coordination* the authors discuss three relevant examples: the Plaza Accord of 1985, the response to the Asian financial crisis of 1997–98 and the more recent responses to the GFC.[77]

I concur with Kahn and Meade that these are the three leading examples of central bank involvement in international *coordination* since the collapse of the Bretton Woods system. I will describe briefly the first two examples and in the following section examine in detail the most recent episode, the GFC.

The Plaza Accord of 1985: The Plaza Accord of 1985 is the result of a meeting held at the Plaza Hotel in New York on 22 September 1985 among the Group of Five (G-5) which comprised of the largest industrialised countries at that time (France, West Germany, Japan, the United States and the United Kingdom). In this accord the countries agreed to act jointly in order to bring down the value of the US dollar through coordinated currency markets intervention.[78] The text of the Plaza Accord signed by the G-5 countries states that:

74 Robert B Kahn and Ellen E Meade, 'International aspects of central banking: diplomacy and coordination' in Peter Conti-Brown and Rosa Maria Lastra (eds), *Research Handbook on Central Banking* (EE 2018).

75 ibid 334.

76 ibid 335.

77 ibid 335–357.

78 Jeffrey Frankel explains the reasons leading to the appreciation of the US dollar in the early 1980's: 'A combination of tight monetary policy associated with Federal Reserve Chairman Paul Volcker during 1980–82 and expansionary fiscal policy associated with President Ronald Reagan during 1981–84 pushed up long-term interest rates, which in turn attracted a capital inflow and appreciated the currency'. Jeffrey Frankel, 'The Plaza

> The Ministers and Governors agreed that exchange rates should play a role in adjusting external imbalances. In order to do this, exchange rates should better reflect fundamental economic conditions than has been the case. They believe that agreed policy actions must be implemented and reinforced to improve the fundamentals further, and that in view of the present and prospective changes in fundamentals, some further orderly appreciation of the main non-dollar currencies against the dollar is desirable. They stand ready to cooperate more closely to encourage this when to do so would be helpful.[79]

The Plaza Accord is widely seen as successful in terms of both international *diplomacy* and international *coordination*. The value of the US dollar fell abruptly after the announcement of the agreement and in the period of two years with concerted intervention ended at 40 per cent of its previous value. Also, as a consequence of this successful cooperation among the G-5 countries, the group was expanded in 1986 to include Italy and Canada. The new Group of 7 (G-7) continues to meet annually since its creation and also includes the European Union as a non-enumerated member. Central banks played without doubt a key role through their involvement both in the debates and studies about foreign-exchange intervention prior to the signing of the Plaza Accord and also with the subsequent execution of the intervention operations in the exchange market.[80]

Despite the success of the Plaza Accord of 1985 and other similar agreements, such as the subsequent Louvre Accord of 1987,[81] they are described by Proctor as agreements of short-term validity and of limited legal force since, 'international law knows of no general obligation to maintain exchange rates at particular levels, and that statements of this kind – whatever their political value- have limited legal force in the monetary sphere'.[82]

Accord, 30 Years Later' (2015) NBER Working Paper 21813 <www.nber.org/papers/w21813> accessed 21 October 2021.

79 Group of 5, 'Announcement the Ministers of Finance and Central Bank Governors of France, Germany, Japan, the United Kingdom, and the United States (Plaza Accord)' (22 September 1985) <www.g8.utoronto.ca/finance/fm850922.htm> accessed 21 October 2021.

80 Kahn and Meade, 'International Aspects of Central Banking' (n 74) 347.

81 In February 1987, the Group of 6 (G-6) finance ministers (consisting of G-5 and Canada) met at Paris, France and agreed that the value of the US dollar had fallen far enough, that future market intervention should occur only when required to ensure exchange rate stability and that they would try to prevent it from falling further. Group of 6, 'Statement of the G6 Finance Ministers and Central Bank Governors (Louvre Accord)' (22 February 1987) <www.g8.utoronto.ca/finance/fm870222.htm> accessed 21 October 2021.

82 Charles Proctor, *Mann on the Legal Aspect of Money* (7th edn, OUP 2012) 888.

The response to the Asian financial crisis of 1997–98: During the 1990's increasing globalisation facilitated the growth of international financial markets with emerging economies taking the lead. However, international diplomacy and coordination in international finance was still dominated by developed economies, mostly accomplished at the G-7 meetings and with the IMF as the leading international organisation for monetary and financial issues. Hence, when the Asian financial crisis erupted in 1997 (when the Thai government decided to stop pegging its currency against the US dollar), the capacity of global policymakers and institutions was challenged.[83]

The Asian financial crisis arose as a combination of macroeconomic factors (most of the Asian region had at that time fixed or semi-fixed exchange rates) and microeconomic problems (associated with balance sheet mismatches).[84] Capital outflows intensified in the region by the end of 1996 and with the end of the peg of the Thai currency (the *baht*) to the US dollar in 1997, countries such as Indonesia and Philippines decided to request for financial assistance from the IMF. These multilateral funds were also complemented with central banks funds.[85]

The increasing global growth of regionalism with the creation of the European Monetary Union and the launch of the Eurozone in 1999 influenced the Asian countries to develop regional financial forums in order to protect and promote their regional interests. Accordingly, the regional responses to the crisis where notable, mostly catalysed through the work of the Association of Southeast Asian Nations Plus Three (ASEAN + 3) and the Executive Meeting of

---

83 For a comprehensive analysis of the Asian financial crisis of the 1990's see Jee-young Jung, 'Regional financial cooperation in Asia: challenges and path to development' (2008) BIS Papers No 42 <https://www.bis.org/author/jee-young_jung.htm> accessed 21 October 2021. See also Takatoshi Kato, 'Can the East Asian Miracle Persist?' (Princeton University's Woodrow Wilson School and East Asian Studies Department, 2 December 2004) <www.imf.org/en/News/Articles/2015/09/28/04/53/sp120204> accessed 21 October 2021; Edwin M Truman, 'Asian and European Financial Crises Compared' (2013) Peterson Institute for International Economics Working Paper No 13-9 <https://papers.ssrn.com/sol3/papers.cfm?abstract_id=2344421> accessed 21 October 2021.

84 Truman explains that: The Asian countries had fixed or semi-fixed exchange rates, which was a source of problems ex ante because the exchange rate regimes encouraged currency mismatches and the buildup of excessive foreign debts by the private sector, including financial institutions. Exchange-rate regimes became an additional source of problems when the pegs broke or were broken, and the sequential collapse of pegs contributed to contagion in the region. The collapse of the pegs magnified recessions in the short run, via balance sheet effects.

Truman, 'Asian and European Financial Crises Compared' (n 83) 9–10.

85 Kahn and Meade, 'International Aspects of Central Banking' (n 74) 349.

East Asia-Pacific Central Banks (EMEAP).[86] These regional financial cooperative efforts resulted in the establishment of regional liquidity support arrangements through the Chiang Mai Initiative (CMI), the creation of the Asian Bond Fund (ABF) and the development of the Asian Bond Market Initiative (ABMI).[87] In this context it can be stated that the role of the central banks was crucial both in terms of diplomacy and cooperation, although they were bolstered by the political support of their governments and the decisive support of the IMF.

Notwithstanding the remarkable regional responses to the Asian financial crisis, they were not sufficient because the crisis escalated and spilled over quickly within the region and beyond. As a consequence, global policymakers recognised that the voices of major emerging economies should be heard and as a result the G20 group of central bank governors and finance ministers was created. According to Kahn and Meade the Asian financial crisis of the 1990's 'created a new appreciation that shocks affecting one country could spill over quickly to others in the region. Increased dependence on foreign capital and bank loans, as well as underdeveloped domestic financial markets, were seen as creating unique regional vulnerabilities from global swings in capital flows'.[88]

2.3 *Responses to the GFC and Its Aftermath*

There is much written about the global financial crisis (the GFC) that erupted in the fall of 2007, bringing about the loss of confidence of investors in the US subprime mortgage market that developed quickly into a global liquidity crisis with the collapse of Lehman Brothers in September 2008 as the inflection point.[89] For the purposes of this chapter, this section examines the responses provided by central banks during the crisis and in its aftermath.

In terms of the categorisation between *diplomacy* and *cooperation*, Kahn and Meade consider that the first set of responses provided by central banks to the GFC fall under the category of *diplomacy*. That is, there were plenty of communications and consultations among central banks about

86 During the crisis Japan proposed to create an Asian Monetary Fund. However, this initiative was rejected on the basis that it would have produced a large freestanding source of external financing unconnected and competing with the IMF and the global policy standards. Truman, 'Asian and European Financial Crises Compared' (n 83) 40.

87 Jung, 'Regional Financial Cooperation in Asia' (n 83). Jung provides an extensive assessment of the Asian regional forums and initiatives undertaken during and after the 1990's Asian financial crisis.

88 Kahn and Meade, 'International Aspects of Central Banking' (n 74) 353.

89 Lastra and Wood, 'The Crisis of 2007–2009: Nature, Causes, and Reactions' (n 14).

the ongoing crisis with sharing of information and market analysis, but the policy responses were not coordinated. However, with the Lehman Brothers collapse central banks moved quickly from the category of *diplomacy* to the category of *cooperation*. That is to say, central banks cooperated with specific actions aimed to alleviate some of the effects of the crisis and also to send a joint signal to the financial markets on the direction that their policies would take.

According to Heath, 'Spontaneous coordination may occur in a global crisis because countries may face similar circumstances that overwhelm other individual country conditions, and so many nations' interests align in seeking action'.[90] Some examples of cooperation during the crisis, or as a response to the crisis, were the synchronised reduction by six central banks of their respective interest rate policies by 25–50 basis points after the collapse of Lehman Brothers, the almost simultaneous start of monetary easing of the major central banks in October 2008[91] and also the establishment of swap lines among the US Fed and various central banks of economies considered to be major and advanced.[92] As highlighted by Kahn and Meade:

> The success of the swap lines in mitigating funding pressures and reducing interbank borrowing rates is considered one of the major successes from central bank coordination during the crisis. In addition to easing funding shortages, these swaps also contributed to an alleviation of market fears and sent a strong signal that central banks were prepared to move outside their comfort zone to address financial stress.[93]

---

90 Daniel Heath, 'International Coordination of Macroprudential and Monetary Policy' (2013–2014) 45 Georgetown Journal of International Law 1093.

91 ibid. The coordinated reduction of the interest rate was taken on 8 October 2008 among the Bank of Canada, the Bank of England, the ECB, the Fed, the Sveriges Riksbank, and the Swiss National Bank. As remarked by James, 'This was the first time that the Fed had ever coordinated a simultaneously announced rate reduction with other central banks'. Harold James, 'International Cooperation and Central Banks' in Youssef Cassis, Catherine Schenk, and Richard Grossman (eds), *The Oxford Handbook of Banking and Financial History* (OUP 2016) 22.

92 The Fed started liquidity lines with the ECB and the Swiss National Bank in December 2007, with twelve more central banks in September to October 2008. Rakesh Mohan and Muneesh Kapur, 'Monetary Policy Coordination and the Role of Central Banks' (2014) IMF Working Paper 14/70 <www.imf.org/external/pubs/ft/wp/2014/wp1470.pdf> accessed 21 October 2021.

93 Kahn and Meade, 'International Aspects of Central Banking' (n 74) 357.

Notwithstanding the above-mentioned examples, most of the solutions adopted to manage the GFC were nation-oriented and uncoordinated. As remarked in a discussion paper by the Bank of England, 'The landscape for international monetary policy co-operation has not changed in any fundamental way since the crisis: with the exception of the co-ordinated monetary easing at the onset of the crisis, conventional monetary policy is still being set by individual central banks without co-ordination'.[94] For example, the setting of key interest rates is one of the main instruments (together with open market operations and reserve requirements) in monetary policy used by central banks in search of monetary stability. As a response to the crisis, central banks resorted to this instrument but used it differently. As remarked by Zimmermann:

> The Fed reacted with a series of interest rate cuts aimed at saving employment while the ECB kept interest rates unchanged for much longer in order not to endanger price stability. This illustrates that the current lack of harmonization in the way interest rates policies are being conducted by central banks may lead to major differences in how similar economic problems are tackled by different countries.[95]

As a reaction to this situation, the IMF Staff Team prepared a discussion note paper about the form monetary policy should have in the aftermath of the GFC. In this discussion paper they argued that in crisis times, 'the potential gains from cooperation are significant. Cooperation reduces the risk of tail events with large international feedback effects, and in those circumstances, central banks have been willing to cooperate'. While in regular times, 'there is insufficient clarity on the size of the welfare gains from monetary policy cooperation'.[96] Moreover, the discussion note remarks that even though the welfare gains were clear during normal times there are several obstacles to cooperation. It listed the obstacles that range from the different economic situations

94 Bank of England, 'One Bank Research Agenda Discussion Paper' (February 2015) <https://www.bankofengland.co.uk/-/media/boe/files/research/one-bank-research-agenda--summary.pdf?la=en&hash=B2C820FBF6A960C4A625C2DAB5B5B6CE4FEDF120> accessed 21 October 2021.

95 Claus D Zimmermann, 'Global Benchmark Interest Rates' in Cottier and others (eds), *The Rule of Law* (n 18).

96 Tamim Bayoumi and others, 'Monetary Policy in the New Normal' (IMF Staff Discussion Note, April 2014) < www.imf.org/external/pubs/ft/sdn/2014/sdn1403.pdf > accessed 21 October 2021.

across countries to the lack of harmonised domestic objectives for the pursuit of monetary stability.

On the obstacles to international monetary policy cooperation, Ostry and Ghosh pointed out that 'the most compelling reasons are asymmetries in country size; disagreement about the economic situation and cross-border transmission effects of policies; and often policymakers' failure to recognise that they face important trade-offs across various objectives'. To address these concerns they proposed on one hand that 'a neutral assessor may play a useful role in helping to bridge the divergent views of national policymakers' and on the other hand 'to buttress international coordination and to provide safeguards when coordination proves impossible to achieve, by implementing two guideposts to limit negative spillovers through the current account and the capital account, respectively'.[97]

Consequently, it is very difficult to foresee under different circumstances what shape international cooperation for the pursuit of monetary stability will take. Kahn and Meade consider that in the GFC aftermath central banks will remain as key actors for global stability and, hence, central bank diplomacy should be maintained and improved.[98] In this regard Coeuré reflects that both formal and informal international institutions and fora must keep a leading role in the further development of central bank diplomacy for three reasons:

> *First*, they achieve a better understanding and a common assessment of the global spillovers from domestic policy actions and the potential policy trade-offs. *Second*, even if the scope for coordination is limited in good times, they make coordination possible in bad times. And *third*, they prompt work at regulatory bodies such as the Basel Committee for Banking Supervision, the International Organization of Securities Commission or the Committee on Payments and Settlement Systems, to establish the standards and infrastructures and create a level playing field, which are necessary for global markets to function in a smooth and safe way.[99]

97 Jonathan D Ostry and Atish R Ghosh, 'Obstacles to International Policy Coordination, and How to Overcome Them' (IMF Staff Discussion Note, December 2013) <www.imf.org/external/pubs/ft/sdn/2013/sdn1311.pdf> accessed 21 October 2021.

98 Kahn and Meade, 'International Aspects of Central Banking' (n 74) 360.

99 Benoît Coeuré, 'The Internationalisation of Monetary Policy' (2016) 67 Journal of International Money and Finance 11.

3 Common Concern as a Guide to Enhanced Cooperation in Monetary Affairs

From all the considerations expressed above, it can be argued that the duty to cooperate in monetary affairs relies mostly on voluntary cooperation. It is here that the potential principle of Common Concern can assist with the new 'obligation to act'.[100] If recognised as a principle of international law, Common Concern will entail the lawful implementation of instruments and incentives supporting international compliance and securing that a recognised Common Concern – such as international monetary stability- is dealt with in priority in domestic and international processes. Hence, it is the responsibility of cooperation emanating from the recognition of international monetary stability as a Common Concern that lays the ground for such new duty at the different levels of governance.

The application of the doctrine of Common Concern to the transboundary public good of monetary stability, suggests different avenues to help solve the cooperation failures. This book, considers the following three areas as examples of enhanced cooperation assisted by the normative claims proposed by Common Concern: IMF surveillance, Global Financial Safety Net (GFSN) and government networks.

3.1 *IMF Mandatory Based Surveillance*

The principle of Common Concern recommends that a progressive move from soft law to hard law in international monetary affairs (top-down approach), might help the national monetary authorities to honor their international legal commitments and engage in further cross-border cooperation. For example, moving from a voluntary to a mandatory based surveillance under the IMF's consultations (made through FSAP and ROSCs). Hence, all policy recommendations made in the context of IMF surveillance could become of mandatory nature.

Therefore, based on the normative claims of the emerging doctrine of Common Concern doctrine, a more effective and impactful IMF surveillance could be promoted. Mark Carney, former governor of the Bank of England, has argued in this regards that '… transparent, evidence-based discussions convened by the IMF can both discipline policy and avoid potentially antagonistic misunderstandings that could lead to de-stabilising tit-for-tat retaliations'. Consequently, the Fund could play a fundamental role in informing

100 Cottier, 'The Principle of Common Concern of Humankind' (n 1) 73.

both domestic and cross-border policies based on its bilateral surveillance performed to individual countries and its multilateral surveillance of the global economy.

3.2 *Improved GFSN*

Another possible option to induce cooperation from a *top-down* approach is to reinforce the GFSN.[101] As described elsewhere in this book, excessive reserve assets accumulation and reliance on few reserve currencies together with the proliferation of regional financing agreements (RFAs) is not only very costly, but also causes potential systemic costs and coordination problems that can affect the stability of the IMS. Consequently, a principle of Common Concern with an enhanced duty to cooperate could promote a stronger and more reliable GFSN. In this regard, Carney remarks that 'Collective action should improve the adequacy of the global financial safety net (GFSN) to reduce the need for EMEs to accumulate reserves of safe assets as insurance against less sustainable capital flows'..[102]

The report published in October 2018 by the G20 Eminent Persons Group on Global Financial Governance (EPG) offers a range of proposals to improve the GFSN with enhanced cooperation from a top-down approach:[103]

> First, we must ensure an adequately-resourced global layer in the IMF through timely conclusion of quota reviews.
>
> Second, the IMF must work with RFAs to enable consistent actions during a crisis so as to achieve the necessary scale and global impact. A properly designed and predictable GFSN can avoid moral hazard, minimize contagion between countries, and promote openness and growth.

---

101 On the topic of GFSN, chapter 1 of this book defines 'reserve assets' as a key element of the IMS and chapter 5 explains that the management of reserve assets is part of the foreign exchange policy of a country. Moreover, chapter 6 of this book analyses the accumulation of reserve assets as a unilateral measure of precautionary nature and contains a note on the proliferation of regional financing agreements as an alternative to manage volatility caused by monetary policy spillovers.

102 Mark Carney, 'Speech' (The Growing Challenges for Monetary Policy in the current International Monetary and Financial System, London, 23 August 2019) 12 <www.bis.org/review/r190827b.htm> accessed 21 October 2021.

103 Eminent Persons Group on Global Financial Governance, 'Making the Global Financial System Work for All' (October 2018) <www.globalfinancialgovernance.org/assets/pdf/G20EPG-Full%20Report.pdf> accessed 21 October 2021.

> Third, it is important to put in place a standing global liquidity facility, drawing on IMF permanent resources, to strengthen countries' ability to withstand global liquidity shocks and avoid deeper crises. A reliable liquidity facility will also help them avoid building up excessive reserves as the price for being open to capital flows, and hence avoid hampering growth. The facility should be designed for countries with sound policies, and to minimize 'IMF stigma' when they draw on it.

These proposals to enhance the GFSN presented by the G20 EPG could only be viable if the members of the international community and specially the IMF member states honor their international legal commitments and engage in further cross-border cooperation.

3.3 *Harness the Commitments Assumed at the Government Networks*

A proposal to promote enhanced cooperation from a *bottom-up approach* can be found in the very influential work on 'government networks' wrote by Anne-Marie Slaughter. In this work Slaughter explains that global governance can occur through government networks that connect domestic government officials to address international problems.[104] She suggests that government networks are the optimal tool of international cooperation to solve global problems that have domestic origins. The main reason for this is that government networks involve directly the participation and the credibility of the government officials who must ultimately be responsible for addressing those common problems at the local level.

Slaughter also remarks that government networks, both as they exist now and as they could exist, exercise different types of power to achieve outcomes. Government networks have access to traditional coercive power (based on 'hard law'). Consequently, she argues that the key role of national government officials in government networks means that when a decision is made and that decision requires implementation, the power to implement already exists at the national level. However, she also recognises that most of the work of government networks depends on 'soft-law' power and, hence, suggests that 'An effective world order needs to harness every kind of power available'.[105]

---

104 Slaughter uses a board concept of a 'network' in order to capture all the different ways that individual government institutions are interacting with their counterparts either abroad or above them, alongside more traditional state-to-state interactions. Anne-Marie Slaughter, *A New World Order* (Princeton University Press, 2005) 14.

105 ibid, 27.

It can be argued that using Slaughter's terminology, 'government networks' in central banking exist in the formal and informal international institutions and *fora* in which central banks participate (most notably, IMF, FSB and BIS).[106] As argued elsewhere in this book, especially in this chapter, central bank diplomacy (based on soft-law commitments) is at the core of such government networks through relationship-building initiatives and information exchange. In concordance with Slaughter, effective central banking cooperation needs to harness the commitments assumed at the government networks. It is here that Common Concern can enable the implementation of such global commitments with the new 'obligation to act' at the domestic level of governance. The adoption at the national level of international standards, like the ones sponsored by the G20 and driven by the FSB, is a successful example on this point. Also, the core principles issued by the International Organisation of Securities Commissions (IOSCO) on securities regulation and the BCBS for banking – while not mandatory – are widely adopted at the national level. The proposed formulation of Common Concern, as a legal doctrine, triggers this enhanced central banking cooperation which then flows into the other aspects of homework and compliance.

4 Conclusion

The recognition of global monetary stability as a Common Concern would imply a reinforcement of the role of the IMF as the central international monetary institution from a *top-down* perspective. In spite of the fact that the regulatory function in global monetary affairs is shared by a number of formal and informal international standard-setters, including most notably the FSB and BIS, the IMF keeps the lead as claimed in this chapter. As asserted by Lastra:

> The IMF is the only institution (other than the BIS and the WTO) that has international legitimacy, an array of tools (surveillance, conditional financial assistance and technical assistance), appropriate financial resources and staffing to assume a formal role as global financial authority. Other informal international standard setters, such as the FSB, the BCBS, or IOSCO, can continue with their rule-making role, but only the Fund can effectively contribute to the enforcement of those standards through its surveillance function.[107]

106 See the graphic of the 'International Financial Architecture' in chapter 4, Annex I of this book.

107 Lastra, *International Financial and Monetary Law* (n 7) 551.

The main reason for this is that the Fund's key surveillance function enables it to monitor the member states' compliance with rules and standards and provide incentives for members to comply with them. Also, beyond bilateral surveillance that is performed by individual countries, the IMF performs multilateral surveillance of the global economy, thus helping to identify the impact domestic policies may have on other countries and the global economy.[108] This analysis may assist with the allocation of burden-sharing of the shared but differentiated responsibilities proposed under the principle of Common Concern.

Notwithstanding the key role of the Fund's surveillance in crisis prevention and enhanced international cooperation, all policy recommendations made in the context of IMF surveillance are of an advisory nature and non-mandatory. Therefore, the *bottom-up* perspective acquires relevance in the pursuit of a Common Concern of global monetary stability. As remarked by Gopinath, recently-appointed chief economist at the IMF, cross-border cooperation efforts among countries from a domestic level approach are welcome developments to support the well-functioning of the international system:

> It is then all the more important for countries to cooperate on financial regulation, to strengthen the global safety net, and to reduce the stigma attached to the lender of last resort role of the IMF. The creation of regional monetary funds like the European Stability Mechanism (ESB) set up in 2012, the Chiang Mai Initiative Multilateralization (CMIM) in 2012, BRICS Contingent Reserve Arrangement (CRA) in 2014 and other smaller regional arrangements that taken together have committed resources of US 1.3 trillion dollars similar to that of the IMF (Denbee et al. (2016)) are welcome developments that complement the IMF in supporting a well functioning international monetary and financial system.[109]

Consequently, the enhanced duty to cooperate proposed by Common Concern would have a positive impact on the promotion of international monetary stability both from a *top-down* and *bottom-up* approach. However, the efficacy of such enhanced duty would still depend on the IMF member states' willingness

---

108 'IMF Surveillance' (2021) <www.imf.org/en/About/Factsheets/IMF-Surveillance> accessed 21 October 2021.

109 Gita Gopinath, 'Rethinking International Macroeconomic Policy' (Conference on 'Rethinking Macroeconomic Policy IV', Peterson Institute on International Economics, 25 October 2017) <https://scholar.harvard.edu/files/gopinath/files/openeconomypolicy100317.pdf> accessed 21 October 2021.

to enhance the Fund's mandate on the premises of Common Concern and also on each state's readiness to engage in further cross-border cooperation under the guidance of the potential principle of Common Concern. Hence, it is under these circumstances that the new obligation to act as proposed by Common Concern acquires relevance.

Annex 1 – International Financial Architecture

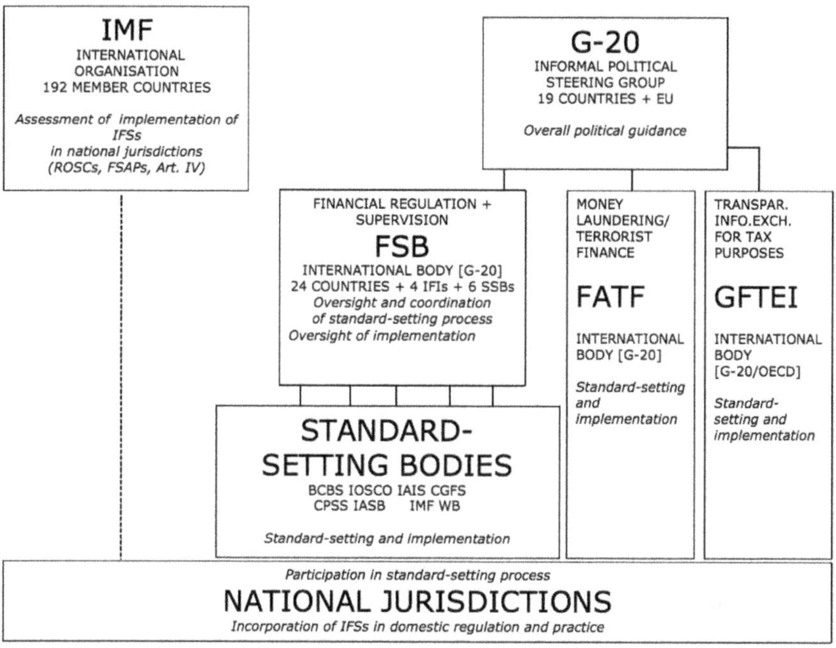

1

Source: Mario Giovanoli, 'A New Architecture for the Global Financial Markets: Legal Aspects of International Financial Standards Setting' in Mario Giovanoli (ed), *International Monetary Law: Issues for the New Millennium* (OUP 2000) 38.

CHAPTER 5

Domestic Obligations concerning Monetary Stability

The Special Role of Central Banks

The second element of the emerging doctrine of Common Concern of Humankind, following the duty to cooperate, introduces the *obligations at the domestic level* or *obligations to do homework*.[1] This element considers not only the duty to promote and protect the Common Concern at the local level but also the duty to implement the international commitments assumed in international agreements and in customary law. As stated by Cottier,

> Common Concern of Humankind calls for action in domestic law and policy. It is at the heart of the principle and amounts to a key obligation under the doctrine of Common Concern of Humankind in order to offset the lack of reciprocity, to avoid free-riding and the endemic tragedy of the global commons (Hardin). The recognition of a problem as a common preoccupation entails the need to engage appropriate domestic resources and activities, again in accordance with equity and distributional justice and shared responsibility, to address the challenge. Think globally – act locally translates into domestic homework. ... Common Concern of Humankind is not limited to implementing international obligations by central government and institutions. Often, the main thrust will be measures undertaken upon own initiatives and bottom up. Depending on the problem and the public goods which need to be produced in response to the challenge, all layers of government may be involved.[2]

1 As explained in detail in chapter 3 of this book, the term 'homework' is introduced by the emerging doctrine as a legal denomination to encompass all the obligations that are attached to the principle of Common Concern of Humankind. For more detail on the normative components of the obligation to do homework as presented by the doctrine of Common Concern see, chapter 3 and Thomas Cottier, 'The Principle of Common Concern of Humankind' in Thomas Cottier (ed) '*The Prospects of Common Concern of Humankind in International Law*' (CUP 2021).

2 ibid 63.

Accordingly, by taking recourse to the doctrines of multilevel governance, Common Concern encourages timely and effective implementation of international commitments and promotes bottom-up initiatives to address the global challenges presented by the Common Concerns. Hence, the *obligations to do homework* comprehend two levels of commitment: the duty to promote and protect the Common Concern at the local level and the duty to implement international commitments assumed in international agreements and in customary law.

For the purposes of the potential Common Concern of monetary stability: the *first level of commitment* encompasses the pursuit and maintenance of monetary stability as a domestic public good and a local Common Concern. This is a clear sovereignty attribute and a state defines what is to be considered as monetary stability locally. The pursuit of monetary stability is usually entrusted to an independent central bank or the relevant monetary authority. Thus, this chapter studies the special role of central banks as the preferred institutional arrangement in the promotion and protection of monetary stability.

1 Domestic Obligations – The Special Role of Central Banks

This section follows up and expands on the preliminary analysis made in chapter 2 of this book concerning the legal and institutional arrangements that promote monetary stability at the domestic level.[3] Such promotion and protection of monetary stability have internal and external dimensions. While the 'internal dimension' of monetary stability refers to the stability of domestic prices (price stability), the 'external dimension' is understood as the stability of the value of a specific currency vis-à-vis other currencies (exchange rate stability).

Sainz de Vicuña, former general counsel of the European Central Bank (ECB), remarks that 'The intrinsic or extrinsic values that a metal equivalent gave to money in the past have been replaced today by the surge of *institutional frameworks* destined to ensure the permanence over time of the purchasing power of money'.[4] He also considers that 'there is a relationship between a currency internal purchasing power (that is, the capacity to acquire goods and services with prices denominated in the national currency), and its external

---

3 The legal and institutional arrangements to promote monetary stability at the domestic level are enshrined in the monetary sovereignty attributes of the states. See chapter 2 of this book.

4 Antonio Sainz de Vicuña, 'An Institutional Theory of Money' in Mario Giovanoli and Diego Devos (eds), *International Monetary and Financial Law, The Global Crisis* (OUP 2010) 525.

purchasing power (that is, acquisition of goods and services invoiced in a foreign currency)'.[5]

Consequently, it can be stated that in modern economies the value of money (or its purchasing power) relies fundamentally on the institutional framework. Therefore, decisions taken by domestic central banks or monetary authorities (through monetary and exchange rate policies) have a direct influence on the currency's purchasing power. Thus, this section starts by examining the institutional framework of central banking. In doing so it studies the main functions and objectives of central banks and monetary authorities in relation to monetary stability. The section continues by analysing the special characteristics of the system of exchange rate control and the management of a country's foreign reserves and its impact on exchange rate stability.

1.1 *Internal Dimension of Monetary Stability – Price Stability*

The design of the international monetary order in the post Bretton Woods era has preferred legal and institutional arrangements at the national level. Independent central banks have been the predominant institutional arrangement since the 1990's, playing a crucial role in the promotion and protection of monetary stability.[6] Monetary policy decisions from major central banks have played a fundamental part in the response to the global financial crisis of 2007–2009 (GFC) and for the valuable role they played in this response central banks have been called the 'only game in town'.[7]

Proctor provides a functional definition of central bank stating that 'A central bank is an institution of a State. In the issue of money, the conduct of national monetary policy, the administration of a system of exchange control, and the management of a country's foreign reserves, it plainly discharges functions of a peculiar sovereign nature'.[8] These central banks functions enumerated by

---

5 ibid.

6 There are other institutional arrangements for the promotion of monetary stability such as currency boards and legislated monetary rules. Rosa M Lastra, *International Financial and Monetary Law* (2nd edn, OUP 2015) 63–64.

7 Raghuram Rajan, 'The Only Game in Town' (2012) <www.project-syndicate.org/commentary/the-limits-of-unconventional-monetary-policy-by-raghuram-rajan> accessed 21 October 2021; Mohamed El-Erian, *The Only Game in Town: Central Banks, Instability, and Avoiding the Next Collapse* (Random House, 2016), among others.

8 Charles Proctor, *Mann on the Legal Aspect of Money* (7th edn, OUP 2012) 573. Proctor also remarks at page 571 that: It may be added that a central bank may have other functions. In some jurisdictions the central bank is responsible for the prudential supervision of the banking sector, whilst in other countries a separate agency is established for this purpose. But these additional features do not add to (or detract from) an entity's legal status as the central bank of a given country.

Proctor have changed over time as acknowledged by the US court in the decision of *NML Capital, Ltd. v Banco Central de la Republica Argentina*, in which it recognised 'that there is no definitive list of activities "normally understood" to be central banking functions. Indeed, the definition of what constitutes a "central bank activity" is likely to change over time'.[9] In this sense, Lastra states that, 'Nowadays the main rationale for central banking is the twin mandate of monetary stability and financial stability'.[10]

1.1.1 Institution of a State

Central banks as institutions of a state are usually established by law or statute which provides legitimacy to operate under a specific mandate. The mandate of a central bank is of a peculiar nature because of its special relationship with the government. As remarked by Lastra:

> Central banks are at the centre, equidistant from the government and the financial system (they are both banker to the government and banker to the banks). Central banking is thus defined by the relationships of the central bank upwards with the government and downwards with the banking and financial system. The law must govern both relationships.[11]

Accordingly, central banks are both regulatory agencies and banks and consequently they carry out public functions governed by administrative law and commercial functions ruled by commercial law.[12] As regulatory agencies most central banks around the world have been granted independence in the pursuit of monetary stability.[13] This movement towards the granting of independence to central banks gained traction in the late 1980's and spread throughout the 1990's with the purpose of combating high inflation. Consequently and in pursuit of domestic price stability, states amended central bank laws to grant independence to central banks to control inflation.[14] The International

9 *NML Capital, Ltd. v Banco Central de la Republica Argentina* 652 F.3d 172, 175 (2nd Cir. 2011).
10 Lastra, *International Financial and Monetary Law* (n 6) 33.
11 ibid.
12 ibid.
13 The legal framework for the independence of central banks is explained in detail in Rosa M Lastra, *Central Banking and Banking Regulation* (Financial Markets Group LSE, 1996).
14 Lastra clarifies that: The phenomenon of independence is not unique to central banking. It is a feature inherent in the administrative law tradition in some countries where functional decentralization is considered an effective way of dividing power, often in combination with geographic decentralization, as is the case in the United States. The rise and rise of agencies or independent regulatory commissions can be explained because of the increasing intricacy of the functioning of the modern state. It is an effective way

Monetary Fund (IMF or Fund), in the context of programs of reforms submitted by its member states, made these changes a necessary condition for such member state to access the Fund's financing. The Treaty on European Union (Maastricht Treaty) also made such changes a condition for a state's entry into the European Monetary Union (EMU).

The consensus that central bank independence is the preferred institutional arrangement was challenged by the expanded goals to be achieved by central banks and rising discontent with the 'status quo', which arose as a result of the GFC.[15] According to Goodhart and Lastra central bank legitimacy is built on the concept of sovereignty, which has two dimensions: formal and societal. The *formal* dimension rests on the democratic foundations of the central bank, usually established by law, treaty or constitution. The *societal* dimension depends upon the support given by the public to the existing system. Therefore, accountability becomes essential to safeguard the legitimacy of central banks over time.[16]

Central bank independence is not absolute but limited to the policy goals set by law, statute or treaty. Hence, central banks are granted independence from the government but at the same time they are accountable to this government. As pointed out by White 'In a democratically ordered society, no government agency, including the central bank, can be wholly "independent" from government'.[17] Therefore, while independent central banks are entitled to

---

of dealing with the regulation of complex realities: money, securities, energy, transport, telecommunications, the environment and others. The skills, expertise and superior qualifications of technocrats (central bankers, energy regulators, etc.) compared to politicians reinforce the case for independence.

Rosa M Lastra 'Central Bank Independence and Financial Stability' (2010) 18 Revista de Estabilidad Financiera 49. On central bank independence also see Lastra (n 6) 64–82; Geoffrey P Miller, 'An Interest Group Theory of Central Bank Independence' (1998) 27 Journal of Legal Studies 433; Douglas Arner and others, 'Central Banks and Central Bank Cooperation in the Global Financial System' (2010) 23.1 Pacific McGeorge Global Business & Development Law Journal, 11; Forrest Capie and Geoffrey Wood, 'Central Bank Independence: Can it Survive a Crisis?' in (2013) 2 Rivista Di Storia Economica 193; Ferdinando Giugliano, Sam Fleming and Claire Jones, 'Central Banks: Peak Independence' *Financial Times* (London, 8 November 2015).

15 According to Goodhart and Lastra the rising discontent with the 'status quo' relates to the increase in populism, understood as 'a major disagreement with the central liberal tenet that allowing the free movement of labour, capital and goods and services between nations would be both generally beneficial and desirable in almost all circumstances'. Charles Goodhart and Rosa Lastra, 'Populism and Central Bank Independence' (2018) 29(1) Open Economies Review 49, 50.

16 ibid 54.

17 William R White, 'Speech' (Central Bank Governor's Club Meeting, Nafplio, 18 October 2012) < www.bis.org/speeches/sp021018.htm> accessed 21 October 2021.

exercise their delegated powers with some degree of discretion in the pursuit of their mandates, they are still accountable to the government and to the electorate on the success or failure to achieve their mandates.

Accountability can take different forms, such as parliamentary accountability, judicial review and cooperation with the executive to coordinate policy.[18] Lastra has pointed out that there are two types of accountabilities – *ex-ante* and *ex-post* accountability. An example of *ex-ante* accountability is where the executive or legislative branch of the government is involved in the appointment of central bank officials. On the other hand, reporting and appearances of central banks officials in front of the legislative branch are considered *ex-post* accountability.[19] In addition, Lastra remarks that the accountability of independent central banks involves both a political dimension and a technical dimension.[20] The political dimension, usually stressed by lawyers, relates to the democratic and institutional legitimacy of independent agencies within the system of checks and balances among the different branches of the state (executive, legislative and judiciary). The technical dimension, mostly emphasised by economists, considers the efficient performance of the independent agencies' objectives and targets and the ex-post disclosure of their actions as a market-based form of accountability.

The judicial review of acts and decisions by central banks was scarce until the GFC. Most notably the Northern Rock case[21] opened in UK the debate on

---

18 As remarked by Fischer, former vice chair of the Board of Governors of the Federal Reserve System: In almost all countries, the central bank's accountability is enforced by requiring regular reporting on monetary policy actions and outcomes to the legislature, to the executive branch, and to the public. The formal centerpiece of the required reporting is generally exercised by the regular publication and presentation to the legislature of an inflation report or monetary policy report, followed by public hearings on the report and related matters.

Stanley Fischer, 'Speech' (Herbert Stein Memorial Lecture National Economists Club, Washington DC, 2015) <www.federalreserve.gov/newsevents/speech/fischer20151104a.htm> accessed 21 October 2021.

19 Lastra (n 6) 90. On the topic of accountable independence see Fabian Amtenbrink and Rosa M Lastra, 'Securing Democratic Accountability of Financial Regulatory Agencies – A Theoretical Framework' in R V de Mulder (ed), *Mitigating Risk in the Context of Safety and Security. How Relevant is a Rational Approach?* (Rotterdam: Erasmus School of Law & Research School for Safety and Security (OMV) 2008) 115.

20 Lastra (n 6) 90–92.

21 Northern Rock, a UK mortgage lender, received liquidity assistance from the Bank of England in September 2017 and this situation triggered a bank run that was followed by nationalisation of the entity and a series of legislative and regulatory responses in UK. Rosa M Lastra, 'Northern Rock, UK bank insolvency and cross-border bank insolvency' (2008) 9(3) Journal of Banking Regulation 165.

discretion, financial stability and the moral hazard associated with the lender of last resort role of the Bank of England. Also, in the EU the Pringle case[22] and the Gauweiler case[23] dealt with the role of the Court of Justice of the European Union (CJEU) in the formation of economic and monetary policy. The Gauweiler case also considered the legality of an unconventional monetary policy measure (the Outright Monetary Transactions (OMT) Programme).[24] As clearly pointed out by Goodhart and Lastra:

> Central bank discretion (a key component of independence) is the freedom to act within the limits of a legal framework. Judicial review does not extend to the 'content of the decision' (the aim of the Court is not to supplant or replace the decision taken or to second guess what central banks should have done), but it does extend to the parameters and legal framework that surround such decision in order to determine whether or not the central bank mandate has been exceeded.[25]

Additionally, the GFC brought to the forefront the issue of transparency of central bank policies, accompanying accountability.[26] This new trend on greater transparency in relation to central bank policies aims to improve the success of the policies by enhancing communication mechanisms and providing clearer expectations for market participants.[27] For example, the minutes of the

---

22 Case C-370/12 *Thomas Pringle v Government of Ireland* EU:C:2012:756.

23 Case C-62/14 *Peter Gauweiler and Others v Deutscher Bundestag* EU:C:2015:400.

24 The technical features of the OMT were published in a press release in September 2012 but were never implemented. European Central Bank, 'Technical Features of Outright Monetary Transactions' (6 September 2012) <www.ecb.int/press/pr/date/2012/html/pr120906_1.en.html> accessed 21 October 2021. The legality of this programme was questioned by German citizens in the German Constitutional Court and the case was brought to the CJEU for a preliminary ruling. On 16 June 2015 the CJEU issued its final ruling that the conditional OMT programme was legal on the basis that the ECB has not exceeded its power concerning monetary policy and did not violate the monetary financing prohibition on EU nations. Case C-62/14 *Peter Gauweiler and Others v Deutscher Bundestag* ibid.

25 Goodhart and Lastra (n 15) 63.

26 A study by Dincer and Eichengreen established a significant movement towards greater central bank transparency in the last decade and also considered that transparent monetary policies are more likely in democratic countries. Nergiz Dincer and Barry Eichengreen, 'Central Bank Transparency: Causes, Consequences and Updates' (2009) NBER Working Paper No 14791 <www.nber.org/papers/w14791> accessed 21 October 2021.

27 Kaufmann and Weber also pointed out that enhanced transparency in relation to central bank policy relates to democratic accountability and thus, is a mechanism to balance central bank independence. Christine Kaufmann and Rolf H Weber, 'Transparency and Monetary Affairs' in Thomas Cottier and others (eds), *The Rule of Law in Monetary Affairs* (CUP 2014) 467.

Federal Open Market Committee in the United States of America (US)[28] and the minutes of the Monetary Policy Committee of the Bank of England in the United Kingdom (UK)[29] must be published within a certain time frame. Also, in its efforts to increase transparency the ECB decided to start publishing an account of the Governing Council's monetary policy meetings minutes since the beginning of 2015, but it does not divulge the details of the vote's records.[30]

1.1.2 Issuance of Money

States exercise monetary sovereignty in the issuance and regulation of money according to the law of the currency (*lex monetae*), which defines what money is and the nominal value that money has in a particular jurisdiction. Hence money, as a creation of the law, is territorial and must be studied within a legal system. The 'state theory of money', adopted in most modern constitutions, claims that money is what the law of the states dictate it to be and as a result falls within the jurisdiction of the issuing state.[31]

The law usually entrusts the central bank with the function of note issuance as a monopoly in the given jurisdiction.[32] In monetary unions this function of note issuance is transferred by treaty from the national authorities of the member states to the supranational authorities of the union, comprising a common central bank or monetary authority.[33] Hence, it can be stated that the legal and institutional arrangements of central banks are at the centre of monetary affairs. Sainz de Vicuña asserts that,

> the concept of money, in a situation of global markets and modern communication technologies, is now inseparable from the institutional set-up of the central banks (that is, their independence, mandate, and instrumentaria) and from the normative framework under which central

28 Federal Reserve Act, s 10 (12 U.S.C. 226).

29 Bank of England Act 1998, s 15.

30 Claire Jones, 'European Central Bank to publish account of meetings' *Financial Times* (Frankfurt, 18 December 2014).

31 For a more detailed analysis on monetary sovereignty and the 'state theory of money' see chapter 2, section 2 of this book.

32 While the monopoly of note issuance by the central bank is the predominant arrangement, there are other arrangements with different levels of competition. Lastra provides a list of some theoretical scenarios of commercial banks competing in the issuance of money. Lastra, *Central Banking and Banking Regulation* (n 13). Also, as remarked in chapter 2, section 2, the expansion of virtual currencies brings some competition to the provision of currency.

33 In the case of the EMU the issuance of money and the conduct of monetary and exchange rate policies has been transferred from national authorities to the European System of Central Banks (ESCB) that includes the ECB and the national central banks.

> banks, credit institutions, financial infrastructures (for example, payments systems), and markets operate, which ensures the stability and the functionality of money.[34]

Central banks, having this monopolist function, can control the volume of the fiat money[35] in circulation and also its seigniorage (that is, the face value of the money minus the cost of their production). The fiat money (physical bank notes and coins) in circulation is *legal tender* as defined by the legislators of the specific monetary system. Proctor remarks that 'only *physical* money is legal tender, whilst the expression "money" embraces a much wider variety of instruments'.[36]

The functions of money as a measure of value, a store of value and a means of payment have evolved over time. For example, during the Bretton Wood system of 1940's the value of money was attached to the value of physical goods (metals, such as gold and silver) and since the collapse of the system in the early 1970's the value of money has been determined by the monetary policy of the relevant central bank and market conditions. The use of fiat money (or cash) as a means of payment has also changed with a decrease in the use of cash over scriptural money. That is, cash payments are used mostly in small amounts while large amounts are settled with scriptural money.[37]

Money issued by a central bank entails a legal claim against it. That is, a credit against a central bank in its deposit account or in cash. As explained by Sainz de Vicuña, 'Money created by central banks is therefore a liability that appears on their balance sheets. It consists of the central bank's duty as deposit-taker to allow the deposit-holder (that is, the commercial banks) to withdraw amounts by way of transfer or cash withdrawal (that is, stock of banknotes)'.[38] He continued by stating that:

> Money is also the credit balance of sight deposits made by the public with credit institutions. These have also the legal nature of being claims against a bank, in this case a commercial bank, but are considered

34 Sainz de Vicuña (n 4) 523.

35 Fiat money is defined as 'Paper money or coins of little or no intrinsic value in themselves and not convertible into gold or silver, but made legal tender by fiat (order) of the government'. Financial Times Lexicon <http://lexicon.ft.com/Term?term=fiat-money> accessed 21 October 2021.

36 Proctor (n 8) 74, fn 51.

37 Scriptural money is dematerialised money such as credit cards, debit cards, online debits, e-money, bank transfers, cheques, computer money (eg paypal), among others.

38 Sainz de Vicuña (n 4) 523.

> 'money' because such claims can be transformed on demand into banknotes, that is, into claims against the central banks.[39]

Consequently, Sainz de Vicuña noted that there is a difference between what is called by the economists 'central bank money' and 'commercial bank money'.[40] While the former entails a central bank liability the latter represents a commercial bank liability.[41]

This note issuance function together with the fractional reserve basis under which most commercial banks operate are the reasons for the 'lender of last resort' (LOLR) function of central banks.[42] In a fractional reserve system only a portion of a bank's assets are liquid. Consequently, banks are not able to convert all of their assets into cash at the same time without losing value or selling them at fire-sale price. This characteristic of a bank's balance sheet makes it fragile to confront a massive liquidity crisis. The central banks, having monopoly of note issuance, are ultimate providers of high-powered money and are

39 ibid.

40 McLeay and others pointed out that, 'Although commercial banks create money through lending, they cannot do so freely without limit. Banks are limited in how much they can lend if they are to remain profitable in a competitive banking system'. Michael McLeay, Amar Radia and Ryland Thomas, 'Money Creation in the Modern Economy' (Bank of England Quarterly Bulletin, 2014 Q1) <www.bankofengland.co.uk/-/media/boe/files/quarterly-bulletin/2014/money-creation-in-the-modern-economy.pdf> accessed 21 October 2021.

41 ibid 524. According to the *Oxford Dictionary of Finance and Banking* a commercial bank refers to: A privately owned bank that provides a wide range of financial services, both to the general public and to firms. The principal activities are operating cheque current accounts, receiving deposits, taking in and paying out notes and coin, and making loans. Additional services include trustee and executor facilities, the supply of foreign currency, the purchase and sale of securities, insurance, a credit-card system, and personal pensions. They also compete with the finance houses and merchant banks by providing venture capital and with building societies by providing mortgages.

Jonathan Law and John Smullen (eds), *A Dictionary of Finance and Banking* (4 rev ed, OUP 2008).

42 Sir Francis Barings was the first to give the name 'the denier resort' to the Bank of England at the end of the eighteenth century. Barings also pointed out that the Bank of England was the only bank that could provide liquidity in times of crisis to the rest of the banks of the system. During the nineteenth century the notion of the LOLR was the focus of much doctrinal debate. From that period, the most relevant writings on the matter emerged from the hands of Thornton in 1802 and Bagehot in 1873. Their contributions, together with those of other scholars of the epoch, have helped to give clarity to the doctrine, improve and detail the main principles and conditions to grant the LOLR assistance either to the market or to individual institutions. Thomas M Humphrey and Robert E Keleher, 'The Lender of Last Resort: A Historical Perspective' (1984) 4(1) Cato Journal 275.

given the final responsibility to ensure the convertibility of a bank's assets into cash.[43]

The fractional reserve banking system under which most commercial banks operate and create the so-called 'commercial bank money' has been subject to a long-standing criticism that acquired new relevance in the aftermath of the GFC and more recently in the debate on the 'Vollgeld' or 'sovereign money' referendum held and rejected in Switzerland on 10 June 2018.[44] The advocates of this referendum proposed a radical reform which purpose was to prohibit commercial banks from issuing commercial money through their traditional business model and to reinstate the central bank as the monopolist provider of all the money in circulation in the given jurisdiction.

1.1.3 Privately Issued Virtual Currencies and Central Bank Issued Virtual Currencies

Other topics that acquired relevance recently in relation to the provision of currency are the proliferation of privately issued virtual or digital currencies (VCs) and the proposals concerning central bank issued virtual or digital currencies (CBVC). Although VCs and CBVCs have common features mostly related to technology – in particular distributed ledgers technology (DLT) and blockchain technology – they are not the same and must be differentiated.[45] While privately issued VCs are 'digital representations of value, issued

43 The GFC has proved that the LOLR remains a vital notion for the central banks in the prevention and management crises. For a comprehensive description of this notion see Andrew Campbell and Rosa M Lastra, 'Revisiting the Lender of Last Resort' (2009) 24 BFLR 453.

44 Ralph Atkins, 'Radical reform: Switzerland to vote on banking overhaul' *Financial Times* (Bern, 29 May 2018); Martin Sandbu, 'Treat money as the public good it is' *Financial Times* (31 May 2018); Martin Wolf, 'Why the Swiss should vote for "Vollgeld" ' *Financial Times* (6 June 2018).

45 Hileman and Rauchs conducted a recent benchmark study on the use of blockchain and DLT and in an effort to clarify the concepts they stated that: the term 'distributed ledger technology' refers to all initiatives and projects that are building systems to enable the shared control over the evolution of data without a central party, with individual systems referred to as 'distributed ledgers'. If one wants to describe a system that has global data diffusion and/or uses a data structure of chained blocks, one should call it a 'blockchain'.

Garrick Hileman and Michel Rauchs, 'Global Blockchain Benchmarking Study' (Cambridge Centre for Alternative Finance 2017) <https://www.jbs.cam.ac.uk/faculty-research/centres/alternative-finance/publications/global-blockchain/#.YXDW157mhdg> accessed 21 October 2021.

by private developers and denominated in their own unit of account',[46] central bank issued CBVCs respond to recent proposals to 'address the direct challenge posed by privately issued VCs by increasing the functionality of central bank money and bolstering public confidence in central bank money',[47] among other considerations.

Lastra and Allen, in a recent paper requested by the European Parliament's Committee on Economic and Monetary Affairs, provide an assessment of the legal aspects of VCs and the implications for central banks' monetary policy and monopoly of note issue.[48] The authors start by considering VCs as financial hybrids that do not fit within established legal concepts but can be differentiated from other types of financial instruments mostly by:

> (i) their use of DLT (in particular blockchain data structures) to facilitate peer-to-peer exchange; (ii) their issuance by an entity outside the traditional monetary system of central banks, commercial banks, and licensed financial intermediaries; (iii) their denomination in a novel unit of account rather than a fiat monetary unit.[49]

These unique characteristics of VCs are a source of concern for regulators worldwide. A variety of regulatory responses have emerged in different jurisdictions and most focus on addressing some of the risks associated with VCs (such as financial integrity, tax evasion and consumer protection). These responses range from the prohibition on usage of VCs, clarifications of existing laws and regulations to consumer warnings.[50] There are also concerns at the international level because VCs operate globally.[51] Thus, a coordinated and

46 Dong He and others, 'Virtual Currencies and Beyond: Initial Considerations' (2016) IMF Staff Discussion Note 16/03, 7 <www.imf.org/external/pubs/ft/sdn/2016/sdn1603.pdf> accessed 21 October 2021.

47 Rosa Maria Lastra and Jason Grant Allen, 'Virtual Currencies in the Eurosystem: challenges ahead' (European Parliament Monetary Dialogue, July 2018) <https://www.europarl.europa.eu/cmsdata/150541/DIW_FINAL%20publication.pdf> accessed 21 October 2021.

48 ibid.

49 ibid 11.

50 An IMF Staff Discussion Note of 2016 includes in its annex a comparison of the different regulatory approaches to VCs opted by a selection of jurisdictions. Dong He and others (n 46).

51 Dong He and others remark that: Regulatory responses are also being developed at the international level. International efforts have focused on achieving consensus on the potential benefits and risks of VCs and identifying areas for future cooperation. A number of international bodies have both provided a forum to discuss issues related to VCs and contributed to the debate through the issuance of reports, guidance and manuals in their areas of expertise. Dong He and others (n 46) 26.

consistent regulatory approach to VCs will be preferable to avoid regulatory arbitrage. However, most jurisdictions have adopted a 'wait and see' strategy in order not to stifle beneficial innovation while the VCs market develops.

Lastra and Allen consider that this 'wait and see' policy strategy is rightly justified on the grounds that VCs do not currently pose any significant implications for the central banks' role on money creation and monetary policy.[52] Some VCs tout that they offer an alternative form of currency in direct competition to the conventional monetary system. However, the authors consider that the growing demand for VCs is motivated more by the interest to invest in a new form of unconventional speculative asset rather than by the desire to obtain a currency substitute outside the traditional monetary system. This consideration together with the current fact that the use of VCs as a medium of exchange (or means of payment) is very low and that VCs possess several technical limitations in their 'medium of exchange' function to qualify as 'money status', weakens the VCs as a potential threat to the central banks' control over money supply. Nonetheless, the authors remarked that this 'wait and see' policy approach to VCs must be regularly re-evaluated to consider new developments in the area.[53]

A recent paper by the Bank for International Payments (BIS) highlighted that CBVCs are 'potentially a new form of digital central bank money that can be distinguished from reserves or settlement balances held by commercial banks at central banks'.[54] Lastra and Allen also reflected on the proposals on the issuance of CBVCs and considered that there are three central reasons for central banks to choose to issue a CBVC:

> The first, and most obvious reason, is that the use of cash is declining in many jurisdictions as electronic payment methods have become more safe and convenient. … The second reason is that central banks currently provide extensive settlement and clearing services for commercial banks, and a CBVC could be used to increase the efficiency of this service with significant costs savings. … The third reason relates to extending central

52 Lastra and Allen (n 47).

53 Lastra and Allen conclude that 'If the VC market continues to grow, central banks such as the ECB may face challenges in their monetary policy role as a large category of money-like payment instruments would be out of their oversight and control'. Lastra and Allen (n 47) 46.

54 BIS Committee on Payments and Market Infrastructures, 'Central bank digital currencies' (March 2018) <www.bis.org/cpmi/publ/d174.pdf> accessed 21 October 2021.

banks' monetary policy toolkit. In particular, CBVC could potentially solve the 'zero lower bound' ('ZLB') problem to encourage spending in the economy during periods of downturn.[55]

These authors continued by stressing that any proposed CBVC will have an effect on the existing monetary system that will vary depending on the choice of design of the instrument. The BIS paper classifies the design choices for a CBVC according to 'access (widely vs restricted); degree of anonymity (ranging from complete to none); operational availability (ranging from current opening hours to 24 hours a day and seven days a week); and interest bearing characteristics (yes or no)'.[56] Recognising that many forms of CBVCs are possible, the BIS paper studies two key alternatives. The first one is titled the *wholesale* alternative because access to CBVCs would be limited to a specific group. The second option is named the *general purpose* alternative because access to CBVCs would be unlimited.

The key properties in the design of a CBVC will have different implications not only on the payments system but also on monetary policy and the stability of the financial system. Therefore, the BIS paper stressed that:

> Any steps towards the possible launch of a CBDC should be subject to careful and thorough consideration. Further research on the possible effects on interest rates, the structure of intermediation, financial stability and financial supervision is warranted. The effects on movements in exchange rates and other asset prices remain largely unknown and also deserve further exploration.[57]

From all the considerations expressed above it can be stated that both VCs and CBVCs present possibilities and threats to the current design of the international monetary and financial order. More remarkably the rise of new technologies like DLT and blockchain structure has the potential to improve existing mechanisms such as the payment, clearing and settlement systems. Hence, regulators must closely monitor the developments in the area while taking care not to stifle beneficial innovation.[58]

---

55 Lastra and Allen (n 47) 39.

56 BIS (n 54) 1.

57 ibid 2.

58 As stated by He, There are both challenges and opportunities for central banks in the digital age. Central banks must maintain the public's trust in fiat currencies and stay in the game in a digital, sharing, and decentralized service economy. They can remain relevant

1.1.4 Conduct of National Monetary Policy

National monetary policy, an essential element of the economic policy of the State, is frequently conducted by a central bank or monetary authority which usually is independent from the government.[59] Most central bank laws assign the central bank with the monetary policy function, listing its objectives and instruments, but do not provide a legal definition of the term. However, it can be stated that 'Monetary policy involves control over the supply of money within the economy and the cost of borrowing that money in terms of its interest rate'.[60] Consequently Gianviti explained the consequences of the implementation of monetary policy as follows, 'The expansion or contraction of the money supply will affect prices. The cost of credit, which affects the level of consumption and investment, varies with the volume of the money supply and with the cost of money available for loans'.[61]

The conduct of monetary policy is directed and also constrained by the objectives or goals set in the central bank's mandate. According to Lastra, 'In the context of the rules versus discretion monetary debate, it is interesting that the advent of central bank independence granted a substantial degree of discretion (technical, not political) to central bankers within the realm of their legal mandate to strive for monetary stability'.[62] These goals are usually determined by the central bank's statute or treaty. In some cases, such as the US Federal Reserve System, central banks are conferred an additional discretion in selecting the objectives to pursue.

The mandate goals of the central banks are generally domestic objectives to pursue the common good. As acknowledged by Gianviti:

> Most countries officially recognise that preserving the value of money is a desirable objective, a 'public good', which has to be attained and preserved to achieve real growth. What this entails, however, is not uniformly

---

by providing more stable units of account than crypto assets and by making central bank money attractive as a medium of exchange in the digital economy.

Dong He, 'Monetary Policy in the Digital Age: Crypto assets may one day reduce demand for central bank money' (2018) 55(2) Finance & Development 13, 16.

59 Independent central banks are in charge of both formulation and implementation of monetary policy. Dependent central banks only deal with the implementation of monetary policy, with the central government retaining control over the design of the policy.

60 Proctor (n 8) 94.

61 François Gianviti, 'Relationship Between Monetary Policy and Exchange Rate Policy' in Cottier and others (eds), *The Rule of Law in Monetary Affairs* (CUP 2014) 545.

62 Rosa M Lastra, 'The Role of Central Banks in Monetary Affairs: A Comparative Perspective' in Cottier and others (eds), *The Rule of Law in Monetary Affairs* (CUP 2014) 91.

> understood. Between preserving the value of the currency in terms of one or more foreign currencies and preserving it in terms of domestic prices, a choice has to be made.[63]

Since the 1990's the objective of domestic price stability prevailed over others in most central bank laws. For example, the ESCB's 'primary objective ... shall be to maintain price stability',[64] the Fed, to 'promote ... stable prices'[65] and the Bank of England, 'to maintain price stability'.[66] Lastra explains that the price stability objective of central banks acquired relevance in the early 1990's as a response to the inflationary conditions of the 1970's and 1980's. She also explains that this objective is backed by economic theory focused on keeping inflation under control and on the empirical proof that independent central banks can control inflationary scenarios better than politicians.[67] A standard definition of inflation is 'A general increase in prices in an economy and consequent fall in the purchasing value of money'.[68] However, domestic price instability can come both from increasing prices (inflation) and decreasing prices (deflation). Thus, White considers that 'there is a growing recognition that "price stability" as an objective of policy implies resisting both rising and falling prices'.[69]

The prevailing goal of domestic price stability on central banks mandates follows the 'Tinbergen Rule'.[70] As explained in chapter 2, this economic rule relies on the assumption that each policy objective correlates to a policy instrument. Hence, multiple policy objectives should be achieved with multiple instruments otherwise some of the objectives will be missed out or under achieved. That said, this rule is applied by central banks (one institution) in the implementation of monetary policy (one instrument) for the pursuit of monetary stability (one goal).

The Tinbergen Rule worked very well for monetary affairs for a long period and helped successfully to contain inflation. However, this rule presented some fissures. For example, in the context of deflation increasing prices are

---

63 Gianviti (n 61) 568.

64 Treaty on the Functioning of the European Union [2008] OJ C115/47 Art 127 and Protocol (No 4) on the Statute of the European System of Central Banks and of the ECB [2010] OJ C326/230 Art 2.

65 12 US Code 226Federal Reserve Act, Section 2 A.

66 Bank of England Act 1998, s 11.

67 Lastra (n 6) 56–59.

68 *Oxford Dictionary of Finance and Banking* (n 41).

69 White (n 17).

70 Jan Tinbergen, *On the Theory of Economic Policy* (North Holland Pub Co 1952).

not a concern (e.g. the case of Japan)[71] and in the context of the most recent GFC the central banks have moved their main concern from price stability to financial stability.[72] With the expanded objectives (financial stability, growth, employment) central banks resorted to a new series of instruments to achieve them. Hence, since the beginning of the GFC central banks have resorted not only to conventional monetary policy instruments (like changes in the interest rate policies) but also unconventional monetary policy instruments. These unconventional tools comprise 'credit support, credit easing, interventions in foreign exchange and securities markets, provision of liquidity in foreign currency and quantitative easing (QE)'.[73]

The expanded goals of central banks together with the recourse to unconventional monetary policies have been subject to much debate and scrutiny since the start of the GFC. The discussion is mainly concerned with the legality of the expansion of central bank mandates and the limits of their emergency powers. In this context, the 'rules *versus* discretion' debate in monetary affairs regained relevance because central banks have discretionary powers within a legal framework.[74] Goodhart and Lastra remind us that:

71 'The Japanese economy has experienced weak inflation for most of the past two decades. ... Continued efforts to reflate the economy have so far fallen short, highlighting the difficulty in escaping a deflation trap once expectations are anchored around a deflation equilibrium'. Samya Beidas-Strom and others, 'Global Disinflation in an Era of Constrained Monetary Policy' in *World Economic Outlook* (IMF 2016) <www.imf.org/en/Publications/WEO/Issues/2016/12/31/Subdued-Demand-Symptoms-and-Remedies> accessed 21 October 2021.

72 The rediscovered objective of financial stability and also the concerns about growth and employment during the GFC triggered regulatory changes for mandates of central banks. For example, in the US, the Dodd Frank Act 2010 reinforced the mandate of financial stability of the Federal Reserve System. In the UK, the law governing the Bank of England was changed to include financial stability together with monetary stability as a dual mandate. In the EU, despite monetary stability remaining as the primary objective in the Treaty, the mandate of the ECB has been expanded through secondary law during the GFC and a new 'banking union' is underway. For a detailed explanation of these regulatory changes and the rediscovered objective of financial stability see Lastra (n 6) 29–110; Rosa M Lastra and Charles E Goodhart, 'Interaction Between Monetary Policy and Bank Regulation' (Monetary Dialogue, September 2015) <www.europarl.europa.eu/committees/en/econ/monetary-dialogue.html?id=20150914CPU05481> accessed 21 October 2021.

73 Lastra (n 6) 1–42. For more detail on conventional and unconventional monetary policies see chapter 2 of this book.

74 This consideration was reflected in the famous statements made by Ben Bernanke, former chairman of the Fed, 'the Federal Reserve has done, and will continue to do, everything possible within the limits of its authority to assist in restoring our nation to financial stability and economic prosperity ...' and by Mario Draghi, president of the ECB, 'Within our mandate, the ECB is ready to do whatever it takes to preserve the euro. And believe me,

> Discretion of course should not mean arbitrariness. It means freedom to act (or not to act) within a framework of rules; and the rules can be changed. ... Some argue that the rules that frame the discretionary decision should be further enhanced. However, it is important to preserve the flexibility to act swiftly in a crisis.[75]

Moreover, the debate concerning central banks mandates and the limits of their emergency powers in crises times have also raised the discussion about the contours between monetary policy and fiscal policy. This debate about the contours among the two policies is not new but has been renewed in the post GFC era and, especially, during the coronavirus disease pandemic (COVID-19) crisis.[76]

According to the 'Annual Economic Report 2020'[77] published by the BIS, monetary and fiscal policies have been very effective since the start of the COVID-19 crisis. As remarked by Borio, 'They rightly worked in close concert leveraging their comparative advantage. Monetary policy deployed its power to create and distribute liquidity; fiscal policy its power to transfer resources and spend. Together, they prevented a much deeper contraction and laid the basis for the recovery'.[78] Borio also states that while blurring the lines among the policies was necessary to provide an effective response to the COVID-19 crisis, it is also relevant to reaffirm the clear boundaries between monetary and fiscal

---

it will be enough'. Ben S Bernanke, 'Speech' (National Press Club Luncheon, Washington, 18 February 2009) <www.federalreserve.gov/newsevents/speech/bernanke20090218a.htm> accessed 21 October 2021; Mario Draghi, 'Speech' (Global Investment Conference, London, 26 July 2012) <www.ecb.europa.eu/press/key/date/2012/html/sp120726.en.html> accessed 21 October 2021.

75 Goodhart and Lastra (n 15) 60.

76 The COVID-19 crisis started in Asia in late 2019 and quickly expanded throughout the rest of the world. As the health crisis worsened, the economic and social crisis also deepened. Equity and credit markets plummeted until major central banks and monetary authorities started injecting liquidity to signal their strong support. See for example Stanley White, Terje Solsvik, Jonnelle Marte, 'Central banks flash the cash as market panic drives liquidity squeeze' *Reuters* (Hong Kong, London, New York, 13 March 2020) <https://www.reuters.com/article/health-coronavirus-liquidity/central-banks-flash-the-cash-as-market-panic-drives-liquidity-squeeze-idINKBN2100NV?edition-redirect=in> accessed 21 October 2021.

77 BIS, 'Annual Economic Report 2020', chapters I and II, <https://www.bis.org/publ/arpdf/ar2020e.htm> accessed 21 October 2021.

78 Claudio Borio, 'Speech: Monetary and fiscal policies at a crossroads: New Normal or New Path?' (2021), Panel remarks at Latvijas Banka Economic Conference, <https://www.bis.org/speeches/sp210920.pdf> accessed 21 October 2021.

policies once the COVID-19 crisis has been left behind and the macroeconomic conditions allow.

1.2 *External Dimension of Monetary Stability – Exchange Rate Stability*

The external dimension of domestic monetary stability – understood as the stability of the value of a specific currency vis-à-vis other currencies (exchange rate stability) – is considered to be part of the foreign exchange policy of a country. Foreign exchange policy encompasses not only the determination of the exchange rate in a given jurisdiction but also the choice of the exchange regime and the management of the reserve assets (monetary reserves). Given these particularities of the foreign exchange policy, the responsibilities of the government and those of the central bank or monetary authority can be confused. Hence, Lastra pointed out that:

> the dividing line of what constitutes foreign exchange policy is often a fuzzy one. In any case, responsibility for the formulation of the exchange rate policy usually rests with the government, while responsibility for its implementation is generally entrusted to the central bank. Accordingly, the central bank has traditionally conducted operations in foreign exchange markets to sustain the national currency's external value, following the guidelines set by the government.[79]

Notwithstanding the major involvement of the government in the direction of the foreign exchange policy, the role of the central bank in this dimension is still crucial. The main reason for this is that nowadays the internal dimension (price stability) and external dimension (exchange rate stability) of monetary stability are intrinsically interrelated. As observed by Gianviti:

> Although the conduct of a country's monetary policy is guided essentially by domestic objectives, such as price stability and/or economic growth and full employment, some decisions may be guided by exchange rate considerations. ... Conversely, in the conduct of a country's exchange rate policy, some decisions may be guided by monetary policy considerations.[80]

79 Lastra (n 6) 51.
80 Gianviti (n 61) 546.

To illustrate the interrelation between monetary policy and exchange rate policy Gianviti described two possible scenarios.[81] In the first case he mentioned the use of instruments of monetary policy to pursue exchange rate stability. That is, for example, a central bank increasing the interest rate for its loans to commercial banks and imposing higher reserve requirements for the extension of credit in order to prevent a depreciation of the exchange rate and to prevent capital outflows.[82] The second case mentioned by Gianviti is the use of exchange rate policy for price stability purposes. That is, for example, a central bank buying all incoming foreign exchange to increase the monetary base and reduce a large balance of payments surplus in the country.

Despite the beneficial effects of coordination between monetary and exchange rate policies, Gianviti also pointed out that these internal and the external dimensions of monetary stability pursue different objectives that can be incompatible in the medium and long term.[83] This conflict between policies was recognised in the text of the Treaty establishing the European Community (EC Treaty) and incorporated later in the Consolidated Version of the Treaty on the Functioning of the European (TFEU). The TFEU provides that the Council can agree on an exchange rate system for non-community currencies subject to a previous recommendation or consultation with the ECB 'in an endeavour to reach a consensus consistent with the objective of price stability …'.[84]

---

81 ibid.

82 This scenario presented by Gianviti was experienced by Argentina during the first week of May 2018 mainly because of the pressure on the Argentinean Peso inflicted by a combination of higher US interest rates, the strong US Dollar and an ongoing domestic conflict with regard to a new legislation to increase the tariff on public services. In order to prevent deeper currency depreciation and capital outflows Argentina's central bank raised the key borrowing rate from 27.25% to 40%. Cat Rutter Pooley and others, 'Argentina Stuns Markets as it pushes interest rates to 40%' *Financial Times* (London, 5 May 2018); John Authers, 'Strong Dollar Poses Big Threat for Emerging Market Investors' *Financial Times* (5 May 2018).

83 See François Gianviti, 'The Objectives of Central Banks' in Mario Giovanoli and Diego Devos (eds), *International Monetary and Financial Law, The Global Crisis* (OUP 2010) 468. On the conflict between monetary and exchange rate policies also see, Manuel Guitián, 'Rules or Discretion in Monetary Policy: National and International Perspectives' in Tomás J T Baliño and Carlo Cottarelli (eds), *Frameworks for Monetary Stability: Policy Issues and Country Experiences* (International Monetary Fund 1994) 33.

84 Consolidated Version of the Treaty establishing the European Community [2002] OJ C325/33 Art 111(1). This provision has been incorporated as Art 219(1) of the Consolidated Version of the Treaty on the Functioning of the European Union OJ C115/47 (TFEU).

1.2.1 Administration of a System of Exchange Control

Countries are free to choose from different exchange rate regimes or arrangements. Since the collapse of the 'fixed exchange rates' system promoted by the Bretton Woods System of 1944 and the subsequent enactment of the Second Amendment to the Articles of Agreement[85] of the IMF in 1978 the era of 'floating exchange rates' began.[86] Countries can choose from a variety of arrangements that include free floating and floating regimes, pegging exchange rates to one currency or to a basket of currencies, using the currency of another state and participating in a currency bloc arrangement.

Notwithstanding the choice of the exchange rate regime Lastra considers that:

> The reality of exchange markets is that exchange rates do fluctuate. Under a system of flexible exchange rates, such variations (appreciation or depreciation of the currency vis-à-vis other currencies) are triggered by market forces. Under a system of government controlled exchange rates, such variations (devaluation or revaluation) are officially imposed decisions.[87]

Concurring with Lastra, Proctor adds that in the era of floating exchange rates the value of a currency in terms of another can be measured in two ways – par of exchange (nominal) and the rate of exchange (real). The par of exchange (nominal) 'is the equation between two money units, each based on a fixed (usually metallic) standard'.[88] This measure is no longer in use since the abandonment of the 'par-value regime' (each currency had a par value with gold or

---

85 As noted by Sir Joseph Gold in 1984: The outstanding characteristic of the provisions on exchange rates in the Second Amendment is that there is no insistence on a unified regime. *Each member is free to choose its exchange arrangement*, with the exception that a member may not maintain the external value of its currency in terms of gold. A member is free also to determine the external value of its currency under the chosen exchange arrangement.

Joseph Gold, 'Public International Law in the International Monetary System' (1984) 38 Sw LJ 819 (emphases added).

86 Notwithstanding this total freedom in the choice of their exchange rate regime the new Article IV, section 1 of the Articles of Agreement of the IMF (Articles of Agreement) created obligations on the conduct of members' policies with the intention to promote exchange rate stability. See IMF, 'Articles of Agreement of the International Monetary Fund' <www.imf.org/external/pubs/ft/aa/index.htm> accessed 21 October 2021. For more detail see chapter 1 section 3 of this book.

87 Lastra (n 6) 425.

88 Proctor (n 8) 495.

with the US gold dollar standard) of the Bretton Woods System of 1944. The rate of exchange (real) refers to the 'market rate' being 'The most frequently quoted rate of exchange is the spot rate, which involves immediate delivery of the currency concerned by means of a credit to the account of the buyer or to its owner'.[89]

Although market forces – ruled by the law of offer and demand – determine the 'market rate' of a currency in relation to another currency, governments retain control over the administration of the system of exchange control and the determination of exchange rate in the given country. The administration of the system of exchange control is not an exclusive function of the central bank and, as mentioned before, usually the central bank implements an exchange rate policy that is decided by the government.[90]

A system of exchange control is usually conducted through domestic regulations that include limitations on capital transfers and/or international payments as artificial boundaries aimed at the protection of national credit markets.[91] While capital transfers relate to the 'capital account' of a country, international payments relate to the 'current account' of a country. As explained in chapter 1 of this book, states are free to adopt 'capital account' restrictions but the rules of international law pose some limitations on 'current account' restrictions. The following chapter 6 detailed the different types of exchange restrictions and capital controls and their corresponding rationales.

1.2.2 Management of a Country's Foreign Reserves

As defined in chapter 1 of this book, the term 'reserve assets' refers to 'external assets that are readily available to and controlled by monetary authorities for meeting balance of payments financing needs, for intervention in exchange markets to affect the currency exchange rate, and for other related purposes …'.[92] This definition explains the economic foundation for countries in holding foreign reserves. That is, exchange rate stability (for both appreciation and depreciation episodes), trade financing and servicing of the country's debts.

89 ibid 503. Proctor also clarifies that the market or commercial rate is not an official rate, which is why commercial documents that involve an exchange rate transaction should detail the institution whose rate is to be referred to and the date and time of the referral.

90 For example in the UK the system of exchange control is a function of the Treasury delegated to the Bank of England. Hence, the Bank of England is independent in the conduct of monetary policy but is dependent in the conduct of exchange rate policy.

91 Lastra (n 6) 54.

92 IMF Statistics Department, 'Balance of Payments Manual', 6th edition (2009) 111 <www.imf.org/external/pubs/ft/bop/2007/pdf/bpm6.pdf> accessed 21 October 2021.

In a recent study on foreign exchange reserves, Goldberg and others explained the official actions taken by central banks in order to influence exchange rates through the accumulation or selling of foreign exchange reserves:

> consider a country that is running a balance of payments deficit – meaning that cash outflows exceed inflows on all transactions between that country and the rest of the world. To avoid a depreciation of the currency, the central bank can sell foreign exchange reserves and buy up the excess supply of the country's currency. Alternatively, in a balance of payments surplus environment, a central bank can avoid a currency appreciation stemming from excess demand for the country's currency by selling domestic currency and accumulating foreign exchange reserves.[93]

Reserve assets can be classified into seven main categories: monetary gold (gold bullions), Special Drawing Rights (SDR) holdings (IMF reserve assets), reserve position in the IMF, currency and deposits, securities (including debt and equity securities), financial derivatives, and other claims (loans and other financial instruments).[94] These categories qualify as reserve assets because they are readily available in unconditional form to the monetary authorities. To be readily available the country's reserve assets must be liquid and denominated in a convertible currency.

The management of a country's foreign reserve assets is usually entrusted with the central bank or relevant monetary authority and is part of the foreign exchange policy dictated by the government.[95] For example, in the US, the Exchange Stabilisation Fund (ESF) of the United States Treasury was established by the Gold Reserve Act of 1934 to contribute to the US dollar exchange rate stability. The ESF operates under the Federal Reserve Bank of New York in its capacity as fiscal agent for the Treasury.[96] In UK, the Exchange Equalisation Account (EEA) was created in 1932 to make available a fund that can be used to

93 Linda Goldberg, Cindy E Hull and Sarah Stein, 'Do Industrialized Countries Hold the Right Foreign Exchange Reserves?' (2013) 19(1) Current Issues in Economics and Finance <www.newyorkfed.org/research/current_issues/ci19-1.html> accessed 21 October 2021.

94 ibid 113–115. The SDR holdings and the reserve position in the IMF only apply as reserve assets for the Fund's members.

95 As noted by Goldberg and others, 'Most often these reserves are held by central banks, although in some cases they may be held by finance ministries or sovereign wealth funds'. Linda Goldberg, Cindy E Hull and Sarah Stein (n 93) 1.

96 Federal Reserve Bank of New York, 'Exchange Stabilization Fund' (Fedpoint, May 2007) <www.newyorkfed.org/aboutthefed/fedpoint/fed14.html> accessed 21 October 2021.

regulate the pound sterling exchange rate stability. The EEA is under the control of the Treasury, which appoints the Bank of England as its agent to manage the reserve assets under the EEA.[97] In Switzerland, the Governing Board of the Swiss National Bank (SNB) decides on the composition of the reserve assets and manages them in order to fulfil the SNB statutory mandate.[98] In the last two decades, the use of reserve assets for exchange rate intervention purposes has been very rare in US and UK.[99] However, Switzerland has been more active in the foreign exchange market with the use of official foreign exchange intervention mechanisms to battle the appreciation of the Swiss franc.[100]

A relevant consideration with regard to foreign reserve assets – or reserve assets held abroad – is the immunities of central banks. The main reason for this is that, within their respective jurisdictions states decide on the level of immunities they provide to their agencies, such as the central bank. However, outside their jurisdictions, states cannot grant immunities to its agents or dependencies. Consequently, the distinction between activities and assets performed and held by central banks for commercial or non-commercial

---

97 HM Treasury, 'Management of the Official Reserves' <https://assets.publishing.service.gov.uk/government/uploads/system/uploads/attachment_data/file/236352/management_of_the_official_reserves_2013_14.pdf> accessed 21 October 2021.

98 Federal Act of 3 October 2003 on the Swiss National Bank (National Bank Act, NBA) Art 5 and Art 46 <www.admin.ch/opc/en/classified-compilation/20021117/index.html> accessed 21 October 2021.

99 With the exception of the collaborative interventions in foreign exchange markets by the US and the UK together with other countries to support the value of the euro in 2000 and the Japanese yen in 2011.

100 In March 2009 the SNB started with a series of interventions in the foreign exchange market to prevent the appreciation of the Swiss franc. Later, in September 2011, the SNB pegged its minimum exchange rate at 1.20 Swiss franc per euro arguing that 'The current massive overvaluation of the Swiss franc poses an acute threat to the Swiss economy and carries the risk of a deflationary development'. After almost four years of maintaining the peg the SNB discontinued the minimum exchange rate and lowered the interest rate into negative territory considering that 'divergences between the monetary policies of the major currency areas have increased significantly … The euro has depreciated considerably against the US dollar and this, in turn, has caused the Swiss franc to weaken against the US dollar. In these circumstances, the SNB concluded that enforcing and maintaining the minimum exchange rate for the Swiss franc against the euro is no longer justified'. Swiss National Bank, *Annual Reports* (2000–2009), <www.snb.ch/en/iabout/pub/annrep/id/pub_annrep> (accessed 21 October 2021); Swiss National Bank, *Swiss National Bank Sets Minimum Exchange Rate at CHF 1.20 per Euro* (2011), <www.snb.ch/en/mmr/reference/pre_20110906/source/pre_20110906.en.pdf> (accessed 21 October 2021); Swiss National Bank, *Swiss National Bank discontinues minimum exchange rate and lowers interest rate to –0.75%* (2015), www.snb.ch/en/mmr/reference/pre_20150115/source/pre_20150115.en.pdf (accessed 21 October 2021).

purposes acquires relevance at this point.[101] As stated before, central banks conduct both commercial and non-commercial activities. In the performance of non-commercial or public functions such as monetary policy and exchange rate policy central banks usually have sovereign immunity.

As noted by Lastra, the theory of sovereign immunity has evolved over time and nowadays 'The new theory of sovereign immunity restricts immunity under certain circumstances, namely when the sovereign engages in acts of a private law or commercial nature'.[102] Nonetheless, Lastra also remarked that central banks and monetary authorities enjoy a distinctive treatment that protect their foreign property from judicial remedies with the presumption that most central bank properties and activities are of a non-commercial nature.[103] This differential treatment is enshrined in the text of domestic laws such as, the State Immunity Act (SIA) of 1978 in the UK,[104] the Foreign Sovereign Immunities Act (FSIA) of 1976 in the US[105] and is also considered by an international treaty, the United Nations Convention on Jurisdictional Immunities of States and Their Property (UNCJIS) of 2004.[106] The presumption of the non-commercial nature of central bank activities and properties is recognised in recent cases like *NML Capital, Ltd. v Banco Central de la Republica Argentina*.[107] As remarked by Proctor, in order to determine whether a particular act is of sovereign or commercial character, it 'is the *nature* of the particular activity, rather than the underlying *purpose* which will be relevant'.[108]

---

101 The law of the state immunity differentiates the acts of the sovereigns (*acta jure imperii*) from acts of a commercial nature (*acta jure gestionis*). The theoretical debate of the law of state immunity is discussed extensively in Hazel Fox and Philippa Webb, *The Law of State Immunity* (3rd edn, OUP 2013).

102 Lastra (n 6) 96–100.

103 ibid.

104 State Immunity Act 1978.

105 Foreign Sovereign Immunities Act of 1976, Pub L 94–583, 90 Stat 2891 (1976) <www.gpo.gov/fdsys/pkg/STATUTE-90/pdf/STATUTE-90-Pg2891.pdf> accessed 21 October 2021.

106 The UNCJIS was adopted in December 2004 during the 65th plenary meeting of the General Assembly by resolution A/59/38 but has not been ratified by enough states in order to become effective. United Nations Treaty Collection, '13. United Nations Convention on Jurisdictional Immunities of States and Their Property' <https://treaties.un.org/Pages/ViewDetails.aspx?src=IND&mtdsg_no=III-13&chapter=3&lang=en> accessed 21 October 2021.

107 *NML Capital, Ltd. v Banco Central de la Republica Argentina* (n 9).

108 Proctor (n 8) 574. Proctor also provides a detailed analysis of the recent cases dealing with the status of monetary institutions before domestic courts and the correspondent procedural immunities. See Proctor (n 8) 572–585.

2 Conclusion

This chapter describes the fundamental role that domestic and regional institutional arrangements have in the promotion of monetary stability. The central banks or relevant monetary authorities are at the centre of this institutional framework both in the pursuit of price stability (internal dimension) and exchange rate stability (external dimension). This chapter also remarks that despite these internal and external dimensions which are interrelated and are better achieved by coordinated actions and policies, they can also present conflicting objectives in the medium and long term.

Beyond the possible conflict between price stability and exchange rate stability, central banks have expanded both their objectives and instruments in the pursuit of stable monetary systems and have also demonstrated themselves to be unique institutions poised to respond to crisis situations such as the GFC. Such unique features are their delegated mandate objectives, instrument independence and accountability, which has allowed them to adapt to changing economic environments and keep their crucial role in the monetary system. As remarked by Arner, 'While central banks adhere to domestic concerns and act autonomously, their independence allows the growth of international cooperation that is increasingly vital to support a state's economic viability'.[109] Notwithstanding the central banks' crucial role in global crisis management scenarios, as remarked in this chapter, they are still institutions of state that are constrained by their domestic goals and mandate. Hence, when it comes to central banks assuming international commitments or engaging with enhanced monetary policy cooperation it rests on unpredictable soft-law commitments that are decided on a case by case situation.

Consequently, it can be argued that under the current circumstances the obligations to do homework promoted by the emerging doctrine of Common Concern in relation to monetary stability are constrained to domestic and regional objectives that do not consider the global dimension. Hence, the aim of Common Concern, if it develops as a principle of law, is to reinforce the role of states as main providers of GPGs not only locally but also globally. As asserted by Cottier, enhanced and shared responsibilities among states beyond existing rights and obligations under international law are of the essence of the legal principle of Common Concern of Humankind.[110]

---

109 Arner and others (n 14) 21.

110 Cottier, 'The Principle of Common Concern of Humankind' (n 1) 84.

These new responsibilities at the domestic level – triggered by the principle of Common Concern and assisted by the multilevel governance theory[111] – may involve an expansion on the mandate goals of central banks to include global stability considerations while deciding domestic policy action. Also, going further, to provide central banks with the possibility to assume international commitments for special situations using as a trigger the Common Concern threshold of the threat to peace, stability and welfare applied to monetary stability. For example, in a liquidity crisis scenario the states which are issuers of reserve currencies may have a commitment to establish bilateral or multilateral swap lines (through their respective central banks) with the central banks of the countries in need of liquidity. Hence, moving from a discretional attribute of central banks to a commitment activated by the principle of Common Concern (resorting to the principle of shared but differentiated responsibility). Furthermore, the emerging doctrine of Common Concern demands increased transparency and accountability. Hence, the implementation of these enhanced obligations of central banks will also involve renewed efforts on transparency, information sharing and accountability, as with more responsibility comes more accountability.

111 For a description of the multilevel governance theory see chapter 3 of this book.

CHAPTER 6

Domestic Obligations concerning Monetary Stability

Unilateral Reactions and Securing Compliance

This chapter follows the previous chapter 5 concerning the second element of the emerging doctrine of Common Concern of Humankind – the obligations at the domestic level or obligations to do homework.[1] While chapter 5 deals with the *first level of commitment* that emerges from the obligation to do homework, that is the pursuit and maintenance of monetary stability as a domestic public good and a local Common Concern, this chapter studies the *second level of commitment* regarding the obligation to do homework within the emerging doctrine of Common Concern. This *second level of commitment* entails compliance with international commitments assumed in international agreements and in customary law. As pointed out by Cottier, the doctrine is not meant to affect the existing obligations under international law but to confer them with the foundations of the emerging principle of Common Concern. That is, encouraging the timely and effective implementation of international commitments.

Beyond the implementation of international commitments, the emerging doctrine aims to inspire autonomous domestic policy-making to address the issues underlying the Common Concerns. That is, to reinforce the role of states as main providers of GPGs not only locally but also globally. In monetary affairs, unilateral actions with extraterritorial effects have proved useful in the pursuit of monetary stability but are limited and temporary in nature. Hence, this chapter analyses this dimension of the obligation to do homework by considering salient examples of domestic unilateral actions with extraterritorial effects regarding monetary affairs. This chapter also offers some remarks on the most controversial element of the emerging doctrine of Common Concern, securing compliance with the obligations that may emerge from an accepted Common Concern of international monetary stability.

1 Thomas Cottier, 'The Principle of Common Concern of Humankind' in Thomas Cottier (ed), *The Prospects of Common Concern of Humankind in International Law* (CUP 2021).

DOI:10.1163/9789004508736_008

1 Domestic Obligations – Unilateral Reactions

As stated in the 1927 Lotus rule,[2] extraterritorial jurisdiction of states requires sufficient attachment to the territory of the State. However, it may be difficult to respect such jurisdictional attachment in the case of common concerns. The nature of the problems considered as Common Concerns are in their nature shared, transboundary problems, often of global reach. Hence, as clarified by Cottier, Common Concern as a principle of international law would not require the territorial linkages but would examine whether the measure and action is able to support the attainment of a Common Concern as defined by the international community during the process of claims and responses.[3]

In monetary affairs, unilateral actions with extraterritorial effects have proved useful in the pursuit of monetary stability but are limited and temporary in nature. The main examples of this point have been brought by the GFC and its aftermath. In order to restore and promote monetary and financial stability and in the absence of appropriate global institutions and adequate international cooperation, states have been implementing a series of conventional and unconventional monetary policy measures. These measures have had and continue to have spillover effects (both positive and negative) beyond their intended borders.[4] The key channels of transmission of monetary policy spillovers are capital flows and exchange rates.[5] Consequently, states have resorted to a set of lawful unilateral measures to limit or repel the unwanted spillovers (or negative externalities) generated by the conventional and unconventional monetary policies in place since the beginning of the GFC. The unilateral measures are comprised mostly by capital controls and exchange restrictions. Additionally, the accumulation of reserves and regional financing agreements have been cited as examples of unilateral measures of a precautionary nature.

---

2 *The Case of the S. S. Lotus* (*France v Turkey*) (1927) PCIJ Series A, No 10. Also see Cedric Ryngaert, *Jurisdiction in International Law* (OUP 2008).

3 Cottier, 'The Principle of Common Concern of Humankind' (n 1) 63.

4 See chapter 2, section 3 of this book for a detailed analysis of the conventional and unconventional monetary policy measures and their corresponding spillovers.

5 The BIS stated in 2012 that the changes in the monetary policy of the major advanced economies 'are being transmitted to emerging economies in the form of undesirable exchange rate and capital flow volatility'. Bank of International Settlements, *BIS Annual Report 2011/2012* ch IV <www.bis.org/publ/arpdf/ar2012e4.pdf> accessed 21 October 2021. The immediate subsequent annual reports for the years 2012–2013, 2013–2014 and 2014–2015 provide an extensive and detailed examination of the spillovers. See Bank of International Settlements, *Annual Report* <www.bis.org/annualreports/index.htm> accessed 21 October 2021.

As mentioned in the previous chapter, the system of exchange control is usually conducted through domestic regulations that include limitations on capital transfers and/or international payments as artificial boundaries aimed at the protection of national credit markets. While capital transfers relate to the 'capital account' of a country, international payments relate to the 'current account' of a country. As explained in chapter 1 of this book, states are free to adopt 'capital account' restrictions but the rules of international law pose some limitations on 'current account' restrictions.[6]

1.1 *Exchange Restrictions*

Viterbo provides a clear and detailed description of the different types of exchange restrictions and their rationale. In doing so Viterbo considers that exchange restrictions are:

> State regulation or administrative practice that limits cross border current transactions in foreign currencies (international payments). When exchange restrictions are in place, residents and non- residents cannot purchase (or sell) foreign currencies and dispose freely of them for current international transactions and transfers (either for goods or services).[7]

These restrictions are usually considered temporary emergency measures that respond to serious balance of payment imbalances.[8] Also, these exchange restrictions are imposed occasionally in order to allocate available foreign currency of a country among different needs (e.g. the purchase of essential imports), to preserve the level of monetary reserves and to monitor the dimension of external debt. These measures may regulate both outwards and inwards international payments and, as a consequence, residents and non-residents may not be able to purchase (or sell) foreign currencies and dispose of them freely for current international transactions and transfers.[9] As an example of

6 As stated elsewhere on this book, this section describes exchange restrictions and capital controls under the IMF legal framework. Hence, trade and investment law considerations regarding exchange restrictions and capital control are not part of this analysis. Those considerations can be found in Annamaria Viterbo, *International Economic Law and Monetary Measures* (EE 2012) ch 5 and 6.

7 Viterbo, *International Economic Law and Monetary Measures* (n 6) 153.

8 See chapter 1 of this book for the definition of the term 'balance of payments'.

9 According to the IMF Articles of Agreement exchange restrictions and exchange controls are not the same: the latter is broader in scope. Hence, not all exchange measures are exchange restrictions. For further discussion on this differentiation see Viterbo, *International Economic Law and Monetary Measures* (n 6) 167.

restrictions on inwards payments Viterbo mentions the repatriation and surrender requirement. This requirement imposes an obligation on residents to repatriate foreign exchange earnings and convert them into local currency at a stipulated exchange rate. Regarding restrictions on outward payments she refers, among others, to the prohibition on the transfer of foreign currency overseas by residents without prior approval of the local authority.

As clearly pointed out by Sir Joseph Gold, general counsel of the IMF from 1960 to 1979, current account convertibility is a key element of the IMS:

> A multilateral system of payments for current transactions among members is another prominent feature of the Articles. This system can be described as one that requires members to make their currencies convertible for the purposes of current international transactions. A member that has been able to make its currency convertible must refrain from imposing restrictions on the making of payment and transfers for current international transactions as defined by the Articles, multiple currency practices, or discriminatory currency arrangements.[10]

Consequently, Article VIII, Section 2(a) of the Fund's Articles of Agreement (Articles of Agreement) prohibits IMF members, without the approval of the Fund, from imposing restrictions on the making of payments and transfers for current international transactions. Notwithstanding that prohibition, the Articles of Agreement recognise some particular exceptions and allow for the introduction of restrictions.

The Articles of Agreement consider four possible exceptions to 'current account convertibility'. The *first exception* is contemplated in Article XIV of the Articles of Agreement and allows member states to a transitional period before committing to the obligations contained in Article VIII of the Articles of Agreement. This provision was meant to facilitate post-war reconstruction. Hence, while member states are allowed to maintain existing currency restrictions at the point of entry into the IMF, new restrictions or the reintroduction of measures must be approved by the Fund. As of December 2017, 'Eighteen IMF members make use of the transitional arrangement under Article XIV. Of these 18 members, three maintain no restrictions but have not yet decided to accept the obligations under Article VIII'.[11]

10 Joseph Gold, 'Law and Reform of the International Monetary System' (1975) 10 Journal of International Law and Economics 376.

11 IMF, 'Annual Report on Exchange Arrangements and Exchange Restrictions 2018' (2019) <www.imf.org/en/Publications/Annual-Report-on-Exchange-Arrangements-and-Exchange-Restrictions/Issues/2019/04/24/Annual-Report-on-Exchange-Arrangements-and-Exchange-Restrictions-2018-46162> accessed 21 October 2021.

The *second exception* requires, under Article VIII of the Articles of Agreement, specific Fund approval to impose a restriction for the purposes of maintaining balance of payments. The aim of this exception was to provide flexibility to the system. However, Article VIII does not provide specific requirements to evaluate the opportunity to introduce such restrictions. In consequence, the Executive Board of the Fund adopted in 1960 the Decision No 1034- (60/27) stating that:

> if members, for balance-of-payments reasons, propose to maintain or introduce measures which require approval under Art. VIII, the Fund will grant approval only where it is satisfied that the measures are necessary and that their use will be temporary while the member is seeking to eliminate the need for them.[12]

Hence, the Fund may approve the imposition of exchange restrictions only if such measures are justified on the grounds of balance of payments needs and they are temporary and non-discriminatory among members.[13] The Fund's decisions on exchange restrictions are not usually published but mentioned in Article IV reports.[14]

The *third exception* concerns national or international security reasons. That is, when a member state requests for the introduction of exchange restrictions on the grounds of essential national or international security reasons pursuant to Article VIII, Section 2(b) of the Articles of Agreement. This exception was not contemplated in the original text of the Articles of Agreement. However, the IMF Executive Board adopted in 1952 the Decision No 144-(52/51), which allows the introduction of exchange restrictions for national or international

12 IMF Executive Board, 'Article VIII and Article XIV' (Decision No 1034-(60/27), 1 June 1960) <https://www.imf.org/external/SelectedDecisions/Description.aspx?decision=1034-(60/27)> accessed 21 October 2021.

13 IMF, 'Article VIII Acceptance by IMF Members: Recent Trends and Implications for the Fund' (2006) <www.imf.org/en/Publications/Policy-Papers/Issues/2016/12/31/Article-VIII-Acceptance-by-IMF-Members-Recent-Trends-and-Implications-for-the-Fund-PP568> accessed 21 October 2021.

14 On this point Viterbo rightly notes that: The publication of the Fund's approval (or advice) and a more transparent process would enable other international organizations and dispute settlement bodies to take into account the position of the IMF in reaching their own decisions. Transparency and exchange of information on exchange restrictions issues would deepen international cooperation and consistency.

Viterbo, *International Economic Law and Monetary Measures* (n 6) 171.

security reasons.[15] Member states depend on this Decision No 144-(52/51) for the imposition of economic sanctions adopted by resolution of the UN Security Council under chapter VII of the UN Charter.[16]

A different procedure applies for restrictions imposed for security reasons than those for maintenance of balance of payments. More specifically, a member state should notify the Fund before imposing such restrictive measures. The notifications are immediately circulated to the Board. The member may assume that the Fund has no objection unless the Fund informs the member otherwise within 30 days of the notification. The Fund's approval of an exchange restriction on security grounds is granted for an unlimited period of time. This exception has been widely invoked by member states since the adoption of the Decision No 144- (52/51). According to the latest annual report on exchange restrictions issued by the Fund:

> In total, 19 members notified the IMF of measures introduced solely for security reasons during 2017, while 10 members did so during January–September 2018. The number of countries notifying the IMF of such measures dropped from 37 in 2015 and 32 in 2016. For the most part, notification came from advanced economies. In general, the restrictions involved take the form of financial sanctions to combat the financing of terrorism or financial sanctions against certain governments, entities, and individuals in accordance with United Nations Security Council resolutions or EU regulations.[17]

The *fourth exception* that permits exchange restrictions is contemplated in Article VII, Section 3(b) and contemplates the case that a currency is declared scarce. This exception was never invoked.

Adopting or maintaining exchange restrictions that do not fall within the above-mentioned exceptions have legal consequences under the Articles of Agreement. As detailed in section 2 of this chapter, Article XXVI, Section 2 of the Articles of Agreement lists exhaustively the three possible sanctions to which a Fund member can be subject in case of breach of its obligations. These sanctions are: ineligibility to use the Fund's resources, suspension of voting

---

15 IMF Executive Board, 'Payments Restrictions for Security Reasons: Fund Jurisdiction' (Decision No 144-(52/51), 14 August 1952) <www.imf.org/external/SelectedDecisions/Description.aspx?decision=144-(52/51> accessed 21 October 2021.

16 United Nations Charter (full text) <www.un.org/en/sections/un-charter/un-charter-full-text/> accessed 21 October 2021.

17 IMF, 'Annual Report on Exchange Arrangements and Exchange Restrictions 2018' (n 11).

rights and expulsion from the Fund. In addition to the sanctions, members that have obtained financial assistance from the Fund cannot impose or intensify exchange restrictions on current international transactions. If the member does not comply with such requirements, further disbursements can be interrupted until a new understanding on the financial assistance is reached with the Fund or the Fund grants a waiver for such non-compliance at the member's petition.[18]

In order to ensure the effectiveness of the exchange restrictions that are approved under the Articles of Agreement, Article VIII, Section 2(b) contemplates that exchange contracts which involve the currency of a member and which are contrary to exchange control regulations applicable to that member in connection with the Articles of Agreement, are unenforceable.[19] Hence, these legitimate exchange restrictions are imbued with legal effectiveness even beyond the jurisdiction imposing the restriction.[20]

1.2 *Capital Controls*

On capital controls Viterbo considers that 'Governments resort to capital controls to regulate the volume, composition, or allocation of international capital flows and to restrict foreign investors' entrance or exit opportunities'.[21] She also mentions that these measures can have a precautionary purpose or an emergency nature and can target capital inflows and capital outflows respectively. According to the Oxford Dictionary of Finance and Banking the term capital inflows relates to 'an increase of a country's foreign assets within its own country or a decrease in its assets held abroad' and on the other hand the term capital outflows means 'a decrease in a country's foreign assets held in its own country or an increase in its assets held abroad'.[22]

On one hand, measures to limit capital inflows are usually precautionary with the intention to prevent the entrance of non-desirable investments such as large and volatile short-term capital investments. As examples of controls

18 Viterbo, *International Economic Law and Monetary Measures* (n 6) 175.

19 François Gianviti, 'Evolving Role and Challenges for the International Monetary Fund' (2001) 35(4) The International Lawyer 1371.

20 In order to clarify the interpretation of Article VIII, Section 2(b) the IMF Executive Board adopted Decision No 446-4. See IMF Executive Board, 'Unenforceability of Exchange Contracts: Fund's Interpretation of Article VIII, Section 2(b)' (Decision No 446-4, 10 June 1949) <www.imf.org/external/SelectedDecisions/Description.aspx?decision=446-4> accessed 21 October 2021.

21 Viterbo, *International Economic Law and Monetary Measures* (n 6) 155.

22 Jonathan Law and John Smullen (eds), *A Dictionary of Finance and Banking* (4th rev edn, OUP 2008).

on capital inflows Viterbo cites the requirement for portfolio investments and foreign direct investments to have at least one year of residence, the prohibition on residents incurring external borrowing beyond certain limits, among others. For example, controls on capital inflows were introduced during the 1990's by Brazil, Chile, Colombia, Malaysia and Thailand, during the GFC of 2007–2009 by Iceland, South Korea and Taiwan, and more recently in 2019 by Argentina.[23]

On the other hand, measures to limit capital outflows are usually reactions to crisis scenarios aimed to prevent capital flight and to 'protect foreign exchange reserves and the ability of the monetary authority to act as a lender of last resort, to manage external debt problems, to prevent large sales of domestic assets as well as investors and lenders flight risk'.[24] As examples of controls on capital outflows Viterbo mentions, among others, the prohibition on transferring capital overseas in relation to the sale of an investment and the obligation imposed on non-residents to maintain their capital for a period of time before repatriation is permitted. For instance, controls on capital outflows were introduced in the 1980's by Latin American countries affected by the debt crisis, during the East Asian crisis of 1997–1998 by Malaysia and Thailand, and in 2008 by Iceland.[25]

Capital controls can also be comprised of direct controls and indirect controls. Direct controls are the administrative controls imposed by governmental regulations. These regulations limit the capital transaction itself and the associated capital movement.[26] Some examples of direct capital controls are quantitative limits on export and import of banknotes, a ban on certain types of investments, compulsory deposit requirement for foreign investors, and restrictions on the repatriation of capital or foreign currency holdings. Indirect controls are market-based controls that discourage capital transactions and their underlying payments and transfers by making them more costly. Some examples of indirect capital controls are taxation on cross-border financial flows, taxation of income on the holding of financial assets (the so-called

23 Since 2012 the IMF publishes annually a document entitled the 'Taxonomy of Capital Flow Management Measures'. This document contains information about measures assessed by Fund staff as capital flow management measures (CFMs) and is discussed in published IMF staff reports. IMF, 'IMF 2019 Taxonomy of Capital Flow Management Measures' <https://imf.org/~/media/Files/Data/2019/imf-2019-taxonomy-of-capital-flow-management-measures.ashx> accessed 21 October 2021.

24 Viterbo, *International Economic Law and Monetary Measures* (n 6) 157.

25 IMF, 'IMF 2019 Taxonomy of Capital Flow Management Measures' (n 23).

26 Viterbo, *International Economic Law and Monetary Measures* (n 6) 157.

Tobin tax[27] or currency taxation) and unremunerated reserve requirement for non-residents.

As stated elsewhere in this book, international capital movements are one of the core elements of the IMS and have evolved over time (as described in Annex I to chapter 1 of this book). International capital movements are intrinsically related to the international payment system and have been subject to the challenges imposed by the liberalisation of current international payments and increased openness of trade and capital flows. While restrictions on making payments and transfers for current international transactions are prohibited under the Articles of Agreement (as described in the previous section), Fund members are entitled to regulate international capital movements. Hence, it can be argued that Fund members have full sovereignty over the regulation of capital flows since the enactment of the original Articles of Agreement to date.[28]

Article VI, Section 3 of the Articles of Agreement expressly recognises the right of the members to regulate capital flows: 'Members may exercise such controls as are necessary to regulate international capital movements, but no member may exercise these controls in a manner which will restrict payments for current transactions or which will unduly delay transfers of funds in settlement of commitments'.[29] This discretion provides the opportunity for the Fund's members to regulate international capital movements both *outwards* and *inwards* as long as their measures do not affect current transactions.[30]

---

27 This tax is named after the economic Nobel laureate James Tobin who suggested the introduction of a currency transaction tax on foreign exchange transactions in order to limit speculative capital flows. James Tobin, 'A Proposal for International Monetary Reform' (1978) 4(3–4) Eastern Economic Journal 153.

28 In 1961 the Organisation for Economic Cooperation and Development (OECD) issued the 'OECD Code of Liberalisation of Capital Movements' (the Code) with the aim to promote the liberalisation of capital account operations. All 36 OECD countries adhere to the Code and since 2012 the Code has also been open to non-OECD countries. The most recent review of the Code in 2016 to 2019 further reinforced the instrument while providing increased flexibility to address financial stability risks. The Code is the only multilateral legal instrument having as its main purpose the regulation of international capital movements. OECD, 'OECD Code of Liberalisation of Capital Movements' <www.oecd.org/investment/codes.htm> accessed 21 October 2021. For an analysis on the Code see Claus D Zimmermann, *A Contemporary Concept of Monetary Sovereignty* (OUP 2013) 45.

29 Rosa M Lastra, *International Financial and Monetary Law* (2nd edn, OUP 2015) 450.

30 The Fund's 'Annual Report on Exchange Arrangements and Exchange Restrictions' differentiates between capital controls based on the type of asset transaction they affect (equity, foreign direct investment and debt holdings or securities) and also by the direction of the flows (outwards or inwards). IMF, 'Annual Report on Exchange Arrangements and Exchange Restrictions 2018' (n 11).

The Second Amendment did not introduce any modification to the framework on capital movements. However, the new Article IV, Section 1(iii) (relating to the stability of the exchange rate system) indirectly limited the right to regulate capital movements through the qualifications established under the new obligations for the Fund's members.[31] In particular the Fund's surveillance decision of 2007 considers that:

> The Fund's assessment of a member's policies will always include an evaluation of the developments in the member's balance of payments, including the size and sustainability of capital flows, against the background of its reserves, the size and composition of its other external assets and its external liabilities, and its opportunities for access to international capital markets.[32]

An amendment to the Articles of Agreement to expand the Fund's jurisdiction over the liberalisation of capital movements was lively debated through the 1990's.[33] This debate was contemporaneous with the liberalisation of capital movements within the EU as it worked towards the adoption of a single currency.[34] In addition, the General Agreement on Trade in Services promoted the removal of capital controls for trade in financial services globally and various bilateral investment treaties included the negotiation of the liberalisation of FDI flows to developing countries.[35] Notwithstanding these developments, the proposed amendment to the Article VI of the Articles of Agreement never came to fruition. The East Asian crisis and the failure of the negotiations on the multilateral framework on investment under the auspices of the OECD weakened the Fund's intentions to expand its jurisdiction over the capital account.[36]

---

31 Hence, the introduction of capital controls may violate the prohibition on manipulation of exchange rates as stated in Article IV, Section 1(iii) of the Articles of Agreement. For more detail about exchange rate manipulation see the following section.

32 IMF Executive Board, 'Bilateral Surveillance over Members' Policies' (15 June 2017) <www.imf.org/en/News/Articles/2015/09/28/04/53/pn0769#decision> accessed 21 October 2021. For more details on the surveillance function of the IMF and Article IV of the Articles of Agreement, see chapter 4 of this book.

33 Stanley Fischer, 'Capital-Account Liberalization and the Role of the IMF' (Essays in International Finance, Princeton University 1998).

34 Lastra, *International Financial and Monetary Law* (n 29) 224; Charles Proctor, *The Euro and the Financial Markets: The Legal Impact of EMU* (Jordans 1999) 6.

35 Viterbo, *International Economic Law and Monetary Measures* (n 6) 187.

36 In the view of some economists the liberalisation of capital movements does not necessarily achieve an optimal allocation of resources, in particular when domestic distortions exist. See Joseph Stiglitz, 'Capital Market Liberalization, Globalization and the IMF' (2005) 20 Oxford Review of Economic Policy 57. On this point Lastra considers that countries,

The longstanding debate about the liberalisation of international capital movements and the benefits of capital controls have been revitalised since the start of the GFC.[37] New capital controls were introduced (e.g. in Brazil, Iceland, Indonesia, Peru, South Korea and Ukraine) and some existing capital controls were tightened (e.g. in Argentina and Russia).[38] Consequently, acknowledging that international capital flows is a key aspect of the IMS provides significant benefits but also carries risks – the IMF approved in 2012 the institutional view on the liberalisation and management of capital flows (the Institutional View).[39] The Institutional View 'provides the Fund with a basis for consistent advice on policies related to capital flows'.[40]

This view states that 'Capital flow management measures (CFMs) are measures that are specifically designed to limit capital flows' and a differentiation is made between residence-based measures (capital controls) and others.[41] On this point Zimmermann makes an interesting observation by considering that:

> the Fund's new institutional view on capital flows may serve as an interesting illustration of how the principle of subsidiarity frames the contemporary exercise of specific sovereign powers on the realm of money. The Fund has eventually given up its quest for shifting the jurisdiction over capital controls to the multilateral level in light of overwhelming

---

such as Chile, that impose controls on short-term capital inflows are less exposed to volatility than countries with unrestricted capital movements. Lastra, *International Financial and Monetary Law* (n 29) 454.

37 For an excellent review on the recent literature on the debate about the liberalisation and management of capital flows see Masahiro Kawai and Mario B Lamberte (eds), *Managing Capital Flows: The Search for a Framework* (EE 2010); Adam Feibelman, 'The IMF and Regulation of Cross-Border Capital Flows' (2015) 15(2) Chicago Journal of International Law 409; Menno Broos and Sebastian Grund, 'The IMF's Jurisdiction Over The Capital Account – Reviewing the Role of Surveillance in Managing Cross-Border Capital Flows' (2018) 21(3) JIEL 489. See also Arvind Subramaniam, Raghuram Rajan and Eswar Prasad, 'Patterns of International Capital Flows and Their Implications for Economic Development' (Proceedings of the 2006 Jackson Hole Symposium, Federal Reserve Bank of Kansas City, 2006); 'Following the Money' (*The Economist*, 22 February 2020) <www.economist.com/finance-and-economics/2020/02/20/cash-sloshes-around-the-world-in-unexpected-ways> accessed 21 October 2021.

38 IMF, 'Annual Report on Exchange Arrangements and Exchange Restrictions 2018' (n 11).

39 IMF, 'The Liberalization and Management of Capital Flows: An Institutional View' (2012) 29–30 <www.imf.org/external/np/pp/eng/2012/111412.pdf> accessed 21 October 2021.

40 IMF, 'Capital Flows – Review of Experience with the Institutional View' (2016) <www.imf.org/en/Publications/Policy-Papers/Issues/2017/01/13/PP5081-Capital-Flows-Review-of-Experience-with-the-Institutional-View > accessed 21 October 2021.

41 IMF, 'The Liberalization and Management of Capital Flows: An Institutional View' (n 39).

> economic evidence showing that outright liberalization of the capital account should not be a one-size-fits-all remedy.[42]

As a consequence, Broos and Grund consider that 'The institutional view can be seen as the most ambitious attempt yet to establish a set of international principles in respect of states' capital account management. Yet it is clear that the institutional view has no intention to prepare the expansion of Fund's formal jurisdiction'.[43] The review of the Fund's mandate over the capital account was again discussed in the context of the IMF's 2014 Triennial Surveillance Review.[44] As a consequence of this debate and based on the results of an external study[45] the IMF staff proposed to extend the Fund's jurisdiction over the members' capital accounts in order to: (i) promote a coordinated response to mitigate any potential risk to the global economy which arises from 'liquidity imbalances' by influencing the combination of countries' policies; and (ii) grant the Fund with additional tools to address risks due to volatile capital flows that threaten the stability of the international monetary system. Ultimately, the IMF Executive Board disagreed with these proposals and rejected the reopening of the 1990's debate on the reconsideration of the Fund's mandate in this field.

In October 2018 the G20 Eminent Persons Group on Global Financial Governance (EPG) launched the report entitled 'Making the Global Financial System Work for All'. In this report, the EPG reopened the debate about the expansion of the Fund's jurisdiction over the capital account. Specifically, on capital flows, the report suggests that:

> the IMF's framework of policy guidance should enable countries to move toward openness as a long-term goal, at a pace and sequence that enables them to preserve financial stability, and to manage episodes of excessive volatility. This involves (i) evolving and extending the IMF's Institutional View as a basis for developing policy options for receiving countries; and (ii) the IMF complementing this by developing a policy framework that

42 Claus D Zimmermann, *A Contemporary Concept of Monetary Sovereignty* (n 28) 44.

43 Broos and Grund, 'The IMF's Jurisdiction Over the Capital Account' (n 37).

44 IMF, '2014 Triennial Surveillance Review-Overview Paper' (2014) <www.imf.org/external/np/pp/eng/2014/073014.pdf> accessed 21 October 2021.

45 Malcolm D Knight and Guillermo Ortiz, '2014 Triennial Surveillance Review-External Study-Multilateral Surveillance: Ensuring a Focus on Key Risks to Global Stability' (2014) <www.imf.org/~/media/Websites/IMF/imported-full-text-pdf/external/np/pp/eng/2014/_073014f.ashx> accessed 21 October 2021.

enables sending countries to meet their domestic objectives while avoiding large adverse spillovers. This is best undertaken with inputs from national authorities and the BIS.[46]

Even though the Fund's members retain the right to impose controls over capital movements, their participation in trade and investment treaties and in regional agreements are subject to liberalisation of capital movements and payments. Hence, the room for states to introduce capital controls in order to promote or protect international monetary stability may be limited.[47]

1.3 *Exchange Rate Manipulation*

Capital flow volatility also put appreciation pressures on the currencies, and thus in order to limit this pressure the spillover-receiving countries took recourse to exchange restrictions. These interventions, in the form of exchange rate manipulation carried out by countries aiming to gain competitive advantage, led to the debate on 'currency wars'[48] or 'exchange rate misalignment'.[49] The debate on exchange rate manipulation is not new and has been a recurrent topic in international relations throughout history.[50] Recent examples are

46 Eminent Persons Group on Global Financial Governance, 'Making the Global Financial System Work for All' (October 2018) <www.globalfinancialgovernance.org/assets/pdf/G20EPG-Full%20Report.pdf> accessed 21 October 2021.

47 During the Obama administration in the US, a group of influential economists issued the 'Statement on Capital Controls and Trade and Investment Treaties' (the Statement) in January 2011. While the Statement argued in favour of the liberalisation of trade in goods and services, they recognised the need for a more prudent approach to capital account liberalisation, allowing countries to implement capital controls when the circumstances demanded them. 'Economists Issue Statement on Capital Controls and Trade Treaties' (11 January 2011) <www.ase.tufts.edu/gdae/policy_research/CapCtrlsLetter.html>.

48 Former Brazilian finance minister Guido Mantega used the term 'currency wars' in 2010 when he denounced what he saw as a deliberate pursuit of weaker currencies. 'How to Stop a Currency War'(*The Economist*, 14 October 2010) <www.economist.com/leaders/2010/10/14/how-to-stop-a-currency-war> accessed 21 October 2021.

49 Exchange rate misalignment refers to deviations in exchange rates from their economic equilibrium levels. For a definition of equilibrium exchange rate see Paul R Krugman, 'Equilibrium Exchange Rates' in William H Branson, Jacob A Frenkel and Morris Goldstein (eds), *International Policy Coordination and Exchange Rate Fluctuations* (University of Chicago Press 1990) <www.nber.org/chapters/c6948.pdf> accessed 21 october 2021.

50 For a detailed and excellent study on exchange rate misalignment and international law, see Claus D Zimmermann, 'Exchange Rate Misalignment and International Law' (2011) 105(3) AJIL 423.

the cases of massive interventions by China[51] and Switzerland[52] to maintain the value of their currencies and avoid appreciation.

As stated elsewhere in this work, countries are free to choose from different exchange rate regimes or arrangements. Since the collapse of the 'fixed exchange rates' system promoted by the Bretton Woods System of 1944 and the subsequent enactment of the Second Amendment to the Articles of Agreement of the IMF, the era of 'floating exchange rates' began. Notwithstanding this total freedom in the choice of exchange rate regime, the new Article IV, Section 1 of the Articles of Agreement imposed obligations on the conduct of members' policies with the intention to promote exchange rate stability. Section 2 of this chapter expands on these obligations.[53]

In addition, Article IV, Section 3(a) mandates the Fund to 'oversee the international monetary system in order to ensure its effective operation' and to supervise the compliance of the members with the general obligations imposed by Article IV, Section 1. To accomplish these functions, the Fund is specifically entitled to exert 'firm surveillance over the exchange rate policies of members' pursuant to Article IV, Section 3(b). Consequently, Article IV, Sections 1 and 3 respectively impose obligations upon members and provide specific powers to the Fund to oversee and monitor the members' compliance with their obligations. The Fund adopted specific principles of surveillance in a decision of April 1977, as replaced by a new decision of June 2007.[54]

The Annex to the 2007 Surveillance Decision aims to clarify the meaning of exchange rate manipulation by considering that 'manipulation of the

---

51 According to Bergsten and Gagnon, it was the massive accumulation of foreign exchange reserves (mostly in US Dollars) by China that resulted in a 'decade of manipulation', through its intervention in the currency market to avoid the appreciation of the renminbi, which had given it large surpluses (reaching almost 10 percent of its GDP in 2017). Consequently, they argued that these large surpluses led to the proposals to include currency manipulation clauses in the new trade agreements to be entered into by the United States. C Fred Bergsten and Joseph E Gagnon, *Currency Conflict and Trade Policy: A New Strategy for the United States* (Peterson Institute for International Economics 2017). For an extended description of the monetary dispute between the US and China see, Charles Proctor, *Mann on the Legal Aspect of Money* (7th edn, OUP 2012) 605.

52 See chapter 5, section 1.2.2 of this book.

53 For an overview of the legal framework of Article IV of the Articles of Agreement see IMF, 'Article IV of the Fund's Articles of Agreement: An Overview of the Legal Framework' (28 June 2006) <www.imf.org/en/Publications/Policy-Papers/Issues/2016/12/31/Article-IV-of-the-Fund-s-Articles-of-Agreement-An-Overview-of-the-Legal-Framework-PP3883> accessed 21 October 2021.

54 Decision of the Executive Board No 5392-(77/63) of 29 April 1977 as replaced by the Decision of the Executive Board of 15 June 2007. See 'Bilateral Surveillance over Members' Policies' (n 32).

exchange rate is only carried out through policies that are targeted at – and actually affect – the level of an exchange rate. Moreover, manipulation may cause the exchange rate to move or may prevent such movement'.[55] It also states that:

> a member will only be considered to be manipulating exchange rates in order to gain an unfair competitive advantage over other members if the Fund determines both that: (A) the member is engaged in these policies for the purpose of securing fundamental exchange rate misalignment in the form of an undervalued exchange rate and (B) the purpose of securing such misalignment is to increase net exports.[56]

The Annex to the 2007 Surveillance Decision then correlates the notion of exchange rate manipulation to the concept of fundamental exchange rate misalignment. However, despite these significant clarifications brought by the 2007 Surveillance Decision a lot of flaws in the determination of manipulation of exchange rate by a Fund's member remain.[57]

As the IMF legal framework on exchange rate manipulation appears to be insufficient to prevent currency manipulation, the debate has been expanded to other international fora and has even been conducted bilaterally.[58] In this context, in the wake of the GFC the G20 has been involved with exchange rate manipulation concerns. It started with an initial commitment made by the G20 Finance Ministers and Central Bank Governors at the meeting held in Korea in October 2010. In this meeting they agreed to:

> move towards more market determined exchange rate systems that reflect underlying economic fundamentals and refrain from competitive devaluation of currencies. Advanced economies, including those with reserve currencies, will be vigilant against excess volatility and disorderly movements in exchange rates. These actions will help mitigate the risk of excessive volatility in capital flows facing some emerging countries. Together, we will reinvigorate our efforts to promote a stable and

---

55 Annex to the IMF Executive Board Decision No 15203-(12/72). See IMF Executive Board, 'Decision on Bilateral and Multilateral Surveillance' (Decision No 15203-(12/72), 18 July 2012) <www.imf.org/external/SelectedDecisions/Description.aspx?decision=15203-(12/72)?> accessed 21 October 2021.

56 ibid.

57 Viterbo, *International Economic Law and Monetary Measures* (n 6) 297.

58 Zimmermann, 'Exchange Rate Misalignment and International Law' (n 50) 437.

well-functioning international monetary system and call on the IMF to deepen its work in these areas.[59]

In subsequent meetings the G20 committed to avoid disorderly movements in exchange rates.[60] However, increasing tensions among the G20 members regarding capital controls and currency appreciation have put into question the forum's ability to reach a consensus on exchange rate manipulation-related issues.[61]

Beyond the IMF and the G20 many experts have considered the suitability of the WTO dispute settlement body as a forum to debate and consider issues related to currency manipulation.[62] In particular, the United States presented three different petitions between 2004 and 2007 under Section 301 of the 1974 Trade Act, to seek recourse through WTO dispute settlement against China, and claiming that China's exchange rate policy was inconsistent with the Fund's Articles of Agreement. The United States Trade Representative rejected the three petitions. Hence, some experts have argued that the WTO is not the suitable forum to discuss exchange rate issues.[63]

1.4 *Other Reactions*

In addition to capital controls and exchange restrictions, Villard Duran remarked that since the 2000's the accumulation of reserves in hard currencies (e.g. US dollar and euro) by emerging market economies (EMEs) has also been a unilateral measure of a precautionary nature in order to increase their monetary independence in times of crisis.[64] While chapter 1 of this book defines

59 Meeting of the G20 Finance Ministers and Central Bank Governors of Gyeongju, Korea (21–23 October 2010). The commitments undertaken at the Korea meeting were reaffirmed at the G20 Seoul Summit during 11–12 November 2010.

60 Zimmermann, 'Exchange Rate Misalignment and International Law' (n 50) 474.

61 The pressure imposed by United States and some European countries over China to remove capital controls and permit the appreciation of the renminbi created tensions among the G20 members. In addition, China and other countries disputed the US dollar's dominance as a reserve currency. Also, in the United States, exchange rate manipulation with special attention on the undervaluation of the Chinese renminbi opened a lively political debate in the last decade. Different legislative proposals have been submitted to the US Congress but none of them were ultimately adopted. Viterbo, *International Economic Law and Monetary Measures* (n 6) 301.

62 Zimmermann, 'Exchange Rate Misalignment and International Law' (n 50) 441.

63 James Bacchus, 'Don't Push the WTO Beyond Its Limits' (*The Wall Street Journal*, 25 March 2010).

64 Camila Villard Duran, 'The International Lender of Last Resort for Emerging Countries: A Bilateral Currency Swap?' (2015) GEG Working Paper 2015/108

'reserve assets' as a key element of the IMS, chapter 5 explains that the management of reserve assets is part of the foreign exchange policy of a country.[65] Hence, the trade-off among the different levels of governance in monetary affairs is also present in the case of reserve assets.[66]

A policy paper published by the IMF in 2016 highlighted that EMEs and developing countries have more than doubled their foreign exchange reserve holdings as a percentage of GDP since the beginning of the 1990's. This policy paper considered that reserves accumulation is not only very costly, but also causes potential systemic costs and coordination problems that can affect the stability of the IMS. It also noted that reserves accumulation has been irregular across countries and has also served other purposes, such as exchange rate management and intergenerational wealth transfer.[67]

It is also interesting to note that beyond the unilateral reactions or as a consequence of the unilateral actions, there has been an emergence and reinforcement of regional financing agreements to manage the volatility caused by monetary spillovers. According to the IMF, regional financing agreements (RFAs) are broadly defined as a financing mechanism through which a group of countries in a region pledges financial support to members that are experiencing, or might experience, a liquidity shortage or balance of payments difficulties.[68] The main examples are the permanent European Stability Mechanism,

---

<www.geg.ox.ac.uk/publication/geg-wp-2015108-international-lender-last-resort-emerging-countries-bilateral-currency> accessed 21 October 2021.

65 As noted by Goldberg and others, usually reserve assets are held by central banks but can also be held by finance ministers or sovereign wealth funds. Linda Goldberg, Cindy E Hull and Sarah Stein, 'Do Industrialized Countries Hold the Right Foreign Exchange Reserves?' (2013) 19(1) Current Issues in Economics and Finance <www.newyorkfed.org/research/current_issues/ci19-1.html> accessed 21 October 2021.

66 Recognising this trade-off, Article VIII, Section 7 of the Fund's Articles of Agreement allows members: to collaborate with the Fund and with other members in order to ensure that the policies of the member with respect to reserve assets shall be consistent with the objectives of promoting better international surveillance of international liquidity and making the special drawing right the principal reserve asset in the international monetary system.

Notwithstanding that the special drawing right (SDR) never assumed the role of principal reserve asset of the IMS, some reserve currencies, especially the US dollar, acquired a *de facto* central role of principal reserve asset. Hence, the Fund's members must observe this provision according to the reserve assets that they hold.

67 IMF, 'Adequacy of the Global Financial Safety Net' (2016) <www.imf.org/en/Publications/Policy-Papers/Issues/2016/12/31/Adequacy-of-the-Global-Financial-Safety-Net-PP5025> accessed 21 October 2021.

68 IMF, 'Stocktaking the Fund's Engagement with Regional Financing Arrangements' (2013) <www.imf.org/external/np/pp/eng/2013/041113b.pdf> accessed 21 October 2021.

with a lending capacity of €500 billion for crisis prevention in the euro area, the Chiang Mai Initiative Multilateralization which was reformed in 2010 and doubled its resources to US$240 billion in 2014, the multilateral Contingent Reserve Arrangement established by the BRICS with total committed resources of US$100 billion, the Eurasian Fund for Stabilization and Development which was established in 2009 with budgetary contributions of US$8.5 billion, and the Arab Monetary Fund and the Latin American Reserve Fund wherein the members' contributions almost doubled.[69]

Notwithstanding the impressive size of these RFAS, these regional initiatives are not the panacea to confront a liquidity crisis because as clearly pointed out by Villard Duran, 'These regional structures are contributing to the fragmentation of the global monetary system without guaranteeing certain and timely access to liquidity in an event of a crisis'.[70]

As pointed out in chapter 1 of this book, the above-mentioned accumulation of foreign reserves and the RFAS are part of the Global Financial Safety Net (GFSN), together with bilateral currency swap lines and financing through multilateral institutions. The G20's EPG report[71] also analysed the GFSN and considered that it has evolved during the last decade as a multi-layered safety net with several key shortcomings:

- The safety nets are highly uneven in scale and coverage across regions. About 70 percent of global RFA resources are concentrated in the Euro Area, which has a political underpinning and a common currency that allows the RFA to function quickly and effectively. Other RFAS lack similar underpinnings. There are also large regions which have no access to RFAS, or on any adequate scale.
- Much of the GFSN's growth has comprised of bilateral swap agreements (BSAS) and RFAS which have not been crisis-tested, and are subject to conditions prevailing in providing countries and regions. The RFAS and BSAS also do not cover several systemically significant countries.
- The system as a whole lacks the necessary coordination to effectively utilise its aggregate financial capacity.[72]

69 IMF, 'Collaboration between Regional Financing Arrangements and the IMF' (2017) <www.imf.org/en/Publications/Policy-Papers/Issues/2017/07/31/pp073117-collaboration-between-regional-financing-arrangements-and-the-imf> accessed 21 October 2021.

70 Camila Villard Duran, 'Voice and Exit: How G20 Emerging Powers are Challenging the Global Monetary Order' (2018) 15 Revista de Direito Internacional.

71 EPG, 'Making the Global Financial System Work for All' (n 46).

72 Ibid (n 46) 63.

Consequently, the G20's EPG report considers it critical to have a strong and reliable GFSN in place before the next crisis arrives. To achieve that, the report presents some proposals including the timely conclusion of the Fund's quota reviews in order to have an adequately-resourced global layer, the joint work of the IMF and the RFAs to enable consistent actions during a crisis and to put in place a standing global liquidity facility drawing on IMF permanent resources.[73]

2 Securing Compliance – Monetary Stability Considerations

Securing compliance with the obligations that emerge from the emerging doctrine and eventually principle of Common Concern is of utmost importance.[74] As remarked by Cottier, there is a fundamental difference between the discretionary right of states to act under the existing mechanism of international law of sanctions and countermeasures and the new obligation to act as suggested by Common Concern. This new obligation to act might be applicable only in the case of a fully-fledged doctrine of Common Concern, determined within the process of claims and responses that is subject to the principles of proportionality and accountability.

The process of claims and responses calls for a multilateral system and appropriate international institutions in order to secure compliance with the obligations that emerge from the collective action problems recognised as Common Concerns of Humankind. These obligations, as laid out in the doctrine of Common Concern, entail an enhanced duty to cooperate globally and the obligations to do homework both within the local jurisdiction and across borders when needed through unilateral lawful measures.

As pointed out elsewhere in this book the stability of the IMS depends on both domestic and international policies. There are clear mandates that attribute responsibility for the promotion and maintenance of monetary stability at the domestic and regional level to the central banks (as state agencies) and for the promotion of monetary stability at the international level to the IMF (a nearly universal institution). These overlapping dominions dealing with monetary stability are not static and interact with each other.

---

73 ibid 22. As proposed in chapter 4, section 3 of this book, the reinforcement of the GFSN from a *top-down approach* of cooperation will be a useful tool to enhance and maintain global monetary stability understood as a Common Concern to be promoted and protected from all levels of governance.

74 Cottier, 'The Principle of Common Concern of Humankind' (n 1) 68.

At the international level the key rules are laid down in the Articles of Agreement of the IMF. The Articles of Agreement contain rights, obligations and sanctions.[75] The legal nature of these rights and obligations create on the one hand, a vertical relationship between each member state and the Fund and, on the other hand, eliminate any possible horizontal relationship among the Fund's members. Consequently, the obligations set forth in the treaty are owed by the Fund's members to the IMF as an institution. There is no bilateral type of obligation among the members of the IMF.[76] Accordingly, if breach of an obligation occurs under the Articles of Agreement, the Managing Director of the Fund is in charge of raising a claim to the Executive Board and there is no possibility for any particular Fund member to bring a claim accusing another member.[77]

The main obligations of the IMF member states are enshrined in Article IV as amended by the Second Amendment.[78] Article IV, Section 1 starts with an introduction (*chapeau*) consisting of a general obligation of the members to collaborate with the Fund and other members and is followed by a non-exhaustive list of specific obligations concerning the members' domestic and external policies.[79] These obligations are considered of a 'soft' nature and would only require the best efforts of the members, with the exception

75 Simmons pointed out that: The Articles of Agreement of the International Monetary Fund ... is the first international agreement in history to obligate signatories to particular standards of monetary conduct. This embodiment of postwar agreements in monetary affairs significantly curtailed decentralized decision making with respect to monetary affairs and created legal and institutional edifice that sharpened obligations, enhanced surveillance, and centralized peer judgement on what constitutes appropriate international monetary policy.

Beth A Simmons, 'Money and the Law: Why Comply with the Public International Law of Money?' (2000) 25(2) Yale Journal of International Law 335.

76 This is the position of the IMF and it is widely accepted in literature with some exceptions. For further detail on this issue see Zimmermann, *A Contemporary Concept of Monetary Sovereignty* (n 28) 131.

77 IMF, 'By-Laws Rules and Regulations' (November 2019) rule K-1 <www.imf.org/external/pubs/ft/bl/blcon.htm> accessed 21 October 2021.

78 For an overview of the legal framework of Article IV of the Articles of Agreement see IMF, 'Article IV of the Fund's Articles of Agreement – An Overview of the Legal Framework' (28 June 2006) <www.imf.org/en/Publications/Policy-Papers/Issues/2016/12/31/Article-IV-of-the-Fund-s-Articles-of-Agreement-An-Overview-of-the-Legal-Framework-PP3883> accessed 21 October 2021.

79 The text of the Article IV, Section 1 reads as follows: Recognizing that the essential purpose of the international monetary system is to provide a framework that facilitates the exchange of goods, services, and capital among countries, and that sustains sound economic growth, and that a principal objective is the continuing development of the orderly underlying conditions that are necessary for financial and economic stability, each member undertakes to collaborate with the Fund and other members to assure

of Article IV, Section 1(iii): 'avoid manipulating exchange rates or the international monetary system in order to prevent effective balance of payments adjustment or to gain an unfair competitive advantage over other members', which is considered of a 'hard' nature and requires the members to achieve results beyond their best efforts.

According to Zimmermann, the 'best effort' obligations under Article IV recognise the full regulatory autonomy of the Fund's members over their economic and financial policies. By contrast, Article IV, Section 1(iii) highlights the international essence of exchange rate policies and consequently the obligation contained therein is of a 'hard' law nature.[80] Hence, it can be stated that in general terms Article IV of the Articles of Agreement gives the Fund's members great regulatory autonomy to implement their domestic policies. However, it should also be noted that this Article IV ought to be read together with the principles adopted by the IMF concerning its reformed bilateral surveillance mechanism.[81]

The principles adopted by the Fund's Integrated Surveillance Decision of 2012 are the following:

> A. A member shall avoid manipulating exchange rates or the international monetary system in order to prevent effective balance of payments adjustment or to gain an unfair competitive advantage over other members.

---

orderly exchange arrangements and to promote a stable system of exchange rates. In particular, each member shall:

(i) endeavor to direct its economic and financial policies toward the objective of fostering orderly economic growth with reasonable price stability, with due regard to its circumstances;

(ii) seek to promote stability by fostering orderly underlying economic and financial conditions and a monetary system that does not tend to produce erratic disruptions;

(iii) avoid manipulating exchange rates or the international monetary system in order to prevent effective balance of payments adjustment or to gain an unfair competitive advantage over other members; and

(iv) follow exchange policies compatible with the undertakings under this Section.

IMF Articles of Agreement.

80 Zimmermann, *A Contemporary Concept of Monetary Sovereignty* (n 28) 92.

81 'Modernizing the Legal Framework for Surveillance – An Integrated Surveillance Decision' (July 2012) para 21 <www.imf.org/external/np/pp/eng/2012/071712.pdf> accessed 21 October 2021. For an extended analysis of these principles see Zimmermann, *A Contemporary Concept of Monetary Sovereignty* (n 28) 94; Nadia Rendak, 'Monitoring and Surveillance of the International Monetary System: What can be learnt from the trade field?' in Thomas Cottier and others (eds), *The Rule of Law in Monetary Affairs* (CUP 2016) 208.

B. A member should intervene in the exchange market if necessary to counter disorderly conditions, which may be characterized inter alia by disruptive short-term movements in the exchange rate of its currency.
C. Members should take into account in their intervention policies the interests of other members, including those of the countries in whose currencies they intervene.
D. A member should avoid exchange rate policies that result in balance of payments instability.
E. A member should seek to avoid domestic economic and financial policies that give rise to domestic instability.

These principles, with the exception of principle A that reinstates the obligation laid down in Article IV, Section 1(iii), are merely recommendations to the Fund's members and, thus, unenforceable. The new mechanism set forth in the Fund's 2007 and 2012 reforms of bilateral surveillance exposed the current limits that the Articles of Agreement impose over the conduct of an IMF member's domestic policies (economic, financial and exchange rates).[82] As argued elsewhere in this book, the surveillance function enables the IMF to monitor compliance with standards and rules and to provide incentives for member states to comply with such standards and rules. Also, as proposed in chapter 4, section 3 of this book, the potential principle of Common Concern will promote an enhanced IMF surveillance based on a stronger commitment to act from the Fund's member states. This enhanced surveillance can be reinforced by explicit recognition of the international spillovers of domestic monetary policies in IMF surveillance.[83]

The Articles of Agreement (Article XXVI, Section 2) detailed in an exhaustive manner the three possible sanctions to which a Fund member can be subject in case of breach of its obligations. These sanctions are: ineligibility to use the Fund's resources, suspension of voting rights and expulsion from the Fund.[84]

82 IMF, 'Modernizing the Legal Framework for Surveillance – An Integrated Surveillance Decision' (2012) <http://imf.org/external/np/pp/eng/2012/071712.pdf> accessed 21 October 2021.

83 Carney remarks that an effective IMF surveillance over the spillover effects of monetary policies may depend on 'the credibility of the monetary policy framework and the transparency with which the strategy is pursued'. Mark Carney, 'Speech' (The Growing Challenges for Monetary Policy in the current International Monetary and Financial System, London, 23 August 2019) 10 <www.bis.org/review/r190827b.htm> accessed 21 October 2021.

84 In addition to these sanctions Zimmermann pointed out that 'the three pillars of the Fund's toolset – conditionality, surveillance, and technical assistance – give the Fund

However, as pointed out by Gianviti, 'there has not been a single instance in which sanctions have been applied or report has been made for breach of obligation under Article IV'.[85] Neither has the IMF ever found a member in violation of the 'hard' nature provision set forth in Article IV, Section 1(iii) concerning exchange rate manipulation.

The determination of whether an IMF member has committed exchange rate manipulation has become a political and economically delicate issue. Especially in recent years several countries such as Brazil, India, Indonesia, Israel, Japan, Korea, Malaysia, the Philippines, Singapore, South Africa, Switzerland, Taiwan, Thailand and particularly China have been accused of exchange market intervention and issuance of capital controls to contrast local currency appreciation.[86] These accusations must be verified using the threshold imposed by Article IV, Section 1(iii). The language of this article requires demonstration that the member had performed exchange rate manipulation with the *intent* to prevent effective balance of payments adjustment or to gain an unfair competitive advantage over other members. Hence, as remarked by Zimmermann 'the requirement of intent renders the key provision of the IMF's code of conduct essentially inoperative'.[87] In this regard Viterbo considers that the *intent* element is focused on a subjective consideration rather than on the economic impact of the measures.[88]

Consequently, it can be argued that the current design of the IMF's Articles of Agreement (in particular, Article IV) and its surveillance mechanism are not

many subtle possibilities, combined with peer pressure, to motivate a member to change a contested policy without even having to formally prove a breach of obligation by that member'. See Zimmermann, *A Contemporary Concept of Monetary Sovereignty* (n 28) 132.

85 Gianviti, 'Evolving Role and Challenges for the International Monetary Fund' (n 19).

86 William R Cline and John Williamson, 'Currency Wars?' (Policy Brief, Peterson Institute for International Economics 2010) <www.piie.com/sites/default/files/publications/pb/pb10-26.pdf> accessed 21 October 2021.

87 Zimmermann, *A Contemporary Concept of Monetary Sovereignty* (n 28) 90. Zimmerman also argues that: The IMF's expanded authority to step in early with policy advice aimed at avoiding external instability might turn out to be a helpful innovation with respect to good faith scenarios of exchange rate misalignment; of special concern here are unsustainable, increasing overvaluations that develop when developing countries adhere for too long to an unrealistic exchange rate peg. However, for any scenario in which an economically and politically powerful IMF member, like China, Japan, or the United States, would deliberately seek to improve its competitive position in an unfair manner by producing and maintaining an artificial undervaluation of its exchange rate in breach of IMF Article IV:1(iii), the IMF is essentially left as powerless as before, in large part because of the political sensitivity of establishing "intent." Zimmermann, 'Exchange Rate Misalignment and International Law' (n 50) 437.

88 Viterbo, *International Economic Law and Monetary Measures* (n 6) 297.

sufficiently equipped to secure compliance with the Fund's members' obligations under Article IV and it is even more uncertain as to whether the sanctions in Article XXVI, Section 2 will ever apply in this context. Accordingly, Viterbo stressed that 'the greater perception that IMF rules are not being enforced the greater is the likelihood that currency issues will be handled bilaterally, or even unilaterally, and outside the IMF framework'.[89] Consequently, state leaders have resorted to diplomatic bilateral discussions in different fora. In particular, since the beginning of the GFC the G20 has assumed a key role in debates concerning international monetary and financial stability. In the US, several legislative proposals have been submitted in order to apply antidumping measures and countervailing duties on imports from countries with undervalued currencies. Also, the possibility of bringing exchange rate issues to the WTO dispute settlement body has been intensively debated.[90]

International monetary law provides, under the premises of the IMF multilateral treaty, a detailed set of obligations for the Fund's members and a list of sanctions applicable on breach of those obligations in order to secure compliance. The obligations set forth in the Articles of Agreement are aimed to promote a prosperous and stable IMS in concordance with the purpose of an accepted Common Concern of global monetary stability. However, as analysed in this section, the obligations laid down in the Articles of Agreement are of a 'soft' nature requiring only the discretional best efforts of the IMF's member states to comply with them, with the notable exception of the case of exchange rate manipulation that is considered of a 'hard' nature. Despite the hard nature of the rule provided by Article IV, Section 1(iii) regarding exchange rate manipulation, the IMF has been severely questioned on its ability to ensure compliance with this obligation. The main reason for this is that the IMF has never found a member in violation of this provision.[91]

The lack of effectiveness of the existing mechanisms of international law to secure compliance with the obligations concerning global monetary stability bring back to the debate the trade-off among the different levels of governance in monetary affairs and how domestic and regional levels prevail over the international dimension. That is, as long as the Fund's members' policies pursue domestic objectives and they do not engage with *intent* on specific beggar-thy-neighbor policies the IMF will not bring them into question.[92] This uncertain scenario has pushed the delicate compliance debate to other

89 ibid (n 6) 301.

90 ibid 315.

91 Gianviti, 'Evolving Role and Challenges for the International Monetary Fund' (n 19).

92 Zimmermann, *A Contemporary Concent of Monetary Sovereignty* (n 28) 133.

diplomatic and political forums outside the IMF. It is in this scenario that the *bottom-up approach* with an enhanced cross-border cooperation among countries becomes more relevant and the emerging doctrine of Common Concern can assist as detailed in chapter 4 of this book.

3 Conclusion

An accepted principle of Common Concern would strengthen the notion that unilateral lawful measures are a valuable tool to mitigate negative spillovers when international cooperative efforts are insufficient. It would also encourage the use of these measures on a regular basis and for long-term purposes if needed but always as a complement to cooperative solutions that remain the best option to accomplish prosperous and stable Common Concerns.

The common concern of humankind is already understood as limiting the policy autonomy of the sovereign states in regard to an area recognized as a shared concern.[93] This limitation, in itself, is an obligation to make policy choices that are aimed at addressing a common concern and not worsening them. The homework obligation as proposed by the doctrine of Common Concern offers to change the current mere encouragement to act (right to act) to a positively articulated obligation to act in response to the problem. For monetary affairs in particular, the principle of Common Concern would reinforce the need for states to recognise and internalise the negative externalities of their policies and to seek to achieve a careful balance between the interests of different jurisdictions (resorting to the principle of shared but differentiated responsibility). As recognized by the G20's EPG report:

> the interplay of international and national initiatives is essential to a stronger future for all. There are several core roles for cooperation in the international monetary and financial system (IMFS), and for the international financial institutions (IFIS) … Policies aimed at growth and financial stability are most effective nationally when they are undertaken widely or coordinated internationally. However, it is also in the nature of today's highly interconnected markets that policies in some economies may have negative spillovers on others or reduce their policy space. A framework is needed to mitigate such spillovers and their effects as

93 Alexandre Kiss, 'The Common Concern of Mankind' (1997) 27 Environmental Policy and Law 244, 246–247.

> much as possible. There is also a role for international commitments to avoid 'beggar-thyneighbor' policies, which benefit one country at the expense of another.[94]

Thus, the recognition of the spillovers inherent in domestic policies may result in a limitation on domestic law by a source of international law (that is, the potential principle of Common Concern).

In addition, a fully-fledged and accepted principle of Common Concern will determine, after a process of claims and responses, whether it is necessary to move from the current 'soft' obligation of conduct under the existing treaty-based obligations to a 'hard' obligation to act in order to secure compliance with international monetary law. This new obligation to act in monetary affairs may demand the commitment of the international community to reform the Articles of Agreement, in particular the provisions in Article IV, so as to move from obligations of conduct to obligations of result to ensure compliance. As stated by Viterbo, 'The provisions of global public goods needs global solutions and a strengthened role of international organizations in economic regulation and supervision'.[95]

94 EPG, 'Making the Global Financial System Work for All' (n 46) 12.

95 Viterbo, *International Economic Law and Monetary Measures* (n 6) 315.

Conclusions

> I would suggest that all those eager to envisage the post-crisis era in constructive terms need to promote the reconstruction of a fully fledged international monetary order. And they need to be fully aware of the fact that this does not just entail questioning what I have called the international monetary system; it also demands that they take a fresh look at our domestic monetary orders, at their 'nationalism' … and at the intrinsic weakness of their aspiration to independence of the outside world.
>
> TOMMASO PADOA-SCHIOPPA, 2010[1]

The starting point and recurrent theme of this book has been to examine whether the promotion and maintenance of international monetary stability can be considered and categorised as a Common Concern of Humankind based on the foundations of, and normative claims made by, the emerging doctrine of Common Concern of Humankind.[2] In doing so, this book has applied the methodological approach proposed by the emerging doctrine – the application of the process of claims and responses, its three-dimensional perspective: international cooperation, domestic obligations and unilateral actions, and securing compliance. Most of the findings in this book lead, without a doubt, to the recognition of international monetary stability as a Common Concern of Humankind.

The analysis undertaken in this book, from a multilevel governance perspective (domestic, regional and international), of the legal and institutional arrangements for the pursuit and maintenance of monetary stability certainly

1 Tommaso Padoa-Schioppa, 'The Ghost of Bancor: The Economic Crisis and Global Economic Disorder' (Lecture, the Triffin International Foundation, Louvain-la-Neuve, 25 February 2010) <www.institutdelors.eu/wp-content/uploads/2018/01/speech-tps-louvainlaneuve-25.02.2010.pdf> accessed 21 October 2021.

2 As stated elsewhere in this book, Cottier develops the emerging doctrine and potential principle of Common Concern of Humankind in Thomas Cottier, 'The Principle of Common Concern of Humankind' in Thomas Cottier (ed), *The Prospects of Common Concern of Humankind in International Law* (CUP 2021).

do not contradict but support this asseveration. Yet, as this book has attempted to show, the recognition of international monetary stability as a Common Concern of Humankind is only the first step in a process that involves enhanced duties to cooperate, consult and negotiate, assumption of responsibilities in domestic law and undertaking homework commitments, and taking appropriate measures to comply with international commitments made. As asserted by Cottier these enhanced and shared responsibilities among states 'go beyond existing rights and obligations under international law and compound the essence of the legal principle of Common Concern of Humankind'.[3] Also, Cottier highlights that while these novel normative claims of the emerging doctrine of Common Concern are mostly controversial and idealistic, they represent 'a new and different realism'.[4]

Assisted by the emerging doctrine of Common Concern, this book has examined not only the *status quo* of the IMS in relation to the potential Common Concern of international monetary stability, but also has looked at the 'new and different realism' that would be envisaged in monetary affairs in the case of a fully fledged principle of Common Concern of Humankind. In that connection, this concluding section summarises the main findings of this book and also discusses the key proposals accompanying a new Common Concern of international monetary stability.

Chapter 1 of this book has explained that today's IMS is governed both by international regulations and domestic and regional policies. While these domains are not static and interact with each other, the GFC has showed that in times of crisis domestic and regional concerns overcome global stability considerations. As claimed in this chapter, the imbalance among the different levels of governance in monetary affairs ought to be assisted and limited by the rules of public international law. However, the chapter also has claimed that the role of public international law in monetary affairs is limited and thus a reconsideration of the role of the states in the pursuit of international monetary stability is required.

Chapter 2 has studied the modern notion of monetary sovereignty and its relationship with the concept of monetary stability from a multilevel governance perspective. It has noted that while states are obliged to recognise the sovereign powers of other states in monetary affairs under the precepts of international law, the monopoly power of states in the domestic monetary field is no longer absolute and has been subject to some limitations (both

3 ibid 84. Also see chapter 3 of this book where the main arguments in support of the principle of Common Concern of Humankind are detailed.

4 ibid 86.

consensual and *de facto*). The chapter has argued that in an integrated global economy the stability of the IMS depends on a delicate balance between the stability of domestic systems and the stability of the overall monetary system. While domestic monetary stability is a fundamental economic goal and an essential regulatory objective based on the monetary sovereignty attributes of the states, international monetary stability comprises the smooth functioning of the core elements of the IMS: international payments system, international capital movements, monetary reserves and access to liquidity. The chapter has recognised that as a result of globalisation and financial integration the borders delineating the different levels of governance in monetary affairs have become blurred. The chapter has also looked into the cross-border spillovers generated by domestic monetary policies and has pointed out that those spillovers can have both stabilising and destabilising effects on the global economy, depending on the business-cycle situation of states globally.

Chapter 3 has argued that the under-provision of GPGs, in particular the GPG of international monetary stability, demands a collective action response with increased international cooperation among the different levels in the multilevel governance structure. It has also stated that international public law and institutions are fundamental to solving collective action problems. However, it has recognised that formal and enforceable international public law in monetary affairs seems to have reached its limits. Consequently, this chapter has introduced the emerging doctrine of Common Concern of Humankind as a valuable methodological approach to analyse the shortcomings associated with the promotion and protection of international monetary stability as a GPG and potential Common Concern.

The chapter has also acknowledged that, after a process of claims and responses, monetary stability fulfils the threshold of *threatening peace, stability and welfare* for an issue to be considered a Common Concern of Humankind. Not all collective action problems can be categorised as Common Concerns but only those that because of their seriousness and magnitude, cannot be solved by states in isolation and demand transboundary cooperation. The potential Common Concern of international monetary stability has been analysed from a three-dimensional perspective in chapters 4, 5 and 6 of this book – firstly, under an enhanced *duty to cooperate, consult and negotiate* (international cooperation among states), secondly, under the basis for *obligations at home* (responsibilities at the state level – homework) that delineates not only the rights but also the duties of the states to act beyond the scope of the territorial application of laws in order to comply with international commitments made (extraterritoriality) and thirdly, *securing compliance* with the obligations that emerge from Common Concerns.

Chapter 4 has examined the *duty to cooperate* globally as the best solution to solve the problems associated with Common Concerns, both from a *top-down approach* (international level of governance) and a *bottom-up approach* (central banking cooperation). From a *top-down approach* the chapter has described the different actors in the International Financial Architecture (IFA) and their governance and normative aspects as integral parts of the IMS. While the chapter recognised that the bundle of soft law instruments in the form of international financial standards issued by the actors of the IFA have been a key success in the development of a more robust and resilient IMS, it has asserted that the IMF is still the crucial central international monetary institution.

The chapter has argued for a reinforcement of the role of the IMF. The Fund's key surveillance function enables it to monitor the member states' compliance with rules and standards and provide incentives for members to comply with them. Also, the IMF performs multilateral surveillance of the global economy, helping to identify the impact domestic policies may have on other countries and the global economy. However, the chapter has also pointed out that all policy recommendations made in the context of IMF surveillance have been non-mandatory and of an advisory nature. It is under these circumstances that the new and enhanced duty to cooperate proposed by Common Concern becomes relevant. In addition, the chapter also noted that the efficacy of such enhanced duty would still depend on the IMF member states' willingness to strengthen the Fund's mandate on the premises of Common Concern.

The chapter has considered that the *bottom-up* perspective has gained relevance in the pursuit of a Common Concern of global monetary stability. Cross-border cooperation efforts among countries from a domestic level are welcome developments to support the well-functioning of the international order. In the particular case of monetary affairs, cross-border cooperation refers to monetary policy coordination and central banking cooperation globally. The chapter has examined the evolution of central banking cooperation throughout history, providing some examples of effective international central bank coordination since the collapse of the Bretton Woods system to date, and observed that central banking cooperation has evolved over time and adapted to the changing economic and financial landscapes. On the responses to the more recent GFC, the chapter has argued that notwithstanding some remarkable examples of monetary policy coordination and cross-border central banking cooperation, most of the responses were nation-oriented and uncoordinated. Hence, while recognising that there is an unsettled debate about the welfare gains to be achieved from monetary policy coordination in regular times as opposed to the established prospect of potential gains from cooperation in crisis scenarios, the chapter has argued in favour of improved central banking cooperation. The chapter has also acknowledged that an improved cooperation and coordination of policies depends upon each state's readiness to engage in further cross-border cooperation under the guidance of the potential principle of Common Concern. Hence, it is under these circumstances that the new obligation to act as proposed by Common Concern acquires relevance.

Chapter 5 has looked into the second element of the emerging doctrine of Common Concern: the *obligations at the domestic level*, with special focus on the *first level of commitment* of this second element that encompasses the pursuit and maintenance of monetary stability as a domestic public good and a potential local Common Concern. The chapter has described the fundamental role that domestic and regional institutional arrangements have to play in the promotion of monetary stability, with central banks or relevant monetary authorities at the centre of this framework both in the pursuit of price stability (internal dimension) and exchange rate stability (external dimension). This chapter has also remarked that central banks are unique institutions poised to respond to crisis situations such as the GFC. Such unique features are their delegated mandate objectives, instrument independence and accountability, which has allowed them to adapt to changing economic environments and keep their crucial role in the IMS. However, the chapter has also noted that central banks are ultimately institutions of state that are constrained by their domestic goals and mandates. Hence, when it comes to central banks assuming international commitments or engaging in enhanced monetary policy cooperation, the result rests on unpredictable soft-law commitments that are decided on a case-by-case basis.

Therefore, the chapter has remarked that the obligations to do homework, promoted by the emerging doctrine of Common Concern in relation to monetary stability, are constrained to domestic and regional objectives that do not always consider the global dimension. While stable domestic and regional constituencies contribute to the stability of the whole IMS, a fully fledged principle of Common Concern aims to encourage states to think beyond their jurisdictions and include global stability considerations in deciding domestic policy action. That is, a principle of Common Concern would reinforce the role of states as main providers of public goods not only locally but also globally. The chapter has argued that this enhanced domestic obligation may involve an expansion of the mandate goals of central banks to include global stability considerations, with the ability to assume international commitments in special situations. That is, moving from discretional attributes of central banks to a commitment to cooperate and coordinate in monetary affairs, activated by the enhanced domestic obligation (based on the principle of shared but differentiated responsibility) with increased transparency and accountability.

Therefore, the implementation of these enhanced obligations of central banks under the premises of Common Concern will improve the results of efforts on transparency, information sharing and accountability. This is because with more responsibility comes more accountability.

Chapter 6 has analysed the *obligations at the domestic level* promoted by the emerging doctrine of Common Concern at its second level of commitment. This *second level of commitment* considers the duty to implement international commitments assumed in international agreements and in customary law and also aims to inspire autonomous domestic policy-making to address the issues underlying the Common Concerns. For existing obligations under international law, the emerging doctrine aims to encourage the timely and effective implementation of international commitments. In relation to autonomous domestic policy-making, the chapter has examined the relevant examples of domestic unilateral actions with extraterritorial effects in the monetary affairs realm: exchange restrictions, capital controls and exchange rate manipulation scenarios. It has also studied briefly the accumulation of reserve assets as a unilateral measure of precautionary nature and has taken note of the increase in regional financing agreements as alternative arrangements.

As the chapter has explained, these domestic unilateral actions have been taken mostly with the aim to limit or repel unwanted spillovers (or negative externalities) caused by both conventional and unconventional monetary policy in place since the start of the GFC. The chapter has stressed that in the pursuit of monetary stability these measures have proven to be useful but have been limited and temporary in nature. Consequently, this chapter has suggested that an accepted principle of Common Concern will strengthen the notion that unilateral lawful measures are valuable instruments to mitigate negative spillovers when international cooperative efforts are not enough. The principle of Common Concern would also encourage the use of these measures on a regular basis and for long-term purposes if needed, but always as a complement to cooperative solutions. In the case of monetary affairs, the novel principle of Common Concern will encourage states to recognise and also internalise the possible negative externalities of their policies in order to achieve a careful balance between the interests of different jurisdictions. Hence, the chapter has claimed that the recognition of the spillovers inherent in domestic policies may result in a limitation on domestic law by the potential principle of Common Concern (as a source of international law).

Finally, the chapter has looked into the third and most provocative element of the emerging doctrine of Common Concern: *securing compliance* with the obligations that may emerge from a fully fledged principle of Common Concern. In doing so, the chapter has described the existing rules relating to compliance at the international level. In the context of monetary affairs, these rules are laid down in the Articles of Agreement of the IMF as rights, obligations and sanctions. The chapter has noted that these compliance rules only apply to the Fund's members and they are mostly of a 'soft' nature, requiring only best efforts of the Fund's members (with the exception of Article IV, Section 1(iii) concerning exchange rate manipulation, which is considered of a 'hard' or enforceable nature). The chapter has also stressed that despite the Fund's rules the compliance situation at the international level is uncertain, and that debate on this issue has moved to other diplomatic and political forums outside the IMF. The chapter has considered that a fully fledged and accepted principle of Common Concern would determine, after a process of claims and responses, whether it is necessary to move from the current 'soft' obligation of conduct under the existing treaty-based obligations to a 'hard' obligation to act in order to secure compliance with international monetary law. This new obligation to act in monetary affairs may demand the commitment of the international community to reform the Articles of Agreement, in particular the provisions in Article IV, so as to move from obligations of conduct to obligations of result to ensure compliance.

Overall, there is little doubt that international monetary stability amounts to a Common Concern of Humankind under the premises of the emerging doctrine and potential principle of Common Concern. The discussion on monetary stability at the different levels of governance together with the analysis of the existing legal and institutional arrangements in this book have emphasised the need for reform of several aspects of the current design of the IMS. This book has claimed on multiple occasions that a fully fledged principle of Common Concern of Humankind can assist in different areas of such reform to achieve a more prosperous and stable monetary order. In particular, the book has presented three specific areas as examples of enhanced cooperation assisted by the normative claims proposed by Common Concern: IMF surveillance, Global Financial Safety Net and government networks.[5]

The GFC has triggered many projects for reform of the international monetary and financial systems in order to achieve the goal of greater resilience globally. According to the latest progress report issued by the Group of 20 in 2019, the new financial regulatory framework is now largely in place but implementation is not yet complete and remains unequal across reform areas mainly because of domestic legislative or rule-making processes, concerns over the pace of implementation in other jurisdictions, and difficulties faced

5 See chapter 4 section 3 of this book.

by regulated entities in adjusting to the new requirements.[6] Hence, while this book has argued that the improvements in the governance aspects of the IFA undertaken as a response to the GFC have enhanced the institutional foundations (particularly in the context of monetary affairs, the noteworthy major overhaul of the IMF's governance structure), it has also remarked that some major challenges concerning the institutional legitimacy of the entities involved in the process of international financial standard setting (IFSs) and the limits of the soft-law approach in IFSs remained unsolved.[7]

This state of affairs brings back the longstanding and classic debate on 'rules *versus* discretion' in monetary affairs.[8] That is, the debate on whether monetary affairs are best conducted under a regime based on rules or a regime where discretion prevails. As detailed in Annex I to chapter 1 of this book the pendulum of 'rules *versus* discretion' has oscillated throughout the different periods in the history of the IMS. It can be argued that the current state of the conduct of affairs under the IMS is discretion-based. Despite the existence of a code of conduct enshrined in the Articles of Agreement of the IMF, the role of public international monetary law is limited.

As remarked throughout this book, the discretion-based IMS that we have today is one of the main causes of the imbalance or trade-off among the different levels of governance in monetary affairs. As the GFC has amply demonstrated, national and regional stability concerns have prevailed over international stability considerations. According to Guitián 'the choice between rules or discretion can also be seen in terms of the importance given to *national* relative to *international* interests in the process of monetary policy implementation'.[9] Thus, it is also in this multilevel governance trade-off context

---

6 Financial Stability Board, 'Progress in implementation of G20 financial regulatory reforms' (25 June 2019) <www.fsb.org/wp-content/uploads/P250619-2.pdf> accessed 21 October 2021.

7 See chapter 4 section 1.1 of this book.

8 This debate was first raised by Henry Simons in the context of monetary policy in 1936. Henry C Simons, 'Rules versus Authorities in Monetary Policy' (1936) 44(1) Journal of Political Economy 1. This debate applies to all levels of governance. Friedman was a strong advocate of rules in the domestic sphere of monetary affairs and of discretion in the international monetary domains. See Milton Friedman, *A Program for Monetary Stability* (Fordham University Press 1959). Guitián remarks that this debate goes beyond the monetary realm and 'It concerns a basic principle of governance that relates to the method of organizing social and economic behavior: should it be based on a well-defined code of conduct, or should it depend on how those in authority judge and interpret events?'. See Manuel Guitián, 'Rules or Discretion in Monetary Policy: National and International Perspectives' in Tomás J T Baliño and Carlo Cottarelli (eds), *Frameworks for Monetary Stability: Policy Issues and Country Experiences* (International Monetary Fund 1994) 33.

9 Guitián, 'Rules or Discretion in Monetary Policy' (n 8) 23.

that a reconsideration of the different sources of international law acquires relevance, in the aim to find an appropriate balance between rules *versus* discretion and among local, regional and international policies in the realm of money. On the different sources of international law in monetary affairs, Lastra clarifies that:

> International law-making relies upon a variety of sources. It is the confluence of 'hard law' (legally enforceable rules), soft law of a 'public law' nature (which can complement, coexist or turn into hard law), and soft law of a 'private law' nature (comprising rules of practice, standards, usages, and other forms of self-regulation as well as rules and principles agreed or proposed by scholars and experts) where the future of international financial and monetary law lies.[10]

Following from the enumeration of the sources of international law in the process of law-making provided by Lastra, this book has considered that Common Concern favours a rationalist approach to the interaction between hard law and soft law, with each one complementing the other in the development of international law.[11] It has also expressed that 'hard law' in the context of the international monetary order has reached its limits and that 'soft law', both of a private and public nature, have proved useful and have worked well in the process of securing a more resilient monetary order. Similarly, as stated by Sir Joseph Gold, general counsel of the IMF from 1960 to 1979, 'It may be that in international economic relations all that can be hoped for in the coming years is "soft law" and more elaborate procedures for consultation, and that firm law will be the work of generations'.[12]

The new normative claims made by the emerging doctrine of Common Concern can be considered part of the soft law of a 'private law' nature (in the form of a principle agreed or proposed by scholars and experts). Moreover, the emerging doctrine aims to develop as a fully fledged principle of international law (hard law) encompassing new and controversial obligations to act and obligations to comply, with a view to promoting and protecting public goods and Common Concerns at the different levels of governance. Though it is still too early to determine if this emerging doctrine will become a source of international law of a 'hard law' nature, this book has showed that the emerging

10 Rosa M Lastra, *International Financial and Monetary Law* (2nd edn, OUP 2015) 554.

11 See chapter 4 section 1.3 of this book.

12 Joseph Gold, 'Public International Law in the International Monetary System' (1984) 38 Sw LJ 849.

doctrine of Common Concern is a most welcome development in the realm of public international law and in the context of international monetary law in particular.

This book has also acknowledged that the proposed novel principle of Common Concern of Humankind will attract criticisms, from the basis of self-determination of states and sovereign prerogatives to the unrealistic or idealistic claims it represents.[13] As remarked by Cottier, these criticisms have raised the question about realism. Realism understands as a fact of life that the current design of the international order fails to provide some public goods that are essential to preserve peace, stability and legal security. In response to that, the emerging doctrine of Common Concern aims to acknowledge the new realism and, in consequence, provide an alternative for the production and protection of those under-provided public goods and potential Common Concerns.[14] It is the recognition of this new realism that makes the emerging doctrine most suitable and attractive in the case of international monetary stability. This book considers that the key reason for this is that the study of international monetary law is the study of a moving target and, hence, the emerging doctrine provides the normative foundations to understand and interpret this constant evolution. As clearly summarised recently by Tharman Shanmugaratnam, deputy prime minister of Singapore, for the IMS:

> There is no going back to the old multilateralism. … We have to build this new multilateralism. It does not need new institutions, multilateral or supranational. But we must create a new system of networked leadership amongst existing bodies – global, regional, bilateral and national. It must be a system of shared responsibilities, of common standards in development finance, and of maximum complementarity between these existing bodies. We also need a system of new global policy norms, including new

13 These criticisms are not new, In the particular context of monetary affairs, Sir Joseph Gold in 1984 in his concluding comments to his article on the role of public international law in the IMS wrote that: Pessimistic views have been expressed on the possibilities for a firmer and broader rule of law on exchange rates and on other aspects of international monetary relations. Some views have been based on the hypothesis that such a development is necessary but insufficient. The interdependence of countries makes it impossible for them to pursue independent policies in either external or domestic monetary matters. Countries are affected by both the external and the domestic policies of other countries. International monetary reform alone would not be successful, because it would not touch such policies. See Gold, 'Public International Law in the International Monetary System' (n 12) 848.

14 Cottier, 'The Principle of Common Concern of Humankind' (n 2) 86.

> norms for national policymaking, to ensure that we can meet our domestic objectives without large spillovers to the rest of the world. … We need a new, collective resolve that recognises that we all have a vested interest in an open, integrated international order. It is a vested interest that we all have nationally. And we are all responsible for the global good.[15]

Looking forward, this book aims to encourage scholars both in the area of international economic law and in other areas of public international law to consider the suitability of the emerging doctrine of Common Concern of Humankind as a useful platform to discuss global problems that demand urgent solutions, to consider how the law can assist on the path to discovering and recognising new realisms with their faults and shortcomings, and to find new normative alternatives to deal with them.

15 Tharman Shanmugaratnam, 'Keynote Address' (Fourth ECOSOC Forum on Financing for Development, 15 April 2019) <www.mfa.gov.sg/Overseas-Mission/New-York/Mission-Updates/Second_committee/2019/04/Press_20190415> accessed 21 October 2021.

Bibliography

Acharya V and others, 'The Financial Crisis of 2007–2009: Causes and Remedies. Financial Markets, Institutions & Instruments' (2009) 18 Financial Markets, Institutions & Instruments 89.

Ahmad Z, 'State Responsibility Aspects of a Common Concern Based Approach to Collective Action' in Samantha Besson (ed), *International Responsibility Essays in Law, History and Philosophy* (Schulthess 2017) 107.

Ahmad Z, 'Trade-Related Measures to Spread Low Carbon Technologies: A Common Concern Based Approach', in Thomas Cottier (ed) *The Prospects of Common Concern of Humankind in International Law* (CUP 2021).

Albagli E and others, 'Channels of US Monetary Policy Spillovers into International Bond Markets' <https://bis.org/events/ccaconf2017/ccaconf2017_12.pdf>.

Alexander K, 'International Economic Law and Macro-prudential Regulation' in Thomas Cottier and others (eds), *The Rule of Law in Monetary Affairs* (CUP 2014) 519.

Ammer J and others, 'International Spillovers of Monetary Policy' (2016) IFDP Notes <https://federalreserve.gov/econresdata/notes/ifdp-notes/2016/international-spillovers-of-monetary-policy-20160208.html>.

Amtenbrink F and Lastra R M, 'Securing Democratic Accountability of Financial Regulatory Agencies – A Theoretical Framework' in R V de Mulder (ed), *Mitigating Risk in the Context of Safety and Security. How Relevant is a Rational Approach?* (Rotterdam: Erasmus School of Law & Research School for Safety and Security (OMV) 2008) 115.

Arner D W and others, 'Central Banks and Central Bank Cooperation in the Global Financial System' (2010) 23(1) Pacific McGeorge Global Business & Development Law Journal 1, 31.

Bacchus J, 'Don't Push the WTO Beyond Its Limits' (*The Wall Street Journal*, 25 March 2010).

Bank for International Settlements, *BIS Annual Report 2011/2012* ch IV <www.bis.org/publ/arpdf/ar2012e4.pdf>.

Bank for International Settlements, *Annual Report* <www.bis.org/annualreports/index.htm>.

Bank for International Settlements, BIS Committee on Payments and Market Infrastructures, 'Central bank digital currencies' (March 2018) <www.bis.org/cpmi/publ/d174.pdf>.

Bank for International Settlements, 'Unconventional monetary policy tools: a cross-country analysis' (October 2019) <www.bis.org/publ/cgfs63.htm>.

Bank of England, 'One Bank Research Agenda Discussion Paper' (February 2015) <www.bankofengland.co.uk/research/Documents/onebank/discussion.pdf>.

Baslar K, *The Concept of Common Heritage of Mankind in International Law* (Martinus Nijhoff Publishers 1998).

Bayoumi T and others, 'Monetary Policy in the New Normal' (IMF Staff Discussion Note, April 2014) < www.imf.org/external/pubs/ft/sdn/2014/sdn1403.pdf>.

Beidas-Strom S and others, 'Global Disinflation in an Era of Constrained Monetary Policy' in *World Economic Outlook* (IMF 2016) <www.imf.org/en/Publications/WEO/Issues/2016/12/31/Subdued-Demand-Symptoms-and-Remedies>.

Beitz C R, 'Human Rights as a Common Concern' (2001) 95(2) American Political Science Review 269.

Bergsten C F and Gagnon J E, *Currency Conflict and Trade Policy: A New Strategy for the United States* (Peterson Institute for International Economics 2017).

Bernanke B S, 'Speech' (National Press Club Luncheon, Washington, 18 February 2009) <www.federalreserve.gov/newsevents/speech/bernanke20090218a.htm>.

Besson S, 'Sovereignty in Conflict' (2004) 8 European Integration Online Papers 13 <https://papers.ssrn.com/abstract=594942>.

Bodansky D, 'What's in a Concept? Global Public Goods, International Law, and Legitimacy', (2012) 23(3) EJIL 651.

Bogdonava I, 'Reshaping the Law of Economic Sanctions for Human Rights Violations: The Potential of Common Concern of Humankind' in Thomas Cottier (ed) *'The Prospects of Common Concern of Humankind in International Law'* (CUP 2021).

Borio C and Toniolo G, 'One Hundred and Thirty Years of Central Bank Cooperation: A BIS Perspective' (2006) BIS Working Papers No 197 <www.bis.org/publ/work197.htm>.

Borio C and Disyatat P, 'Unconventional Monetary Policies: An Appraisal' (2009) BIS Working Paper No 292 <www.bis.org/publ/work292.pdf>.

Broos M and Grund S, 'The IMF's Jurisdiction Over The Capital Account – Reviewing the Role of Surveillance in Managing Cross-Border Capital Flows' (2018) 21(3) JIEL 489.

Brown Weiss E, 'Rethinking compliance with international law' in Eyal Benvenisti and Moshe Hirsch (eds), *The Impact of International Law on International Cooperation* (CUP 2004).

Brummer C, 'Why Soft Law Dominates International Finance – and not Trade' in Thomas Cottier and others (eds), *International Law in Financial Regulation and Monetary Affairs* (OUP 2010).

Bummer C, *Soft Law and the Global Financial System – Rule Making in the 21st Century* (CUP 2011).

Brummer C, *Soft Law and the Global Financial System – Rule Making in the 21st Century* (CUP 2015) 69.

Brunnée J, 'Common Interest – Echoes from an Empty Shell?' (1989) 49 Heidelberg Journal of International Law 791.

Brunnée J, 'Common Areas, Common Heritage and Common Concern' in Daniel Bodansky, Jutta Brunnée and Ellen Hey (eds), *The Oxford Handbook of International Environmental Law* (OUP 2007).

Camdessus M, 'International Financial and Monetary Stability: A Global Public Good? – Remarks by Michel Camdessus' (IMF/Research Conference, May 28 1999) <https://www.imf.org/en/News/Articles/2015/09/28/04/53/sp052899>.

Campbell A and Lastra R M, 'Revisiting the Lender of Last Resort' (2009) 24 BFLR 453.

Capie P and Wood G, 'Central Bank Independence: Can it Survive a Crisis?' in (2013) 2 Rivista Di Storia Economica 193.

Carney M, 'Speech' (The Growing Challenges for Monetary Policy in the current International Monetary and Financial System, London, 23 August 2019) <www.bis.org/review/r190827b.htm>.

Caruana J, 'Central bank cooperation: reflections on the experience of the last eight decades' (CEMLA's 60th Anniversary Commemorative Conference on 'Central bank cooperation at the beginning of the 21st century', 20 July 2012) <www.bis.org/speeches/sp120724.htm>.

Charnovitz S, 'Addressing Government Failure through International Financial Law' in Cottier and others, *International Law in Financial Regulation and Monetary Affairs* (OUP 2010), 205.

Cline W R and Williamson J, 'Currency Wars?' (Policy Brief, Peterson Institute for International Economics 2010) <www.piie.com/sites/default/files/publications/pb/pb10-26.pdf>.

Cœuré B, 'Domestic and Cross-Border Spillovers of Unconventional Monetary Policies' (SNB-IMF Conference 'Monetary Policy Challenges in a Changing World', Zurich, May 2015) <https://ecb.europa.eu/press/key/date/2015/html/sp150513.en.html>.

Coeuré B, 'The Internationalisation of Monetary Policy' (2016) 67 Journal of International Money and Finance 11.

Cottier T, 'Challenges Ahead in International Economic Law' (1999) 12(1) JIEL 3, 15.

Cottier T and Hertig M, 'The Prospects of 21st Century Constitutionalism' (2003) 7 *Max Planck Yearbook of United Nations Law* 261.

Cottier T, 'Multilayered Governance, Pluralism and Moral Conflict' (2009) 16(2) IJGLS 647.

Cottier T and Matteotti S, 'International Environmental Law and the Evolving Concept of "Common Concern of Mankind"' in Thomas Cottier, Olga Nartova and Sadeq Z Bigdeli (eds), *International Trade Regulation and the Mitigation of Climate Change* (CUP 2009), 21.

Cottier T, Jackson J H and Lastra R M (eds), *International Law in Financial Regulation and Monetary Affairs* (OUP 2010).

Cottier T, 'Towards a Five Storey House' in C Joerges and E U Petersmann (eds), *Constitutionalism, Multilevel Trade Governance and International Economic Law* (Hart Publishing 2011).

Cottier T and Satragno L, 'The Potential of Law and Legal Methodology in Monetary Affairs' in Thomas Cottier and others (eds), *The Rule of Law in Monetary Affairs* (CUP 2014) 411.

Cottier T and others, 'The Principle of Common Concern and Climate Change' (2014) 52(3) Archiv des Volkerretchts 293.

Cottier T and others (eds), *The Rule of Law in Monetary Affairs* (CUP 2014).

Cottier T, 'Improving Compliance: Jus Cogens and International Economic Law' (2015) 46 *Netherlands Yearbook of International Law* 329.

Cottier T (ed) '*The Prospects of Common Concern of Humankind in International Law*' (CUP 2021).

Cottier T, 'The Principle of Common Concern of Humankind' in Thomas Cottier (ed) '*The Prospects of Common Concern of Humankind in International Law*' (CUP 2021).

Crawford J, 'State Responsibility', *Max Planck Encyclopedias of Public International Law* <https://opil.ouplaw.com/view/10.1093/law:epil/9780199231690/law-9780199231690-e1093>.

Crockett A, 'What Have We Learned in the Past 50 Years about the International Financial Architecture?' (Reserve Bank of Australia 50th Anniversary Symposium, Sydney, February 2010) <www.rba.gov.au/publications/confs/2010/pdf/crockett.pdf>.

Crotty J, 'Structural Causes of the Global Financial Crisis: A Critical Assessment of the "New Financial Architecture"' (2009) 33 Cambridge Journal of Economics 563.

De Larosiere J and others, 'Report of the High Level Group on Financial Supervision in the EU' (2009) <http://ec.europa.eu/internal_market/finances/docs/de_larosiere_report_en.pdf>.

De Stefano C, 'Reforming the Governance of International Financial Law in the Era of Post-Globalization' (2017) 20(3) JIEL 509.

Dicey A V and others (eds), *Dicey, Morris and Collins on the Conflict of Laws* (15th edn, Sweet & Maxwell 2012), rule 259.

Dincer N and Eichengreen B, 'Central Bank Transparency: Causes, Consequences and Updates' (2009) NBER Working Paper No 14791 <www.nber.org/papers/w14791>.

Draghi M, 'The International Dimension of Monetary Policy' (ECB Forum on Central Banking, Sintra, 28 June 2016) <www.ecb.europa.eu/press/key/date/2016/html/sp160628.en.html>.

Draghi M, 'Speech' (Global Investment Conference, London, 26 July 2012) <www.ecb.europa.eu/press/key/date/2012/html/sp120726.en.html>.

Drahos P, 'The Regulation of Public Goods' (2004) 7(2) JIEL 321.

Dorrucci E and McKay J, 'The International Monetary System After the Financial Crisis' (February 2011) 123 ECB Occasional Paper Series.

Durlauf S N and Blume L E (eds), *The New Palgrave Dictionary of Economics* (2nd edn Palgrave Macmillan, 2008) <https://link.springer.com/referenceworkentry/10.1057/978-1-349-95121-5_2742-1>.

Dworkin R M, 'The Model of Rules' (1967) 35(1) The University of Chicago Law Review 14.

Eichengreen B, 'Hegemonic Stability Theories of the International Monetary System' (March 1987) NBER Working Papers No 2193.

El-Erian M, *The Only Game in Town: Central Banks, Instability, and Avoiding the Next Collapse* (Random House, 2016).

Eminent Persons Group on Global Financial Governance, <https://www.globalfinancialgovernance.org/about-g20-epg/>.

Eminent Persons Group on Global Financial Governance, 'Making the Global Financial System Work for All' (October 2018) <www.globalfinancialgovernance.org/assets/pdf/G20EPG-Full%20Report.pdf>.

European Central Bank, 'Technical Features of Outright Monetary Transactions' (6 September 2012) <www.ecb.int/press/pr/date/2012/html/pr120906_1.en.html>.

European Central Bank, 'Virtual Currency Schemes' (2012) <https://ecb.europa.eu/pub/pdf/other/virtualcurrencyschemes201210en.pdf>.

Federal Reserve Bank of New York, 'Exchange Stabilization Fund' (Fedpoint, May 2007) <www.newyorkfed.org/aboutthefed/fedpoint/fed14.html>.

Feibelman A, 'The IMF and Regulation of Cross-Border Capital Flows' (2015) 15(2) Chicago Journal of International Law 409.

Ferran E and Alexander K, 'Can Soft Law Bodies be Effective? The Special Case of the European Systemic Risk Board' (2010) 35(6) European Law Review 751.

Financial Stability Board, 'About the FSB' <www.fsb.org/about/>.

Financial Stability Board, 'Implementation and Effects of the G20 Financial Regulatory Reforms: Fourth Annual Report' (28 November 2018) <www.fsb.org/2018/11/implementation-and-effects-of-the-g20-financial-regulatory-reforms-fourth-annual-report/>.

Financial Stability Board, 'Progress in implementation of G20 financial regulatory reforms' (25 June 2019) <www.fsb.org/wp-content/uploads/P250619-2.pdf>.

Financial Times, Lexicon <http://lexicon.ft.com/Term?term=fiat-money>.

Financial Times, Jones C, 'European Central Bank to publish account of meetings' (18 December 2014).

Financial Times, Ferdinando Giugliano, Sam Fleming and Claire Jones, 'Central Banks: Peak Independence' (8 November 2015).

Financial Times, Authers J, 'Strong Dollar Poses Big Threat for Emerging Market Investors' (5 May 2018).

Financial Times, Rutter Pooley C and others, 'Argentina Stuns Markets as it pushes interest rates to 40%' (5 May 2018).

Financial Times, Atkins R, 'Radical reform: Switzerland to vote on banking overhaul' (29 May 2018)'.

Financial Times, Martin Sandbu, 'Treat money as the public good it is' (31 May 2018).

Financial Times, Wolf M, 'Why the Swiss should vote for "Vollgeld" ' (6 June 2018).

Fischer S, 'Capital-Account Liberalization and the Role of the IMF' (Essays in International Finance, Princeton University 1998).

Fischer S, 'Speech' (Herbert Stein Memorial Lecture National Economists Club, Washington DC, 2015) <www.federalreserve.gov/newsevents/speech/fischer20151104a.htm>.

Fleming M J, 'Domestic Financial Policies under Fixed and under Floating Exchange Rates' (1962) 9(3) Staff Papers International Monetary Fund, 369.

Fox H and Webb P, *The Law of State Immunity* (3rd edn, OUP 2013).

Frankel J, 'The Plaza Accord, 30 Years Later' (2015) NBER Working Paper 21813 <www.nber.org/papers/w21813>.

French D, 'Common concern, common heritage and other global(-ising) concepts: rhetorical devices, legal principles or a fundamental challenge?' in Michael Bowman, Peter Davies and Edward Goodwin (eds), *Research Handbook on Biodiversity and Law*, 344 (EE 2016).

Friedman M, 'The Case for Flexible Exchange Rates', published in *Essays in Positive Economics* (University of Chicago Press, 1953).

Garber P M, 'The Collapse of the Bretton Woods Fixed Exchange Rate System' in Michael D Bordo and Barry Eichengreen (eds), *A Retrospective on the Bretton Woods System: Lessons for International Monetary Reform* (University of Chicago Press 1993), 461.

Gianviti F, 'Evolving Role and Challenges for the International Monetary Fund' (2001) 35(4) The International Lawyer 1371.

Gianviti F, 'Current Legal Aspects of Monetary Sovereignty' in IMF (ed), *Current Developments in Monetary and Financial Law*, vol 4 (2005).

Gianviti F, 'The Objectives of Central Banks', in Mario Giovanoli and Diego Devos (eds), *International Monetary and Financial Law: The Global Crisis* (OUP 2010), 465.

Gianviti F, 'Relationship Between Monetary Policy and Exchange Rate Policy' in Cottier and others (eds), *The Rule of Law in Monetary Affairs* (CUP 2014) 545.

Giovanoli M, 'A New Architecture for the Global Financial Markets: Legal Aspects of International Financial Standard Setting' in Mario Giovanoli (ed), *International Monetary Law: Issues for the New Millennium* (OUP 2000) 9.

Giovanoli M and Devos D (eds) *International Monetary and Financial Law: The Global Crisis* (OUP 2010).

Giovanoli M, 'The International Financial Architecture and its Reform After the Global Financial Crisis' in Mario Giovanoli and Diego Devos (eds), *International Monetary and Financial Law: The Global Crisis* (OUP 2010) 3.

Giovanoli M, 'The International Monetary and Financial Architecture – Some Institutional Aspects' in Thomas Cottier and others (eds), *The Rule of Law in Monetary Affairs* (CUP 2014) 45.

Gold J, 'Law and Reform of the International Monetary System' (1975) 10 Journal of International Law and Economics 371.

Gold J, 'Public International Law in the International Monetary System' (1984) 38 Sw LJ 799.

Goldberg L and others, 'Do Industrialized Countries Hold the Right Foreign Exchange Reserves?' (2013) 19(1) Current Issues in Economics and Finance <www.newyorkfed.org/research/current_issues/ci19-1.html>.

Goodhart C, *The Regulatory Response to the Financial Crisis* (EE 2009).

Goodhart C, *The Basel Committee on Banking Supervision: A History of the Early Years 1974–1997* (CUP 2011).

Goodhart C and Lastra R M, 'Populism and Central Bank Independence' (2018) 29(1) Open Economies Review 49, 50.

Gopinath G, 'Rethinking International Macroeconomic Policy' (Conference on 'Rethinking Macroeconomic Policy IV', Peterson Institute on International Economics, 25 October 2017) <https://scholar.harvard.edu/files/gopinath/files/openeconomypolicy100317.pdf>.

Group of 5, 'Announcement the Ministers of Finance and Central Bank Governors of France, Germany, Japan, the United Kingdom, and the United States (Plaza Accord)' (22 September 1985) <www.g8.utoronto.ca/finance/fm850922.htm>.

Group of 6, 'Statement of the G6 Finance Ministers and Central Bank Governors (Louvre Accord)' (22 February 1987) <www.g8.utoronto.ca/finance/fm870222.htm>.

Group of 20, 'What is the G20 Summit?' <https://g20.org/en/summit/about/>.

Group of 20, 'Declaration Summit on Financial Markets and the World Economy' (15 November 2008) <www.mofa.go.jp/policy/economy/g20_summit/2008/declaration.pdf#action>.

Group of 20, 'London Summit – Leaders' Statement' (2 April 2009) <www.mofa.go.jp/policy/economy/g20_summit/2009-1/communique.pdf>.

Guitián M, 'The Unique Nature of the Responsibilities of the International Monetary Fund' (1992) Pamphlet Series No 46 <https://imf.org/external/pubs/ft/pam/pam46/pam46con.htm>.

Guitián M, 'Rules or Discretion in Monetary Policy: National and International Perspectives' in Tomás J T Baliño and Carlo Cottarelli (eds), *Frameworks for Monetary Stability: Policy Issues and Country Experiences* (International Monetary Fund 1994) 33.

He D and others, 'Virtual Currencies and Beyond: Initial Considerations' (2016) IMF Staff Discussion Note 16/03, 7 <https://imf.org/external/pubs/ft/sdn/2016/sdn1603.pdf>.

He D, 'Monetary Policy in the Digital Age: Crypto assets may one day reduce demand for central bank money' (2018) 55(2) Finance & Development 13, 16.

Heath D, 'International Coordination of Macroprudential and Monetary Policy' (2013–2014) 45 Geo J Int'l L 1093.

Hileman G and Rauchs M, 'Global Blockchain Benchmarking Study' (Cambridge Centre for Alternative Finance 2017) <www.jbs.cam.ac.uk/fileadmin/user_upload/research/centres/alternative-finance/downloads/2017-global-cryptocurrency-benchmarking-study.pdf>.

Hirsch M, 'Compliance with international norms in the age of globalization' in Eyal Benvenisti and Moshe Hirsch (eds), *The Impact of International Law on International Cooperation* (CUP 2004).

HM Treasury, 'Management of the Official Reserves' <https://assets.publishing.service.gov.uk/government/uploads/system/uploads/attachment_data/file/236352/management_of_the_official_reserves_2013_14.pdf>.

Horn L, 'The Implications of the Concept of Common Concern of a Human Kind on a Human Right to a Healthy Environment' (2004) 1 Macquarie Journal of International and Comparative Environmental Law 233.

Howse R, 'Sovereignty, Lost and Found' in Wenhua Shan, Penelope Simons and Dalvinder Singh (eds), *Redefining Sovereignty in International Economic Law* (Hart Publishing 2008), 61–75.

Humphrey T M and Keleher R E, 'The Lender of Last Resort: A Historical Perspective' (1984) 4(1) Cato Journal 275.

International Law Commission, 'Draft articles on responsibility of States for internationally wrongful acts' (2001) 2(2) *Yearbook of the International Law Commission* 26.

International Law Commission, 'Provisional summary record of the 3246th meeting' (A/CN.4/SR.3246, 67th Session (first part), 11 January 2016) 4–5.

International Monetary Fund, 'Article IV of the Fund's Articles of Agreement: An Overview of the Legal Framework' (2006), para 3.2 <https://www.imf.org/external/np/pp/eng/2006/062806.pdf>.

International Monetary Fund, 'Article VIII Acceptance by IMF Members: Recent Trends and Implications for the Fund' (2006) <www.imf.org/en/Publications/Policy-Papers/Issues/2016/12/31/Article-VIII-Acceptance-by-IMF-Members-Recent-Trends-and-Implications-for-the-Fund-PP568>.

International Monetary Fund, 'Bilateral Surveillance over Members' Policies' (21 June 2007) <www.imf.org/en/News/Articles/2015/09/28/04/53/pn0769#decision>.

International Monetary Fund, IMF Statistics Department, 'Balance of Payments Manual', 6th edition (2009) <www.imf.org/external/pubs/ft/bop/2007/pdf/bpm6.pdf>.

International Monetary Fund, 'Lessons of the Financial Crisis for Future Regulation of Financial Institutions and Markets and for Liquidity Management' (4 February 2009) <www.imf.org/en/Publications/Policy-Papers/Issues/2016/12/31/Lessons-of-the-Financial-Crisis-for-Future-Regulation-of-Financial-Institutions-and-Markets-PP4316>.

International Monetary Fund, 'The Fund's Role and Mandate – An Overview' (2010) <https://imf.org/external/np/pp/eng/2010/012210a.pdf>.

International Monetary Fund, 'The Fund's Mandate – The Legal Framework' (2010) <http://imf.org/external/np/pp/eng/2010/022210.pdf>.

International Monetary Fund, 'Understanding Financial Interconnectedness' (2010) <http://imf.org/en/Publications/Policy-Papers/Issues/2016/12/31/Understanding-Financial-Interconnectedness-PP4503>.

International Monetary Fund, 'Strengthening the International Monetary System: Taking Stock and Looking Ahead' (2011) <https://imf.org/external/np/pp/eng/2011/032311.pdf>.

International Monetary Fund, 'Modernizing the Legal Framework for Surveillance – An Integrated Surveillance Decision' (2012) <http://imf.org/external/np/pp/eng/2012/071712.pdf>.

International Monetary Fund, 'The Liberalization and Management of Capital Flows: An Institutional View' (2012), 29–30 <www.imf.org/external/np/pp/eng/2012/111412.pdf>.

International Monetary Fund, 'Stocktaking the Fund's Engagement with Regional Financing Arrangements' (2013) <www.imf.org/external/np/pp/eng/2013/041113b.pdf>.

International Monetary Fund Statistics Department, 'Clarifying the Concept of Reserve Assets and Reserve Currency' (2015), 3 <www.imf.org/external/pubs/ft/bop/2015/pdf/15-14.pdf>.

International Monetary Fund, 'Adequacy of the Global Safety Net' (2016) <https://imf.org/external/np/pp/eng/2016/031016.pdf>.

International Monetary Fund, 'Capital Flows – Review of Experience with the Institutional View' (2016) <www.imf.org/en/Publications/Policy-Papers/Issues/2017/01/13/PP5081-Capital-Flows-Review-of-Experience-with-the-Institutional-View>.

International Monetary Fund, 'Strengthening the International Monetary System – A Stocktaking' (2016), <www.imf.org/external/np/pp/eng/2016/022216b.pdf>.

International Monetary Fund, 'Collaboration between Regional Financing Arrangements and the IMF' (2017) <www.imf.org/en/Publications/Policy-Papers/Issues/2017/07/31/pp073117-collaboration-between-regional-financing-arrangements-and-the-imf>.

International Monetary Fund, 'IMF Quota and Governance Publications' (9 August 2018) <www.imf.org/external/np/fin/quotas/pubs/index.htm>.

International Monetary Fund, 'IMF Surveillance' (8 March 2018) <www.imf.org/en/About/Factsheets/IMF-Surveillance>.

International Monetary Fund, 'IMF Lending' (25 February 2019) <www.imf.org/en/About/Factsheets/IMF-Lending>.

International Monetary Fund, 'Annual Report on Exchange Arrangements and Exchange Restrictions 2018' (2019) <https://www.imf.org/en/Publications/Annual-Report-on-Exchange-Arrangements-and-Exchange-Restrictions/Issues/2019/04/24/Annual-Report-on-Exchange-Arrangements-and-Exchange-Restrictions-2018-46162>.

International Monetary Fund, 'IMF Capacity Development' (5 March 2019) <www.imf.org/en/About/Factsheets/imf-capacity-development>.

International Monetary Fund, 'Currency Composition of Official Foreign Exchange Reserves' (2019), <http://data.imf.org/?sk=E6A5F467-C14B-4AA8-9F6D-5A09EC4E62A4>.

International Monetary Fund, 'IMF Conditionality' (5 March 2019) <www.imf.org/en/About/Factsheets/Sheets/2016/08/02/21/28/IMF-Conditionality>.

International Monetary Fund, 'IMF Quotas' (8 March 2019) <www.imf.org/en/About/Factsheets/Sheets/2016/07/14/12/21/IMF-Quotas>.

International Monetary Fund, 'Special Drawing Right (SDR)' (2019) <http://www.imf.org/external/np/exr/facts/sdr.htm>.

International Monetary Fund, *The IMF at a Glance* (2019) <http://imf.org/About/Factsheets/IMF-at-a-Glance?pdf=1>.

International Monetary Fund, 'IMF 2019 Taxonomy of Capital Flow Management Measures' <https://imf.org/~/media/Files/Data/2019/imf-2019-taxonomy-of-capital-flow-management-measures.ashx>.

International Monetary Fund, 'Financial Sector Assessment Program (FSAP)' (3 June 2019) <www.imf.org/en/About/Factsheets/Sheets/2016/08/01/16/14/Financial-Sector-Assessment-Program>.

International Monetary Fund, 'Reports on the Observance of Standards and Codes (ROSCs)' (21 June 2019) <https://www.imf.org/external/NP/rosc/rosc.aspx>.

International Task Force on Global Public Goods, *Meeting Global Challenges: International Cooperation in the National Interest* (Final Report, Stockholm, 2006) 13 <https://ycsg.yale.edu/sites/default/files/files/meeting_global_challenges_global_public_goods.pdf>.

Jackson J H, 'Sovereignty Modern: A New Approach to an Outdated Concept' (2003) 97 AJIL 782.

Jackson J H, *Sovereignty, the WTO and Changing Fundamentals of International Law* (2006 CUP).

James H, 'International Cooperation and Central Banks' in Youssef Cassis, Catherine Schenk, and Richard Grossman (eds), *The Oxford Handbook of Banking and Financial History* (OUP 2016) 22.

Jung J, 'Regional financial cooperation in Asia: challenges and path to development' (2008) BIS Papers No 42 <https://www.bis.org/author/jee-young_jung.htm>.

Kahn R B and Meade E E, 'International aspects of central banking: diplomacy and coordination' in Peter Conti-Brown and Rosa Maria Lastra (eds), *Research Handbook on Central Banking* (EE 2018).

Kato T, 'Can the East Asian Miracle Persist?' (Princeton University's Woodrow Wilson School and East Asian Studies Department, 2 December 2004) <www.imf.org/en/News/Articles/2015/09/28/04/53/sp120204>.

Kaufmann C and Weber R H, 'Transparency and Monetary Affairs' in Thomas Cottier and others (eds), *The Rule of Law in Monetary Affairs* (CUP 2014) 467.

Kaul I and others (eds), *Global Public Goods: International Cooperation in the 21st Century* (OUP 1999).

Kaul I and others (eds), *Providing Global Public Goods: Managing Globalization* (OUP 2003).

Kaul I and Conceiçao P, *The New Public Finance: Responding to Global Challenges* (OUP 2006).

Kaul I, 'Global Public Goods and Responsible Sovereignty' (*The Broker*, 1 July 2010) <http://www.thebrokeronline.eu/Articles/Special-report-Collective-self-interest >.

Kaul I, 'Global Public Goods: Explaining their Underprovision' (2012) 15(3) JIEL 729.

Kawai M and Lamberte M B (eds), *Managing Capital Flows: The Search for a Framework* (EE 2010).

Keller H, 'Friendly Relations Declaration (1970)', *Max Planck Encyclopedias of Public International Law IV* (2012) 250.

Kingsbury B and others (eds), 'The Emergence of Global Administrative Law' (2005) 68 Law and Contemporary Problems 1.

Kirgis F L, *Prior Consultation in International Law* (University Press of Virginia 1983).

Knight M D and Ortiz G, '2014 Triennial Surveillance Review-External Study-Multilateral Surveillance: Ensuring a Focus on Key Risks to Global Stability' (2014) <www.imf.org/~/media/Websites/IMF/imported-full-text-pdf/external/np/pp/eng/2014/_073014f.ashx>.

Kolb R, 'Principles as Sources of International Law (With Special Reference to Good Faith)' (2006) 53(1) Netherlands International Law Review.

Kontolemis Z, 'Exchange rates are a matter of common concern: policies in the run-up to the euro?' (No 191 Economic Papers, Directorate-General for Economic and Financial Affairs Publications 2003).

Krugman P R, 'Equilibrium Exchange Rates' in William H Branson, Jacob A Frenkel and Morris Goldstein (eds), *International Policy Coordination and Exchange Rate Fluctuations* (University of Chicago Press 1990) <www.nber.org/chapters/c6948.pdf>.

Krugman P R, 'Equilibrium Exchange Rates' in William H Branson, Jacob A Frenkel and Morris Goldstein (eds), *International Policy Coordination and Exchange Rate Fluctuations* (University of Chicago Press 1990) <www.nber.org/chapters/c6948.pdf>.

Lastra R M, *Central Banking and Banking Regulation* (Financial Markets Group LSE, 1996).

Lastra R M, 'Northern Rock, UK bank insolvency and cross-border bank insolvency' (2008) 9(3) Journal of Banking Regulation 165.

Lastra R M, 'Central Bank Independence and Financial Stability' (2010) 18 Revista de Estabilidad Financiera 49.

Lastra R M and Wood G, 'The Crisis of 2007–2009: Nature, Causes, and Reactions' (2012) 13 JIEL 531.

Lastra R M, 'Do We Need a World Financial Organization?' (2014) 17 JIEL 787.

Lastra R M, 'The Role of Central Banks in Monetary Affairs: A Comparative Perspective' in Thomas Cottier and others (eds), *The Rule of Law in Monetary Affairs* (CUP 2014), 98.

Lastra R M, *International Financial and Monetary Law* (2nd edn, OUP 2015).

Lastra R M and Goodhart C A E, 'Interaction Between Monetary Policy and Bank Regulation' (2015) Monetary Dialogue Papers – European Parliament <www.europarl.europa.eu/committees/en/econ/monetary-dialogue.html?id=20150914CPU05481>.

Lastra R M and Allen J G, 'Virtual Currencies in the Eurosystem: challenges ahead' (European Parliament Monetary Dialogue, July 2018) <www.europarl.europa.eu/cmsdata/150541/DIW_FINAL%20publication.pdf >.

Law J and Smullen J (eds), *A Dictionary of Finance and Banking* (4 rev ed, OUP 2008).

Lowenfeld L, *International Economic Law* (2008 OUP).

Lupo-Pasini F, 'Financial Stability in International Law' (2017) 18(1) MJIL 52.

Lupo-Pasini F, 'Financial Stability as a Common Concern of Humankind' in Thomas Cottier (ed), *The Prospects of Common Concern of Humankind in International Law* (CUP 2021).

McLeay M and others, 'Money Creation in the Modern Economy' (Bank of England Quarterly Bulletin, 2014 Q1) <www.bankofengland.co.uk/-/media/boe/files/quarterly-bulletin/2014/money-creation-in-the-modern-economy.pdf>.

Miller G P, 'An Interest Group Theory of Central Bank Independence' (1998) 27 Journal of Legal Studies 433.

Mohan R and Kapur M, 'Monetary Policy Coordination and the Role of Central Banks' (2014) IMF Working Paper 14/70 <www.imf.org/external/pubs/ft/wp/2014/wp1470.pdf>.

Mundell R A, 'Capital Mobility and Stabilization Policy under Fixed and Flexible Exchange Rates' (1963) 29(4) The Canadian Journal of Economics and Political Science 475.

Murase S, 'Second report on the protection of the atmosphere' (A/CN.4/681, International Law Commission, 67th session, Geneva, 2 March 2015) 25, 49.

Musgrave R A, 'Public Goods' in Brown E Cary and Robert M Solow (eds), *Paul Samuelson and Modern Economic Theory* (McGraw Hill 1983).

Nakavukaren Schefer K and Cottier T, 'Responsibility to Protect (R2P) and the Emerging Principle of Common Concern' in Peter Hilpold (ed), *The Responsibility to Protect; A New Paradigm of International Law?* (Brill Nijhoff 2014).

Nanda V P and Ris W, Jr, 'The Public Trust Doctrine: a Viable Approach to International Environmental Protection', (1976) 5(2) *Ecology Law Quarterly* 291.

Nollkaemper A, 'Issues of Shared Responsibility before the International Court of Justice' in Eva Rieter and Henri de Waele (eds), *Evolving Principles of International Law; Studies in Honour of Karel C. Wellens* (Martinus Nijhoff Publishers 2012).

Organisation for Economic Co-Operation and Development, 'OECD Code of Liberalisation of Capital Movements' <www.oecd.org/investment/codes.htm>.

Ostry J D and Ghosh A R, 'Obstacles to International Policy Coordination, and How to Overcome Them' (IMF Staff Discussion Note, December 2013) <www.imf.org/external/pubs/ft/sdn/2013/sdn1311.pdf>.

Padoa-Schioppa T, 'The Ghost of Bancor: The Economic Crisis and Global Economic Disorder' (Lecture, the Triffin International Foundation, Louvain-la-Neuve, 25 February 2010) <www.institutdelors.eu/wp-content/uploads/2018/01/speech-tps-louvainlaneuve-25.02.2010.pdf>.

Palais-Royal Initiative, 'Reform of the International Monetary System: A Cooperative Approach for the Twenty First Century' (2011) <http://global-currencies.org/smi/gb/telechar/news/Rapport_Camdessus-integral.pdf >.

Pardo A and Christol C Q, 'The Common Interest: Tension Between the Whole and the Parts' in R Macdonald and D Johnston (eds), *The Structure and Process of International Law* (Martinus Nijhoff Publishers 1993).

Peters A, 'Compensatory Constitutionalism: The Function and Potential of Fundamental International Norms and Structures' (2006) 19 Leiden Journal of International Law 579.

Peters A and others (eds), *Non-State Actors as Standard Setters* (CUP 2009).

Petersmann E U, 'International Economic Law, 'Public Reason', and Multilevel Governance of Interdependent Public Goods' (2011) 14(1) JIEL 30.

Petersmann E U, *International Economic Law in the 21st Century: Constitutional Pluralism and Multilevel Governance of Interdependent Public Goods* (Hart Publishing 2012).

Petersmann E U, 'Framework of Analysis: Multilevel Governance' in Thomas Cottier and others (eds), *The Rule of Law in Monetary Affairs* (CUP 2014).

Prasad E, 'The Dollar Reigns Supreme by Default' (2014) 51(1) Finance & Development <http://www.imf.org/external/pubs/ft/fandd/2014/03/prasad.htm>.

Proctor C, *The Euro and the Financial Markets: The Legal Impact of EMU* (Jordans 1999) 6.

Proctor C, 'Indexation and Value Clauses' in Mario Giovanoli and Diego Devos (eds), *International Monetary and Financial Law, The Global Crisis* (OUP 2010), 576.

Proctor C, *Mann on the Legal Aspect of Money* (7th edn, OUP 2012).

Rajan R G, *Fault Lines: How Hidden Fractures Still Threaten the World Economy* (Princeton University Press 2010).

Rajan R G, 'The Only Game in Town' (2012) <www.project-syndicate.org/commentary/the-limits-of-unconventional-monetary-policy-by-raghuram-rajan>.

Rendak N, 'Monitoring and Surveillance of the International Monetary System: What can be learnt from the trade field?' in Thomas Cottier and others (eds), *The Rule of Law in Monetary Affairs* (CUP 2014) 204.

Rey H, 'Dilemma not Trilemma: The Global Financial Cycle and Monetary Policy independence' (2013) Proceedings – Economic Policy Symposium – Jackson Hole, Federal Reserve of Kansas City Economic Symposium, 285–333.

Rodrik D, *The Globalization Paradox: Democracy and the Future of the World Economy* (W W Norton & Company 2011) 204.

Roubini N and Mihm S, *Crisis Economics: A Crash Course in the Future of Finance* (Penguin Press 2010).

Ryngaert C, *Jurisdiction in International Law* (OUP 2008).

Sainz de Vicuña A, 'An Institutional Theory of Money' in Mario Giovanoli and Diego Devos (eds), *International Monetary and Financial Law, The Global Crisis* (OUP 2010) 525.

Samuelson P, 'The Pure Theory of Public Expenditure' (1954) 36 Rev Econ Stat 387.

Sarooshi D, 'The Essentially Contested Nature of the Concept of Sovereignty: Implications for the Exercise by International Organizations of Delegated Powers of Government' (2004) 25 Mich J Intl L 1107.

Satragno L, 'Responsibility for International Monetary Stability in the Post-Crisis Era' in Samantha Besson (ed), *International Responsibility: Essays in Law, History and Philosophy* (Schlthess 2017) 77.

Satragno L, 'International Monetary Stability as a Common Concern of Humankind' in Thomas Cottier (ed), *The Prospects of Common Concern of Humankind in International Law* (CUP 2021).

Schoenmaker D, *Governance of International Banking: The Financial Trilemma* (OUP 2013).

Schwartz H M, *Subprime Nation: American Power, Global Capital and the Housing Bubble* (Cornell University Press 2009).

Shaffer G and Pollack M A, 'Hard vs. Soft Law: Alternatives, Complements, and Antagonists in International Governance' (2010) 94 Minn L Rev 706.

Shaffer G, 'International Law and Global Public Goods in a Legal Pluralist World' (2012) 23(3) EJIL 692.

Shan W and others (eds), *Redefining Sovereignty in International Economic Law – Studies in International Trade Law (No.7)* (Hart Publishing 2008).

Shanmugaratnam T, 'Keynote Address' (Fourth ECOSOC Forum on Financing for Development, 15 April 2019) <www.mfa.gov.sg/Overseas-Mission/New-York/Mission-Updates/Second_committee/2019/04/Press_20190415>.

Siegel D, 'Legal Aspects of the IMF/WTO Relationship: The Fund's Articles of Agreement and the WTO Agreement' (2002) 96 AJIL 561, 600.

Simmons B A, 'Money and the Law: Why Comply with the Public International Law of Money?' (2000) 25(2) Yale Journal of International Law 335.

Simons H C, 'Rules versus Authorities in Monetary Policy' (1936) 44(1) Journal of Political Economy 1.

Slaughter A, *A New World Order* (Princeton: Princeton University Press 2004).

Steil B, The Battle of Bretton Woods: John Maynard Keynes, Harry Dexter White, and the Making of a New World Order (Princeton University Press 2014).

Stiglitz J, 'Capital Market Liberalization, Globalization and the IMF' (2005) 20 Oxford Review of Economic Policy 57.

Subramaniam A and others, 'Patterns of International Capital Flows and Their Implications for Economic Development' (Proceedings of the 2006 Jackson Hole Symposium, Federal Reserve Bank of Kansas City, 2006).

Swiss National Bank, *Annual Reports* (2000–2009), <www.snb.ch/en/iabout/pub/annrep/id/pub_annrep>.

Swiss National Bank, *Swiss National Bank Sets Minimum Exchange Rate at CHF 1.20 per Euro* (2011), <www.snb.ch/en/mmr/reference/pre_20110906/source/pre_20110906.en.pdf>.

Swiss National Bank, *Swiss National Bank discontinues minimum exchange rate and lowers interest rate to –0.75%* (2015), <www.snb.ch/en/mmr/reference/pre_20150115/source/pre_20150115.en.pdf>.

The Economist, 'How to Stop a Currency War' (*The Economist*, 14 October 2010) <www.economist.com/leaders/2010/10/14/how-to-stop-a-currency-war>.

The Economist, The Next Recession (11 October 2018).

The Economist, 'Following the Money' (*The Economist*, 22 February 2020) <www.economist.com/finance-and-economics/2020/02/20/cash-sloshes-around-the-world-in-unexpected-ways>.

Tietje C, 'The International Financial Architecture as a Legal Order' (2011) 54 German Yearbook of International Law (2011).

Tietje C, 'The Role of Law in Monetary Affairs: Taking Stock' in Thomas Cottier and others (eds), *The Rule of Law in Monetary Affairs* (CUP 2014).

Tinbergen J, *On the Theory of Economic Policy* (North Holland Pub Co 1952).

Tobin J, 'A Proposal for International Monetary Reform' (1978) 4(3–4) Eastern Economic Journal 153.

Tolba M, 'The Implications of the "Common Concern of Mankind" Concept on Global Environmental Issues' (1991) 13 Revista Instituto Interamericano de Derechos Humanos 237, 240.

Toniolo G, *Central Bank Cooperation at the Bank for International Settlements 1930–1973* (CUP 2005).

Trachtman J P, 'The International Economic Law Revolution' (1996) 17(1) University of Pennsylvania Journal of International Economic Law 1.

Trindade A A C, *International Law for Humankind: Towards a New Jus Gentium* (2nd ed, Martinus Nijhoff Publishers 2013).

Truman E M, 'Asian and European Financial Crises Compared' (2013) Peterson Institute for International Economics Working Paper No 13–9 <https://papers.ssrn.com/sol3/papers.cfm?abstract_id=2344421>.

Turpin J, 'Bitcoin: The Economic Case for a Global, Virtual Currency Operating in an Unexplored Legal Framework' (2014) 21 Indiana Journal of Global Legal Studies 335.

Villard Duran C, 'The International Lender of Last Resort for Emerging Countries: A Bilateral Currency Swap?' (2015) GEG Working Paper 2015/108 <www.geg.ox.ac.uk/publication/geg-wp-2015108-international-lender-last-resort-emerging-countries-bilateral-currency>.

Villard Duran C, 'Voice and Exit: How G20 Emerging Powers are Challenging the Global Monetary Order' (2018) 15 Revista de Direito Internacional'.

Viterbo A, *International Economic Law and Monetary Measures* (EE 2012).

Walker N, 'The Idea of Constitutional Pluralism' (2002) 65 Modern Law Review 317.

White W, 'Speech' (Central Bank Governor's Club Meeting, Nafplio, 18 October 2012) <www.bis.org/speeches/sp021018.htm>.

Wolfrum R, 'The Principle of Common Heritage of Mankind', (19983) 43 Heidelberg Journal of International Law 312.

Wouters J and others, 'The Influence of General Principles of Law' in Sanford E Gaines and others (eds), *Liberalising Trade in the EU and the WTO – A Legal Comparison* (Cambridge University Press 2012).

Yellen J L, 'Improving the International Monetary and Financial System' (Banque de France International Symposium, Paris, 4 March 2011) <https://www.federalreserve.gov/newsevents/speech/files/yellen20110304a.pdf>.

Yellen J L, 'Speech' (The Elusive 'Great' Recovery: Causes and Implications for Future Business Cycle Dynamics, Boston, 14 October 2016 <https://federalreserve.gov/newsevents/speech/yellen20161014a.htm>.

Zimmermann C D, 'Exchange Rate Misalignment and International Law' (2011) 105(3) AJIL 423.

Zimmermann C D, *A Contemporary Concept of Monetary Sovereignty* (OUP 2013).

Zimmermann C D, 'Global Benchmark Interest Rates: conflicting objectives and increasing hybridisation' in Thomas Cottier and others (eds), *The Rule of Law in Monetary Affairs* (CUP 2014), 153.

Zimmermann C D, closing statement in Thomas Cottier (ed) *The Prospects of Common Concern of Humankind in International Law* (CUP 2021).

Index

www.ingramcontent.com/pod-product-compliance
Lightning Source LLC
Chambersburg PA
CBHW071322230926
51849CB00002B/294
* 9 7 8 9 0 0 4 5 0 8 7 2 9 *